CODE WORD: CATHERINE

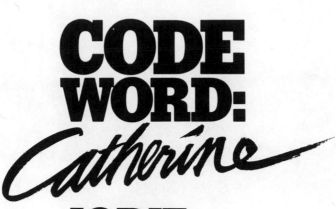

CODE
WORD:
Catherine

JODIE
COLLINS

TYNDALE HOUSE
PUBLISHERS, INC.
WHEATON, ILLINOIS

CODE WORD: CATHERINE
Second printing, July 1985
Library of Congress Catalog Card Number 84-51056
ISBN 0-8423-0301-4
Copyright © 1984 by Jodie Collins
Printed in the United States of America

CONTENTS

GENEALOGY
*of the ten royal children
rescued by the Collinses*

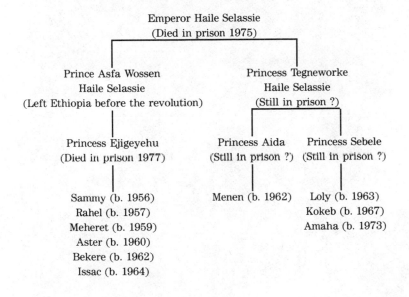

Emperor Haile Selassie
(Died in prison 1975)

Prince Asfa Wossen
Haile Selassie
(Left Ethiopia before the revolution)

Princess Tegneworke
Haile Selassie
(Still in prison ?)

Princess Ejigeyehu
(Died in prison 1977)

Princess Aida
(Still in prison ?)

Princess Sebele
(Still in prison ?)

Sammy (b. 1956)
Rahel (b. 1957)
Meheret (b. 1959)
Aster (b. 1960)
Bekere (b. 1962)
Issac (b. 1964)

Menen (b. 1962)

Loly (b. 1963)
Kokeb (b. 1967)
Amaha (b. 1973)

Foreword

The imprisonment of Ethiopia's Emperor Haile Selassie in the mid-1970s and the subsequent Marxist revolution shocked many in Congress, including myself. Ethiopia had been a long-standing ally of the United States, while Emperor Selassie had been a personal friend. The plight of the royal family came to my attention during this time and I joined efforts to ensure their admission to the U.S., while seeking mercy for those members of the government and of the family still in jail.

Code Word: Catherine, Jodie Collin's incredible firsthand escape story, not only makes for fascinating reading, but provides a uniquely intimate version of events of which I became aware only after the fact. She vividly portrays the stark contrast of life under Emperor Selassie with that under the Marxist government currently in power in Ethiopia. Unfortunately, a decade after the revolution, the situation she describes has not changed, as poverty and starvation are still pervasive and the suppression of human rights continues.

But there is a brighter picture within this story of the escape of the royal children. It is that of the steadfast faithfulness of God and the trust in Him shown by Denton and Jodie Collins in the face of the great risks they took in behalf of the royal family. By continually reminding her to trust, God guided Jodie through many doubts and uncertainties as He unfolded every detail of her plan for the rescue of all of the Emperor's great-grandchildren.

The suspense kept me enthralled as the escape plan grew and reached its climax. *Code Word: Catherine* was an inspiration to me and is worthy of wide readership.

Senator Mark O. Hatfield
June 1984

PART ONE

PART ONE

CHAPTER ONE

"Cancel Catherine's Surgery!"

My heart pounded with excitement and my hands trembled as I sat on the edge of the bed in my motel room in Oklahoma City, waiting for the telephone to ring—willing it to ring. It was almost an hour since I had placed the call to Addis Ababa. I could hardly wait to share my joy with my husband. All our dreams were finally going to be realized, and six months of planning, plotting, and preparing would soon culminate in the successful escape of Denton and the four royal children in his care. Their secret airlift out of Ethiopia was confirmed.

I had spent nearly six weeks in England, making all the arrangements, then had come on to the United States to visit family members and join our son and daughter who had come earlier. Denton had risked his life to remain in Africa with the royal children. Now that I had everything in order, it remained only to let Denton know the plans—but I must remember the code we had worked out. We could never speak openly over the telephone about our dangerous plan to whisk four great-grandchildren of Haile Selassie out of the country right under the noses of the Marxists who now held the country in their grip.

The code. I had been afraid to write it down until now, but now I would jot down the secret words and plan just what I would say to Denton when my call came through. *Catherine:*

that stood for Denton and the four children. *Surgery:* the escape. I would give Denton the date and time of Catherine's surgery, and he would understand it was the date and time of the escape. *The doctor:* he was the man we wanted to fly to East Africa to meet with Denton and explain the details of the planned escape, or "Catherine's surgery!" Good! I remembered it all.

I wrote out my message just as I would read it to Denton. My heart beat fast as I read over my note. The telephone rang. I grabbed my paper and pencil from the bedside table and sat down by the telephone, trying to calm myself. I let the phone ring once more, then lifted the receiver slowly.

"Hello," I began, my voice trembling.

"Hello, is this Mrs. Jodie Collins?"

"Yes, it is."

"I have Denton Collins on the line from Addis Ababa, Ethiopia. Did you place this call?"

"Yes, I did, Operator. Thank you."

"Go ahead, please."

"Denton, are you there? Can you hear me?"

I felt as if all of Oklahoma could hear me, I was shouting so loudly, but all that I heard was static. Finally I caught my husband's voice fading in and out.

"Yes, Jodie. How are you? How are Shellie and Brent?"

He sounded tired and strained.

"The kids are fine. I'm well, too. How are you and the children?"

"We are all right. Things are about the same here."

His voice sounds depressed, I thought.

"Denton, listen." I held my note up to the light and began to read: "Catherine's surgery is scheduled. It is scheduled for April 22, eight o'clock in the morning. The doctor will contact you with all the details about Catherine's surgery."

I listened intently for his reply. It seemed like forever before I heard his voice again.

"Jodie, listen to me."

"I'm listening, Denton, what is it?"

"Cancel Catherine's surgery."

I screamed into the receiver, "What are you talking about, Denton! I can't cancel Catherine's surgery! Don't be silly! If I cancel her surgery, she will die! What do you mean?"

"Jodie, listen!" His voice was steady and firm now. He repeated again, "Jodie, listen to me! Catherine will die if you *don't* cancel the surgery! Cancel it! I will write the details. Trust me." And he hung up.

I was dumbstruck. I sat with the receiver in my lap. I felt as though the earth had just opened up, and I was falling into a deep abyss. *This can't be happening! What am I going to do? Can I stop everything in time?*

I burst into tears and fell on my knees beside the bed. "God, how can this be happening to me?" Just an hour before, I had been one of the happiest people on earth. We had the money, the airplane, and the pilot, and the contact man was ready to leave for Ethiopia to explain all the details to Denton. Now our plans had collapsed.

With my face in my hands, I sobbed until I had no breath left. My head throbbed, but I knew I had to pull myself together and phone London. My hands trembled as I dialed the number.

"Hello, Michael, this is Jodie. Listen to me, Michael. We must cancel Catherine's surgery. I don't know why. I only know that I talked to Denton just a few minutes ago, and something was terribly wrong. He said to cancel the surgery or Catherine would die. Yes, I'll call you when I've heard something. Just tell our contact man not to go in there. He shouldn't try to get in touch with Denton until I find out what is happening."

That was my second transatlantic call of the day. I felt exhausted and emotionally drained. My Bible lay open on the table beside me. I picked it up and began to leaf through the pages. My silent tears fell on the onion skin pages, wrinkling the paper as the tears splashed here and there. My eyes burned so badly I could hardly focus on the words. Again I knelt beside my bed with my face in my hands. I felt so alone. I slammed my clenched fists into the soft blankets and cried, "God, what's going on? Didn't I ask you to save these children's lives? And now what? Am I going to lose my husband and the children!"

Denton and I had talked on many occasions about escaping with the four royal children. We had tried to calculate and anticipate the many risks involved. We knew several people's lives, as well as their careers, were in jeopardy. But what was the alternative? Staying in Ethiopia meant that the four children left in our care after the late Emperor Haile Selassie and the royal family were imprisoned, would be returned to prison with their already imprisoned parents. The rumors were that the new Marxist government planned to execute the entire royal family. It was a matter of life and death either way.

I had prayed that the escape plan wouldn't get to first base if anyone was going to get killed. I tried desperately to console myself with the thought that cancelling the escape might have saved someone's life, but nothing could stop the avalanche of tears.

I tried to smooth the wrinkled pages of my Bible with the palm of my hand. "God, why do things like this have to happen?"

My eyes finally focused, and they fell upon verses I had marked with my pink highlighter. "Trust in the Lord. . . ."

That's ironic, I thought angrily. There's that word again: "Trust!" Denton had just said, "Trust me," when he told me to cancel the escape. It rang another familiar bell in my mind. How could I forget it! I could still see Loly's helpless little face as she stood there in the airport.

We had received word suddenly that the children were going to be arrested and returned to prison. Within one week's time I had resigned my teaching position at the English School, applied for an exit visa, and explained to the children that my mother was ill and in need of surgery, and I wanted to be with her during the surgery. Shellie and Brent would be going with me. Although I didn't say it directly, I implied that I was planning to come back. The three older royal children and our own two were quite shaken by the news of our sudden departure. During the last few days they barely talked to me. Just a few minutes before Shellie, Brent, and I were to board the airplane, I knew I had to say something to them. I was holding Amaha. For a two-year-old he was unusually sensitive and perceptive. He nestled his warm little face into my neck and hugged me tightly. I felt his tears on my neck and heard him whisper again and again, "Bye-bye, Mommy. Bye-bye."

I knew I had to say something to the girls before I left. I handed Amaha to Denton and walked toward them. They were all crying. Loly was holding onto Brent and crying. Shellie had her arms around Kokeb and Menen. I put my arm on Loly's shoulder and gently turned her toward me. Embarrassed that she was crying, she kept her head down. I lifted her face. I wasn't sure I could trust my voice. I, too, was on the verge of tears.

"Loly, aren't you going to say goodbye to me?"

For a moment she kept her eyes downcast, refusing to look at me. I held her in front of me, hoping I would not have to leave her like this. Suddenly she looked straight into my eyes.

"Mommy, my mother is in prison. Menen's mother is in prison. You are the only mom we have, and now you are leaving us!"

Her words cut me to the quick. How would I answer her accusations? I could not say what I wanted to say: "Loly, I'm leaving here to plan your escape. . . ." Instead, I continued to hold her and look into her accusing eyes. My voice was barely audible as tears finally spilled down my face.

"Loly, sweetheart, do you have any idea how much I love you children? Don't you know I love you like my very own? Loly, please . . . please . . . trust me!"

She looked at me for a moment. I thought she was going to say something more. Then she turned and walked away.

I didn't think I could stand the hurt that welled up in my throat. It felt as if it would strangle me. My emotions gave way like a giant earthslide. Fumbling in my pocket for a tissue, I walked slowly toward the girls. I kissed Loly, Menen, and Kokeb on their tear-streaked faces and said softly, "See you soon."

I kissed Denton and Amaha goodbye. Shellie, Brent, and I walked toward the plane. I didn't look back. The truth was, I didn't know if I *would* ever see them again. It all depended on an escape plan that had not yet been formulated.

I had asked Loly to trust me. Denton had asked me to trust him. As I stared at the wrinkled, well-worn page in my Bible, I understood that God was asking me to trust Him. I continued reading the verses I had marked at some previous reading.

"Trust in the Lord and do good; dwell in the land and enjoy safe pasture. Delight yourself in the Lord and he will give you the desires of your heart. Commit your way to the Lord; trust in him and he will do this. He will make your righteousness shine like the dawn, the justice of your cause like the noonday sun. Be still before the Lord and wait patiently for him; . . . do not fret" Psalm 37:3-7, NIV.

I remembered how badly I had wanted Loly to trust me. I knew I was leaving Ethiopia to plan her escape. Vaguely I began to understand. I had Loly's best interest at heart even though she didn't understand it at the moment. God had my best interest at heart, too. Even though it didn't appear that He did, He was asking me to trust Him just as I had asked Loly to trust me. I was scared, disappointed, angry, and confused. I had no idea if the children were dead or alive. I was uncertain about Denton. Perhaps his life was in jeopardy. Could I trust God to help me even though the situation looked impossible?

I got up from my knees and sat on the edge of the bed. I took a deep breath, looked up, and whispered, "I do want to trust you, God. Please help me. I'm so confused!"

CHAPTER TWO
Dark Days in Ethiopia

Early the next morning I left Oklahoma City. The five-hour flight to California gave me ample time to think about my reunion with my children, Shellie and Brent. I was certain Mom, my stepfather, Ben, and our good friends Jean and Moses Hernandez would be at the airport, too. It would be great to see them all again, but how would I ever explain this past year, much less the last six weeks!

I wondered how much Shellie and Brent had understood about what I was doing in England during the three weeks they were with me. Denton and I had decided that we should not risk telling the children about our ideas for an escape, but, after all, Shellie and Brent were old enough to listen and observe a great deal that I was doing in England. I was sure they had heard many of the conversations even though they always appeared busy doing other things. There were meetings where we discussed strategy, as well as our train trip to Oxford where I discussed the financial arrangements for the airplane we planned to use. There had been the frightful evening when Michael had come to our hotel to warn us about the eight assassins that had been sent to England to search for members of the Ethiopian royal family. Certain he had seen two of the assassins in the hotel bar as he was coming to our room, he insisted that we make a hasty exit out the fire escape and run down a dark alley to escape being seen. I must admit I had had some second thoughts about the whole scheme that evening.

Now, sitting securely on a commercial plane, safe within the United States, the experiences of the last six weeks seemed very remote, almost like a dream, far removed and distant.

Shellie and Brent had enjoyed their three weeks in England. When I wasn't in meetings, we enjoyed visiting museums, the Tower of London, taking a ride on the Thames. When I was meeting with people, they either stayed in the hotel and watched television or struck out on their own sightseeing trips.

When I had suggested to them that they fly to the States ahead of me, they were quite eager to go. I couldn't imagine what Shellie had told her grandma and grandpa or Jean and Moses about the past year. I smiled, thinking about my phone call to Jean the day I planned to put Shellie and Brent on the plane in London.

"Hi, Jean, this is Jodie."

"Jodie!" she screamed excitedly. "Where in the world are you?"

"London."

"London! Whatever are you doing there? Where are Denton and the children?"

"Shellie and Brent are here with me. Denton is still in Ethiopia. I'm putting the kids on a plane this afternoon. They will go through customs in Los Angeles and fly PSA flight 24, arriving at four o'clock tomorrow afternoon in San Francisco. Will you pick them up, and settle them into school? I'll explain everything when I get home. I'll be home in a few weeks. I still have business to settle here in London."

Only Jean would have taken it all so calmly with no prying questions.

"All right, Jodie. We'll take care of everything. Are you OK?"

"Yes, I'm fine. Thanks so much, Jean. Oh, listen! I called my Mom and Ben and told them to meet you at the San Francisco airport, but it will help a lot if the kids can stay with you and go to school. Mom and Ben will keep them on weekends if you need a break. You can work all of that out when you get together with them at the airport. OK?"

"Shellie and Brent will be just fine, Jodie. We'll take care of everything," she said reassuringly.

Jean and Moe were marvelous. So were Mom and Ben. I hadn't had to explain details to Mom or Jean. They were both just willing to do whatever was necessary. Did everyone have such supportive friends and family, or was I just specially blessed?

When the seat belt sign flashed off, I reclined my seat. I closed my eyes, wishing I could sleep on airplanes, but it was useless. Instead, my mind reeled with thoughts of Denton and the four children that were, I hoped, still in his care.

Or had the children been arrested? Could that be why he had cancelled the escape plan? This question had nagged me for the last twenty-four hours, but I wouldn't know until Denton was able to get some word to me.

I fought back tears again as I thought of those four precious children. Loly and Kokeb were the ages of our own two children, Shellie and Brent. I recalled how surprised I had been when Loly told me that her birthday was October 15.

"Oh," I exclaimed when she first told me, "we will have fun celebrating your birthday and Shellie's together, particularly since you will both be teenagers this year! Shellie's birthday is October 14."

Brent and Kokeb were eight, and their birthdays were in July. Menen, the cousin of Loly, Kokeb, and Amaha, was the oldest. She had her thirteenth birthday just three months after they first came to live with us. I smiled to myself as I thought of how shy Menen was when we had all sung "Happy Birthday" to her. She was such a quiet, reticent child. Amaha. What a cuddly little teddy bear he was—so gentle and soft-spoken for a two-year-old child. Although he had come to live with us several months after the girls, I could hardly remember what it was like without him. I thought of Kokeb and how she giggled and squealed each night when I tucked her into bed. She was so petite, almost fragile, but her eyes danced with vitality and mischief. Unlike Loly, who was so ladylike and proper, Kokeb was a gangling youngster full of fun and laughter.

The thought that they might have been imprisoned was

more than I could cope with at this moment. I tried to remember happier moments.

So much had happened during the last year. It had all seemed so simple in the beginning.

It had all begun when Mrs. Casbone, the Headmistress of the English School where I was teaching, called me aside in the teachers' lounge before school.

Mrs. Casbone's round, wrinkled face was filled with concern as she stood beside me that morning in the teachers' lounge of the English School.

The old brick fireplace was aglow, but the warmth did little to dispel the early morning cold. The fire snapped and crackled its protest against the February chill, and a steady hum of voices filled the room as the teachers' arrivals signaled a new day.

I was busy correcting papers when I felt someone standing beside me. I looked up into Mrs. Casbone's drawn face. She glanced nervously about the room; then, leaning down, she lowered her deep, resonant voice and said, "Jodie, may I see you after school today?" Her voice was firm but I sensed her emotion.

"Why, yes, of course, Mrs. Casbone," I stammered, a little surprised that she even knew my name. I had been teaching at the English School for only four months, and I had never had an occasion to talk to her. Mr. Casbone was the director of the school, and he had interviewed me for my job. I had seen Mrs. Casbone on many occasions. She was usually so jovial, a gregarious lady in the center of a lively conversation, but today she appeared worried and strained. Why did she want to talk with me, I pondered curiously.

The first bell sounded as I stuffed my papers into my big straw basket. Weaving my way through the maze of children of all nationalities running toward their classrooms, I soon forgot my strange encounter with Mrs. Casbone. It was the lunch bell that reminded me of our afternoon appointment.

During my two-hour lunch break I decided to drive to the American embassy snackbar and visit my friend Carol.

Driving toward the American embassy, I was well aware of the soldiers milling about on nearly every street corner.

Their rifles were slung carelessly over their shoulders as they stood talking to one another. Tanks were positioned in strategic places along the tree-lined boulevard leading to the university campus.

A Marxist revolution in its infancy, I thought bitterly. I didn't appreciate the changes that the revolution had brought into my life. I was weary of the shooting, food rationing, shortages, bread lines, early curfew, unannounced house searches, executions, and daily arrests of anyone the government suspected of antirevolutionary activities. There seemed to be no such thing as a routine day anymore.

I saw a young boy selling newspapers. I stopped beside him and bought a copy of the English newspaper, *The Ethiopian Herald*. Dated February 2, 1976, the headlines depressed me. "Eleven Antirevolutionary Individuals Executed," "Tentacles Crippled: Four U. S. Organizations in Ethiopia Closed Down," "The Integrity, Valour of Our Country Shall Not Be Transgressed Today," "Revolutionary Ethiopia or Death!" "Two Confirmed CIA Agents Expelled from Ethiopia."

After awhile it all started sounding the same. Disgustedly I folded the newspaper, shifted the car into low gear, and continued toward the embassy.

It had been only seventeen months since the Ethiopian military had toppled the eighty-three-year-old monarch, Haile Selassie, and imprisoned him and his family.

During our thirteen years in Ethiopia there had always been rumors regarding attempted coups, and almost everyone speculated about what would happen "after the Emperor was gone."

I doubted that anyone had guessed accurately how it would all come about. Certainly, in January 1974 the Emperor appeared to be well in control of the country. In September of the same year, he was languishing in a prison cell.

It appeared to me that the Emperor, whose titles included The King of Kings, Elect of God, Conquering Lion of the Tribe of Judah, must have thought of himself as infallible and indestructible.

Too late he had tried to negotiate and make compromises with the demands of his military and civilian antagonists.

Like so many other leaders, he underestimated the determination and patience of his people.

No single event triggered the revolution, although it seemed to gather momentum after a military mutiny among the rank-and-file soldiers over poor food, shortages of drinking water, and inadequate wages. A ripple-like effect of unrest and uprising began on different military posts around the empire. The unrest quickly spread to the civilian population. Unprecedented waves of strikes, demonstrations, and violence broke out in every sector of the population. Shortages, outrageous food and gasoline prices, meager salaries, student and teacher unrest, and discontent over educational reform all added fuel to the fire that was about to engulf the nation. Taxi drivers and bus drivers went on strike in Addis Ababa, paralyzing life in the capital city. The chaos could not be quickly suppressed, because the military's loyalty was in doubt.

Not least among the issues was the Emperor's refusal to acknowledge the drought in northern Ethiopia, allowing more than 100,000 peasants to die of starvation.

After nearly two months of military and civilian uprisings, the Emperor made a long series of concessions. In early April it appeared that the soldiers were returning to their barracks and that some stability would return to the country. It was short lived.

In April a Coordinating Committee surfaced and issued its first statement announcing that the military intended to ensure peace, and as a first step they arrested some of the Emperor's closest ministers and officials. The Coordinating Committee became known as the Derg. At first they pledged loyalty to the Emperor, but at the same time they began making much more widespread arrests of officials in high power.

By July the Emperor had been reduced to a figurehead who could no longer protect even his closest associates. They were being arrested one by one. In a thirteen-point statement, the Derg's position began to take form, and within two months it had become obvious that their intent was the deposition of Emperor Haile Selassie and the scrapping of the imperial system of government. Even the Emperor's palace was nationalized from under him. The state-run media that had for decades sung his daily praise now began to undermine his prestige and authority, publishing articles detailing the horrors and corruption of his imperial order.

Thus, on September 12, 1974, just nine months after the first winds of civil and military unrest began to blow, there was no public outcry when the Emperor, The Elect of God, was taken off to prison in a small Volkswagen—without a shot being fired or a cry raised in his defense.*

There was little doubt in my mind that the military was the prime mover of the revolution, and their omnipresence was a constant reminder that they had no intention of letting their prize slip out of their hands. With the same tenacity as the Lion of Judah, they clung to their hard-won gains with claws of iron.

On my way to the embassy, I drove past two army jeeps with machine guns mounted on pivoting stands. The young soldiers peered through their goggles, their fingers poised on the triggers, as they watched suspiciously for any sign of rebellion among the crowds of young people milling near the university.

I shivered as I thought of the students I had seen slaughtered just two weeks ago. I had been driving near the Tobacco Monopoly where I intended to shop at a small vegetable stand and bakery. There had been no sign of trouble, although I never left home without wondering what I might do if something serious erupted.

Normally the sight of military jeeps would not have aroused my suspicion; however, when one sped by me nearly forcing my car into a gaping ditch, I had my first clue that something was amiss. I pulled to the side of the road to gather my wits. Moments later I noticed a students' demonstration and heard their chants against the government. Truckloads of soldiers suddenly appeared. It was obvious that they had no intention of peacefully dispersing the crowd of young people. Spilling from the backs of the cavernous trucks, hundreds of uniformed, armed soldiers ran in

*Details of the history of the revolution are found in *Ethiopia, Empire in Revolution,* by Marina and David Ottaway; © 1978 Africana Publishing Company, a division of Holmes and Meier Publishers, Inc.

all directions with their rifles blazing. The noise was deafening. I began to feel sick at my stomach and dizzy with fear. Traffic stood still, pedestrians fled in all directions, pack animals stood dumb as their owners ran for cover. The students, like limp rag dolls, began slumping onto the ground in scarlet pools of blood.

I felt the blood drain from my own face, and I became lightheaded. I thought I might faint. I covered my eyes and rested my head on the steering wheel of my car. I wanted to plug my ears so I couldn't hear the screaming and confusion, but I didn't want to uncover my eyes. I was mesmerized by fear. The thought of trying to start my car and flee from the scene didn't cross my mind.

Suddenly it was silent. Only then did I peer between my ice-cold fingers. Soldiers were lifting the limp, bloody bodies and throwing them carelessly into the trucks. I heard the huge engines turning over, and the gears grinding as the soldiers disappeared back into the canvas-covered trucks. The roadway was empty and silent. It was over.

My body shook involuntarily. My stomach began its own revolt. I opened the car door and the sour vomit spewed over the curb beside me. My hands shook as I turned the key in the ignition. Like a robot I drove away from the scene. I forgot about my shopping list and turned the car toward home.

The farther away I drove from the Tobacco Monopoly, the angrier I became. Didn't the students realize they were no longer demonstrating against the Emperor, who, like a benevolent old grandfather, had nervously tolerated their demonstrations?

Annually for as long as we had been in Ethiopia, the students had demonstrated every spring. I remembered it well, because during our first six years in Ethiopia we had lived in our Mission Headquarters two blocks from the university. I would watch the students from our fourth-floor apartment as they carried their placards and marched down the main street below our window, chanting communist slogans: "Land to the tiller. Free the masses!" The Emperor would dispatch the police backed up by a few soldiers. A few canisters of tear gas sent the students scurrying. Armed with their riot shields and clubs, the soldiers would hit a few heads, gather up the students, put them into huge military trucks, and drive them to a large, fenced-in fairground. The students were unloaded like cattle, then their heads were shaved and their shoes confiscated. After a few days of hard labor the students were sent home to frightened parents. The Emperor would make a radio speech, or, in later years, a television speech, imploring the young people to take their education more seriously, and admonishing them not to listen to the theories of the Marxists, who knew nothing about the practicalities of making a Marxist system work in Ethiopia. After his reprimand the students returned to school, and everything remained quiet until the following spring.

It was different now. Since the Derg had taken power and outlawed any type of demonstration, any move of dissent was dealt with swiftly and harshly.

I was happy that today the roads to the embassy appeared peaceful, and I felt relieved as I pulled up in front of the stalwart-looking gates of the American embassy. The neatly groomed Ethiopian guard pushed open the heavy iron gate as I shifted my little Volkswagen into low gear and waited for him to check my identification. As he walked toward my car, he recognized me and waved me through the gate.

The snack bar was noisy as usual. Hamburgers and hot dogs sizzled on the grill, the French fries bubbled in the deep fryer, making me hungrier than ever. After placing my order for lunch, I spotted an open table toward the back of the room and made my way through the maze of tables and talking people. Laughter rang out in the small room as a group of American men shared a joke. I liked to come here. It was like a small slice right out of America. I settled into my chair, waiting for my order. I was happy for a little time to recoup for my afternoon arts and crafts class and my meeting with Mrs. Casbone. I glanced around the room to see if I recognized anyone.

I spotted Carol's blonde hair behind the counter. She must have been back in her office when I ordered my lunch. She was the snack bar manager and had a small office behind the kitchen. Now she was busy with the phone orders. This was her busiest time of the day, but I knew that if she had a minute to spare she would come over and chat. She looked across the room, saw me, and waved. There had been many managers in the snack bar during our years in Ethiopia, but as far as I could recall, Carol was the friendliest. She knew almost everyone by name and had a big smile for all who came through the door. Carol's husband was an air force colonel and they had been stationed in Ethiopia for two years.

Waving again, she called across the crowded room, "Jodie, your hot dog and fries are ready."

"Here you go," she said, handing me my plate. "What can I get you to drink?"

"A Coke is fine. Can you get away for a few minutes?" I asked hopefully, as she handed me my Coke.

"Sure. Things are slowing down a bit now. Most of the phone orders are in. I'll be over in a couple of minutes. Anything wrong?" she asked, lowering her voice.

"No, I just wanted to chat for a few minutes before I have to go back to school."

I had just popped the last bite of hot dog into my mouth as she pulled out the chair next to me and flopped down.

"Whew! that feels good," She stretched her legs out in front of her. "What's new?"

"Not much really. This morning Mrs. Casbone, the Head-mistress at school, said she wanted to talk to me right after school today. For the life of me, I can't figure out what she wants to see me about. She seemed sort of upset."

Carol's giggle was contagious. "Do you have a guilty conscience, Jodie?" she asked jokingly. "It's probably nothing serious."

I laughed, too. "I'm more curious than worried, I guess."

Her smile and good nature made me feel better.

"Well, I'd better get back to school and get ready for my thirty little charges. We are painting this afternoon."

"Call me, Jodie, and let me know what Mrs. Casbone wanted to see you about."

"Sure. I'll call you this evening."

"Be careful going back to school, Jodie. Keep your head down." I knew she was reminding me about the shooting incident two weeks ago.

"I'll be careful; don't you worry."

C H A P T E R   T H R E E
Always Room for More

I survived finger painting with my afternoon class of first
graders. Just before the final bell, I sent the children to the
playground with my assistant, Elizabeth, so I could clean
and straighten my room. The final bell of the day found me
all packed and ready to turn the big skeleton key in the
ancient lock of my classroom door. Waving goodbye to the
children on the playground, I headed up the hill to the teachers' lounge to find Mrs. Casbone.

I was breathing deeply when I reached the office. I slowed
my pace the last few steps to catch my breath. The squeaky
wooden floor of the teachers' lounge announced my entrance. Mrs. Casbone was the only one in the room.

"Good afternoon, Mrs. Casbone. You wanted to see me?"

"Yes, Jodie, please come and sit down." She pointed to a
chair opposite hers.

I put my basket on an empty table and settled myself in a
chair across the table from her. She appeared much more
relaxed this afternoon.

"Jodie," she began slowly, "thank you for coming." The
furrows between her eyebrows deepened as she contemplat-
ed how to proceed. I waited.

She began haltingly at first. "Jodie, how long have you
and your husband been in Ethiopia?"

"Twelve years," I answered quickly, wishing she would get
directly to the point.

"You speak Amharic quite fluently, I understand?"

"Yes, Denton and I studied Amharic in the Cooperative Language Institute here in Addis when we first came to Ethiopia."

Then, almost without a breath, she poured out the reason she had wanted to see me.

"Jodie, do you think that you and your husband would be able to take three of the late Emperor's great-granddaughters into your home and care for them for a short time? Their parents were arrested with other members of the royal family and are in prison. The girls have been staying with Woz. Tsige, their aunt, since they were released from house arrest. Woz. Tsige described to me how the children were arrested along with their mothers and placed under house arrest. When they transferred the women to the women's prison, the children were released into the custody of their aunt. She has been caring for four children. Loly and Kokeb are sisters. They have an infant brother, Amaha. The fourth child is the oldest. She is a cousin to Loly, Kokeb, and Amaha. Her name is Menen."

She paused briefly, and I asked, "How long have the children been with Tsige?"

"She has had them for seventeen months. I'm certain Tsige would have continued to care for the girls; however, she had an accident several weeks ago. A light bulb exploded in her face, and she is going to require eye surgery. She will continue to care for Amaha, but she feels it would be much better if the girls were in a home with a family, and she prefers that whoever takes the children take all three of them. She would hate to see them divided up. Tsige is in the process of transferring the girls to the English School from Bingham Academy where they have been attending since their release from house arrest. Perhaps you are familiar with Bingham. It is a boarding school for missionary children."

I nodded, and decided not to distract her by adding that Shellie and Brent were students there.

She continued. "I understand it is not popular to identify with the Emperor's family at this time, but these are children, and perhaps you would be willing to help them?"

She paused again, and I understood she was waiting for my response. I was nearly speechless—something unusual for me! My usual response would have been to gather the children into my arms and head for home, but I checked my natural instinct and thought momentarily of the impact it might have on my husband and children if I walked into the house with three more children.

"Mrs. Casbone, perhaps I should discuss this with my husband and children and give you an answer tomorrow morning."

Relief flooded her face, and she grasped my hand. "Oh, yes, of course. Thank you, Jodie. Yes, indeed, talk it over with your family, and I will look forward to your answer tomorrow."

When she stood, I knew our meeting was over. "I will see you in the morning then," she concluded graciously.

"Yes, I will come to your office as soon as I arrive at school," I assured her.

I picked up my basket. Somehow it felt heavier than when I had walked into the room an hour earlier.

The little Volkswagen engine churned noisily as I headed out of the empty school parking lot. Making its third appearance of the day, the sun poked through the threatening monsoon clouds. Its warmth on my shoulder felt like a friendly companion.

The outside noises were only muffled sounds inside my car. It felt good to be alone and quiet. An interlude between my busy day in the classroom and my motherly responsibilities at home. Quiet! I smiled, thinking of the word. How could anyone be quiet on a busy boulevard with cars rushing by, trucks grinding their noisy gears, motorcycles darting in and out of traffic, their harsh engines insulting the environment, bicycle bells clanging as their erratic drivers zigzagged through the labyrinth of traffic congestion? These sounds I could shut out, unlike the voices of the children, husband, and servants: "Mom, where are you? Have you seen my reading book? Honey, where are my car keys? Mrs. Collins, did you bring home the milk we need for supper?"

Yes, the noise and confusion on the city streets could be ignored, but within the comfortable confines of my car, I wrestled with Mrs. Casbone's unusual request. How would Denton respond? Would he be as eager to take three more children into our home as I was? Would Shellie mind sharing her room with three more girls? I thought of the children's parents, locked away in some dark, dank prison cell. My heart went out to them. If I ever faced such a tragic upheaval in my life, I would hope and pray that Shellie and Brent would be well cared for, and that was what I wanted to do for these parents and children. Would my family understand?

How would Tolessa react? Even more than Shellie and Brent, Tolessa should understand. We had found him sleeping on the doorstep of our mission when he was only six or seven years old. Certainly the sight of starving, homeless children was common in Addis Ababa. It was just one of the most difficult adjustments I had had to make when I first went to Ethiopia. Overwhelming poverty faced us each time we left the mission compound. This time it had arrived right on our doorstep. It was our first morning of Vacation Bible School, so it must have been in July, nearly ten years ago now. We lived in the Headquarters building then. The monsoon rains had begun in June, and the weather was cold and damp.

The night guard was just leaving, and Berhanu, the day guard, was just opening the front doors of the mission. As I passed by on the way to my office, I saw a bundle lying on the steps. It wasn't until I walked closer to it that I saw it was a young child, still sleeping. As if he sensed me standing there looking at him, he sat up, rubbing his red, infected eyes. He pulled the tiny, ragged cloth around his shivering body and eyed me suspiciously. Although it hurt me even to look at him, I tried to smile and greet him. He quickly looked away and ignored my greeting.

We began our Bible classes for the children at nine o'clock. The singing had just begun when I heard a child screaming at the top of his lungs in the church foyer. I quickly left the room to see what was happening. Just as I entered the foyer, I saw the guard walking toward the door, carrying the little boy who had been sleeping on the steps.

"What's wrong, Berhanu?"

"This little urchin was trying to come into the church, Mrs. Collins."

"Oh, I see. Well, let him down, and I will talk to him."

"He doesn't speak Amharic, Mrs. Collins, only Gallenia."

That suddenly explained why the child had ignored my greeting earlier that morning. Not wanting to turn the child away, I asked Berhanu to tell him to follow me into Joseph's office. Joseph was Galla and would be able to talk to him. I took the youngster's hand in mine, and he followed along quietly.

I knocked gently on Joseph's office door. I was not sure he would be there, since he sometimes went directly to the government ministries if Denton had some errand for him to do before he came to work. He had been Denton's assistant for nearly ten years. I was relieved to hear Joseph's voice.

"Come in," he called in Amharic.

He greeted me warmly. Joseph and I were good friends. He was such a kind, caring person. I hadn't always understood that; in fact, when I had first met him, during my first months in Ethiopia, we had had quite an argument. Neither of us could recall what it was about, but we were to the point that we could laugh about it whenever either of us recalled the incident. He loved our whole family, and Shellie tagged after him, begging him for pencils, paper, paper clips, anything that would occupy her while she sat at his desk or at a small desk-like table he arranged for her beside his desk.

Joseph looked at the young boy beside me, and I explained where I had found him and that he didn't speak Amharic. The boy stared at the floor. Joseph began talking to him slowly and gently. The child's voice was barely audible.

Finally Joseph turned back to me. "He says his name is Tolessa, and his village is far from the city. He isn't certain of his age, but he said that his father left home right after he was born, and that his mother had many other children besides him. A man came to their village and promised to bring Tolessa to the city to attend school. Instead, he made a slave out of Tolessa. For months Tolessa has done nothing but carry sheep to the marketplace."

Joseph lifted the threadbare wrap from the child's shoulders. I gasped at the gaping, red, infected flesh obviously worn away by the weight of the heavy sheep he had been carrying to the market.

"He says he hasn't eaten for several days, Mrs. Collins. What should we do?"

"Keep him here with you for a minute," I said as I turned to leave the office. I hurried upstairs to our apartment, returning a few minutes later with a few coins.

"Take him next door to the restaurant and order him something to eat, Joseph."

I had been warned by veteran missionaries never to become involved in a situation like this. It was possible that tomorrow morning I would find dozens of hungry, homeless children sleeping on the mission steps if word got out that I had fed Tolessa. No matter! I could not stand the sight of this hungry, pitiful child.

That was just the beginning. That night Denton gave Tolessa a clean blanket and money to buy food. He allowed Tolessa to sleep inside the locked doors where he would be safe.

During the days that followed, Denton found odd jobs for Tolessa around the mission. We cleared out a storeroom in the basement, and made him a comfortable room to stay in. We bought him two new outfits of clothes, and he began eating all of his meals with us. I couldn't believe how rapidly he learned Amharic. In September we registered him in a private mission school near our Headquarters building.

Tolessa had lived with us more than a year when Brent was born. He and Tolessa were like brothers. Brent called him Titi. By the time we moved out of the Headquarters building six years later, Tolessa was like a family member, and, of course, he moved with us. He was in tenth grade now. It seemed impossible that this tall, lean, handsome young man who could communicate in fluent English could be the same little boy we had found sleeping on our doorstep ten years ago.

I didn't think Tolessa would particularly object to the three girls' coming to live with us, but I did wonder if he might feel somewhat threatened, considering the fact that they were members of the royal family. I guessed I would find out soon enough.

I pulled up in front of our big black gate and honked for Assefa, our day guard, to open the gate. Nearly everyone in Ethiopia lived within the confines of a compound surrounded by a tall fence of some kind. In the countryside it might only be thorn bushes circling a cluster of thatched roof huts or corrugated tin nailed to a eucalyptus frame to ward off hyenas that preyed upon the cows, sheep, and chickens. In Addis Ababa most homes and embassies had a six-foot stone wall. Thieves were prevalent in the city, and the walls alone would not keep them out. A night and day guard were usually employed, and along with two or three guard dogs, they guarded against intruders.

In spite of all our precautions—high walls lined with jagged glass, guards, four dogs—we were robbed on one occasion. It wasn't unusual for the night guard to awaken us with his whistling or calling to a neighboring night guard. This was usually a sign that he suspected thieves nearby and it served to warn us as well as to alert the thief that the guard was awake and watching for any intrusion. Occasionally Assefa would suspect a gang of thieves working together. One thief would distract the dogs, another the guard, and a third would try to scale the wall. If Assefa suspected such a situation, he would knock on our door and Denton would go out on the porch and fire his shotgun. This was the best deterrent, and would send the thieves scurrying off to some less suspecting compound. Since the revolution, however, it was illegal to own a gun, and Denton was reluctant to use his to discourage thieves. In fact, he kept it well hidden in case our house was searched.

As Assefa pushed open the heavy gate for me, our four dogs bolted through the opening, chasing the grazing animals outside our gate. In Ethiopia, homes are fenced, not pastures. The people's animals graze wherever they can find grass. Young shepherd children were playing in the meadow next to our house. When the dogs charged toward their unsuspecting sheep and cows, the children chased the dogs back to our compound.

I glanced toward our garage as I pulled into the driveway. Denton's car was not there, so I knew he and the children weren't home yet. Feyesa came running out of the back door to help me carry my paraphernalia into the house. During our twelve years in Ethiopia, I had hired and fired many servants. I considered them a necessary bother. I had difficulty living with them, but life was worse without them. However, Feyesa was different and was by far the family's favorite. He had worked for us seven years now, and we got along beautifully.

He shooed the dogs away from the car and lifted my cumbersome basket from the back seat.

"Has Mr. Collins called to say when he will be home, Feyesa?"

"Yes, Mrs. Collins, he said he was going to get Shellie and Brent at school, and he would be home by six o'clock," he answered in Amharic.

Feyesa knew only a few words of English. He had worked for an American military family stationed in Addis Ababa before he had come to work for us. His favorite English saying was directed at Shellie and Brent when they had been naughty. Waving my wooden spoon, which served as the household paddle, he would say, "If you don't be good, Mommy is going to get you with the B-52 when she come home!" There was always a twinkle in his eye, and though he tried to keep a straight face, it lasted only until Shellie and Brent broke into laughter. As hilarious as it was, the children usually refrained from any more mischief, knowing Feyesa wasn't reluctant to report their misdeeds.

Feyesa carried my things into the house. After I had washed my hands, changed clothes, and settled into my favorite chair in the living room, Feyesa brought me a steaming cup of lemon tea. Sipping the hot liquid, I watched the tall eucalyptus swaying like graceful Ethiopian folk dancers. Just beyond the trees the swollen brown river wound its rumbling way through the forest while the sloping hillsides angled gently downward to meet the river's muddy edge. I watched as the farmers worked the deep, rich soil, coveting the final few minutes of daylight and enjoying the brief respite from the rain showers that had pummeled their fields off and on all day. Their crops of cabbage and chard lay in neat little furrows ready for harvest. Early Saturday morning the farmers would pile their vegetables onto their donkeys' backs and herd them across town to the marketplace.

There are so many paradoxes in this country, I mused. The ancient and the modern exist side by side, and nowhere is it more evident than right here, visible from my living room window. I sat in my warm, comfortable, modern home and watched these hardworking men coax their very existence from the soil with handhewn wooden plows drawn by cantankerous brahma bulls, the farmer's most costly possession. They harvested with their sharp, crudely made scythes and transported their wares on the backs of donkeys each Saturday to the largest outdoor market in East Africa.

Would communism be able to close the gap between the rich and the poor, the old ways and the new? "*Hebrettesebawinet*," the people chanted whenever they gathered in Red Square. It meant "Ethiopian socialism." The Derg had defined *Hebrettesebawinet* as equality, self-reliance, the dignity of labor, the supremacy of the common good, and the indivisibility of Ethiopian unity.

I thought of Mao of China and his unsuccessful cultural revolution. Ethiopia, like China, was an ancient culture, and I could think of nowhere outside of India where a society was more stratified than Ethiopia. Equality in any culture is a noble goal. However, Ethiopia's class and status consciousness would make it difficult to achieve quickly. From an Emperor who had considered himself the elect of God to the freed slaves, there were numerous degrees of rank—the landowning peasants, peasants who did not own lands, tennants living on the estates of the wealthier peasants, nobles, agricultural laborers. Below all of these were the weavers, minstrels, common soldiers, and beggars. Lower yet were the metalsmiths, potters, and tanners. Of course, the recent land reform, more sweeping in its scope than anyone had anticipated, had certainly equalized everyone on that score. All land had been nationalized. No one could own land.

When it came to self-reliance I couldn't help wondering if any third-world country could be self-reliant. The Emperor had been as dependent on the United States as his successors were on the Soviet Union and Cuba.

I heard the horn of Denton's car and my mind was brought sharply back to the moment at hand and my earlier conversation with Mrs. Casbone. I hurried into the kitchen through the swinging door. I watched from the kitchen window as Denton's large frame emerged from his car. Shellie and Brent wrestled the dogs to the ground, as Feyesa ran to greet them and carry their school bags into the house.

Shellie is getting so tall and thin. She is going to be a beautiful young lady, I thought proudly, as I watched her run to the horse corral and rub her horse's nose. Brent was still on the ground, surrounded by all four dogs. I could see only his blond hair as he pulled one dog after another down around him.

Waiting for Denton to come into the house, I busied myself at the stove, stirring the mashed potatoes and checking the delicious roast chicken Feyesa had prepared for dinner.

"Hi, hon," Denton said, coming into the kitchen. "How was your day?"

"It was different," I responded, as he gave me a gentle hug and kissed me on the cheek. "Why doesn't Feyesa fix us some hot tea, and we can talk while he gets dinner on the table?" I suggested, eager to share my news with him.

"That sounds good. I'll be right in as soon as I wash my hands and put on my slippers."

I felt like a lioness waiting for her prey as I went back into the living room.

"You said your day was different," Denton remarked, settling his tall frame into his favorite green swivel chair. He stretched his long legs out in front of him as I handed him a cup of tea.

"What did you mean?" he coaxed curiously.

Denton listened intently to my recounting of my conversation with Mrs. Casbone. I watched him carefully as I concluded, hoping he would give me some clue to what he was thinking. He was very thoughtful and quiet for a few minutes, and neither one of us spoke. Unable to wait any longer, I broke the silence.

"Well, what do you think about having them come and stay with us for awhile, Denton?"

Instead of telling me what he thought, he returned the question to me.

"What do you think about it?"

"I want to do it!" I answered excitedly and without hesitation.

"You are working full time now. Don't you think three more children would be a little too much for you to handle?"

"No, Denton. We have Feyesa, and if it is too much work for him, we can hire someone else to help him. Just how much work can three little girls add, anyway?"

Before Denton had time to say anything else, Feyesa called us to dinner. Hoping for an answer before we went to the kitchen, I asked, "Do you really object to their coming to stay for awhile, Denton? Mrs. Casbone said it would be for only a short time."

"I'm wondering if there would be any political ramifications against the Mission."

"Political ramifications! Denton, we are discussing three little girls. They aren't adults!"

As we went into the kitchen, I knew the decision had still not been made. Tolessa, Shellie, and Brent were seated at the table when we walked into the kitchen. When I sat down, Tolessa leaned over and kissed me on the cheek.

"How was your day, Mom?" he asked in perfect English.

"It was interesting. How about yours?"

After Denton asked the blessing, all the family started to talk about their various activities during the day. I waited for a lull in the conversation to tell them about mine.

When my chance came, I explained the whole conversation in as much detail as I could remember and concluded by saying, ". . . and they go to your school, Shellie and Brent. Do you know them?"

"Oh, I know them, Mom," Shellie said in her usual enthusiastic way. "I see their chauffeur drop them off each morning when Daddy takes Brent and me. The little one is in Brent's class. She is really cute. I think her name is Kokeb. Her sister, Loly, is stuck up. She's in my class. I don't know the other one very well, but she is in my class, too. She's quiet and doesn't talk to anyone but Loly and Kokeb. She is their cousin, isn't she? Oh, I remember. Her name is Menen."

"Well, if you don't like Loly, you wouldn't want her sharing your bedroom," I reasoned.

"Oh, I don't mind, Mommy. Can they all sleep in my bedroom?" she asked eagerly.

"There would be nowhere else for them to sleep."

"Mom," Brent interjected, "why do we have to get all girls? Can't we get some boys, too?"

I couldn't help but laugh. As usual, Brent's sense of humor made us all chuckle. I saw the twinkle in his eye and knew he was teasing. His half-smile always gave him away.

Tolessa, like Denton, said very little.

I'm not certain when the decision was made about the girls' coming. After dinner no one brought it up again.

The next morning at breakfast I waited for some reaction. Only Shellie asked where they would all sleep, since she only had a single bed.

Looking at Denton I said, "I was thinking of asking Mrs. Casbone to lend us two sets of bunk beds. The English School used to be a boarding school, and they have all the old dorm furniture in the storeroom. I've seen it there. What do you think about that, Denton? Would two sets fit into Shellie's room?"

"I don't see any problem with that. We have an old dresser up at the Headquarters building that would probably fit in there, too. I could bring that home."

I assumed the decision had been made at that point, and I could hardly wait to get to school to tell Mrs. Casbone.

She received the news enthusiastically. The worry and strain I had seen in her face yesterday were gone. She made a list of the things I suggested to her that I might need to accommodate the three youngsters and offered to have the school driver deliver them. After I gave her directions to our home, she told me that another aunt of the children wanted to meet with me and discuss the final details. I suggested we meet together during my lunch break at her earliest convenience.

A week later I met with Kali. She was younger than I had imagined she would be, possibly in her thirties. It was difficult to tell the age of Ethiopian women. They rarely looked as old as they were. Kali spoke impeccable English and was very pleasant and gracious. She explained briefly how difficult it had been on the children, particularly Menen, since they had been separated from their mothers. The day-to-day uncertainty about their mothers' and fathers' future was a great strain on the children, she said.

"When people come to Woz. Tsige's, where the children are living now, they inevitably talk about the parents. The children hear this constantly, and I personally think it will be good for them to be completely removed from this atmosphere for a time. They are so weary of it all. I cannot tell you, Mrs. Collins, how much we appreciate what you are doing."

"Please, Kali, it is no more than what anyone would do, given the same opportunity to help. I am pleased that I was asked to do it. When is it best for the girls to come to us?"

"Would a week from today be too early for you, Mrs. Collins?"

"No, not at all. Mrs. Casbone is making arrangements for us to get additional beds and a larger kitchen table."

"Oh, that is fine. Perhaps it would be more convenient for everyone involved if Woz. Tsige brings the children on Saturday week."

I knew she meant a week from Saturday, and I quickly agreed. That was the last time I saw Kali for nearly a year.

CHAPTER FOUR
Our Family Increases

The whole family was excited about the girls' imminent arrival. I suspected even Tolessa was caught up in the excitement of the day. He hadn't left to visit his friends as he usually did on Saturday morning. In fact, he had been helping Denton set up bunk beds, give them a fresh coat of paint, and rearrange Shellie's bedroom with all the freshly painted furniture.

Hagop and Hrip, our Armenian friends, owned a drapery and upholstery shop. The new curtains and bedspreads were their labor of love. They had no children of their own, but they had virtually adopted Shellie and Brent, and the children called them Aunt Hrip and Uncle Hagop. They had been as excited as we were about the children coming to stay with us.

Shellie had been fluttering around her room all morning. She had already decided which bunk she wanted. Like a sentinel, Brent paced up and down in front of the kitchen window, then paused to survey the tree-lined lane. As Feyesa worked in the kitchen, Brent plagued him with questions, "When are they coming, Feyesa? Where are they? How come they don't get here?" Brent's vigil continued until Feyesa said teasingly in broken English. "You big boy now. You have three new sisters. You the big brother."

Before Brent had time to contradict Feyesa he saw a car

coming down the road. "Here they come. Mom, Dad! Quick, here they come!" We all hurried into the kitchen and watched the big Land Rover as it approached our gate. The dogs began barking as they heard the car approaching. Assefa opened the gates, and the dogs disappeared in search of the grazing animals.

I called to Assefa, "Tie up the dogs, Assefa." I didn't want them to frighten the girls or their aunt.

Bowing politely and shaking our hands as we welcomed her to our home, the aunt greeted us warmly and introduced herself. The three little girls sat quietly in the back seat of the Land Rover, reluctant to get out of the car. Their bright Byzantine eyes took in all of their new surroundings.

I wondered what their thoughts were about coming to live with a new family. Were they frightened or angry? I wanted to take them into my arms and tell them everything was going to be fine, but I knew I would have to wait for the right time.

"Come in. Come in," Denton said cheerfully, leading the way into our home with an armful of suitcases and shopping bags he had helped Woz. Tsige lift from the back of the Land Rover. Feyesa ran to help him. Shellie coaxed the girls from the back seat, offering to help them carry their last few items into the house.

"You are staying in my room with me," she said, trying to start a conversation. "Come and let me show you." She was so excited and radiant. The girls followed her into the house. They seemed so fragile, like porcelain dolls. Their hair was cut short, and under their beautiful eyes there were dark circles, the only hint of strain or anxiety that they must have been feeling with the constant changes taking place in their young lives. My heart ached for them.

As I led the way into the living room, Shellie and the girls disappeared into the bedroom to unpack and settle in. Feyesa bustled around the kitchen, fixing coffee and cookies. He loved company as much as I did, and even though it always meant extra work for him, he seemed to thrive on it.

Woz. Tsige was dressed in black with her hair tied neatly in a black scarf. I assumed she was still in mourning for the Emperor and other family members who had been executed. Most middle-aged Ethiopian women never wore any other color. When a family member or friend died, custom required that they wear black for one year. By middle age it seemed someone would pass away every year, and the woman was constantly in mourning. Woz. Tsige wore her sunglasses even in the house, and I was reminded of her eye injury, sustained when the light bulb exploded in her face. When I asked her about the surgery, she was still uncertain about the date. We spoke only in Amharic.

Late in the afternoon she asked me to call the girls into the living room. They came quietly and stood respectfully before her. With great dignity and sincerity, she admonished them to be on their best behavior and reassured them that they were in the care of a wonderful Christian family where they would be loved and well cared for. The girls stood bravely until she kissed them goodbye, and then silent tears rolled down the delicate golden cheeks. I went to their side and put my arms around them as I had wanted to do all day. "We will be fine. We are going to have a wonderful time together. We will be one big, happy family."

We all walked with Woz. Tsige to her car and said our final goodbyes. She told me that she would pick the girls up at the English School on Friday afternoon so they could spend the weekend with her.

We watched her drive down the lane, and then the girls followed Shellie back into their bedroom. I followed them in and asked if they had everything they needed. They were very shy and quiet, but Loly, obviously the spokesperson for the other two, assured me they were very comfortable and needed nothing.

After dinner that evening, Denton went into the girls' room and read them a bedtime story. I smiled as I saw Brent follow his dad into the bedroom and crawl up beside Shellie on her new top bunk.

Much later, as I lay in bed, I realized how tired I was. As the tension eased from my body and I began to doze, I heard the children giggling in the hallway. I listened carefully, wondering what they were doing. As their laughter came closer to our bedroom, I sat up in bed. Suddenly Shellie poked her head into our room and whispered, "Mom, are you asleep?"

"No, Shellie, what is it?"

"Mom, the girls want to know what to call you and Dad."
"Oh." I smiled to myself. "Well, they can call us Mr. and
Mrs. Collins, or Aunt Jodie and Uncle Denton. Or maybe
they want to call us Mom and Dad. Whatever they are comfortable with is fine with us."

With that, I heard them all giggling again as they returned
to their bedroom, "Mom, Dad, Mom, Dad," they whispered
again and again—and then more giggles.

On that February night in 1976, no one could have fore-
seen that we would be like parents to them for many years
to come.

It was a new beginning for all of us. It wouldn't be our last
beginning.

The children's transition was not abrupt. For several weeks
the girls spent each weekend with their Aunt Tsige, who
was now settled into one of Princess Sebele's homes in Addis
Ababa. The new government had confiscated Tsige's home
and coffee plantation in the countryside as well as her other
properties. The Derg had impounded all of the royal family's
personal property and possessions. They had, however,
made an exception and allowed Tsige to live in one of Princess Sebele's homes since she was caring for the Princess's
children, Loly, Kokeb, and Amaha, and her niece, Menen.

Each Friday afternoon Tsige dispatched Menen's elderly
nanny, Ruth, to the English School to bring the girls home by
taxi. Ruth's wrinkled old face bobbed up and down as she
bowed respectfully each time I approached her. I usually
volunteered to drive Ruth and the children to Tsige's house
unless I had a previous appointment.

On the way home, Ruth's chatter would provide me with
interesting insights into the royal family. Her loyalty to the
family remained undiminished in spite of their present dilemma. She had recently visited the women in prison, and
she told me with horror of their surroundings and physical
condition. Always aware of the children's presence in the
back seat, she talked in hushed tones, hoping they would not
overhear her.

"The Princesses have been in prison since September
1975. That's when they transferred them from the Villa

where they were under house arrest to that horrible Akaki prison. It's called 'The End of the World' prison, you know!" She shook her head in utter disgust as she continued to describe the women's sordid living conditions.

"They are being held in a former clinic, a white stone house with a cement floor and bars on the window, and they all suffer from arthritis, you know. There are only two small rooms and there are fifteen women of the royal family imprisoned in there. Neither of the rooms has beds, only mattresses spread out on the floor, and no other furniture or heating. It's too cold, much too cold for them. They have been sick the whole time. And their rooms are full of rats, lice, and cockroaches. The toilet is a primitive hole in the floor with a barrel of water sitting beside it. Can you imagine! No matter how much they scrub, clean, and disinfect it, they say there is a terrible stench. They always ask us to send them bathroom spray, but it helps very little."

During another drive home on Friday afternoon she complained bitterly, "They are not allowed weekly visitors like the common prisoners. We have been allowed into the prison only once, and they can receive their food only once a day."

Ruth explained to me that the aunt received 120 Ethiopian dollars per month, approximately $60 U.S., supposedly in compensation for their confiscated property. This was to provide the prisoners with food, since the prison took no responsibility for feeding the prisoners.

"Only a few books, magazines, and materials for needlework and knitting are permitted to be brought into the prison," Ruth continued. "And visits from priests are forbidden, too."

When Ruth told me of the women's continued request for tranquilizers, painkillers, and sleeping pills, it confirmed my worst fears and suspicions regarding their physical and mental state. *Just how long could these women survive under such gruesome and depressing conditions?* I asked myself. I felt certain that a day didn't pass when Loly, Kokeb, and Menen didn't ask themselves the same question. The women had been in prison for eighteen months now, and it didn't appear likely that they would ever be brought to trial but rather left to die of neglect, much like the rumored death of the Emperor on August 22, 1975, after a serious prostate surgery.

I knew that most of the women political prisoners were wives, daughters, and mothers of former government ministers and other prominent people, many of whom had been imprisoned as "hostages" against the behavior of their relatives. Some of the prisoners had no political significance other than that their husband, father, or brother was wanted for conspiring against the new government. That was the case with approximately twenty-five girls aged twelve through nineteen, held in the Akaki prison in the room next to Princess Sebele and her sisters, Princesses Sophie, Ruth, Sara, and Aida, Menen's mother. Also imprisoned in the same cell with her daughters was the Emperor's daughter, Princess Tegneworke. How a woman in her seventies could endure such harsh treatment was beyond my comprehension!

I had a secret list of the names of 362 political prisoners, all fairly well known, held in Addis Ababa, mostly in three prisons. Most of us suspected this was only a partial list of the total number of political prisoners throughout Ethiopia. Besides the ones in prisons there were political prisoners being held in police stations, military camps, and "correction centers." The labor camps or "correction centers" were established to punish students during the rural literacy campaign of 1974-1975. I had heard of one maximum security concentration camp just recently completed in the Ogaden Desert where conditions were much harsher than in Addis Ababa. Unlike the bitter cold of Russia's Siberia, the devastating temperatures of the Ogaden soared to 120 or 130 degrees. It was a waterless wilderness covered with thorns, scorned by most Ethiopians, who preferred the cooler highlands.

I had also heard reports about two hundred prisoners at the Fourth Army Division Headquarters where they had imprisoned the Emperor. These were mostly actors and theater workers arrested after a demonstration. I thought it was funny that they were allowed to take their own beds and some books and magazines to prison with them. They were allowed to go to the toilet only twice a day, once in the early morning and again in the late afternoon. At these times they were marched single file to a latrine outside their cells. At other times they had to use bottles left in their cells, and these became full very rapidly and overflowed. Often those who made special requests for medical treatment or refused to obey orders of the guards were severely punished. I had heard most of these reports of the prison conditions first hand when detainees were released from the tightly guarded prisons. Occasionally such news was reported by a prison guard. Only a few released prisoners told of torture of the prisoners. They said not all political prisoners were tortured, and probably very few prominent Ethiopians suffered physical torture, but in my mind, the emotional torture was as cruel.

The alleged leaders of members of the secessionist movements or anti-government groups were the most likely to suffer physical torture. Torture was rumored to take place at the Third Police Station in Addis Ababa, the Security office headquarters in Addis, and in certain other police stations and military detention centers in different parts of Ethiopia.

Young people, particularly students, told of cruel, inhumane, and degrading treatment carried out against them. Some told of severe beatings with rifle butts, truncheons, sticks, clubs, and rubber hose and kicking with heavy boots, also the use of electric shocks, various degrading punishments, and sexual abuse, as well as the pulling out of toe and finger nails.

When I heard of such atrocities, anger welled up within me until my stomach burned as if an unquenchable fire roared through my intestines. There seemed to be no way to fight such cruel, degrading treatment.

One Sunday afternoon not long after the children came to live with us, they returned from their aunt's with exciting news. Hurrying into the house to greet me, they were radiant.

"Mommy, Enataye has seen our father."

I knew "Enataye" was what they called Tsige, and I joined them in their excitement.

All three gathered around me and talked at once. When

Shellie and Brent heard their excited voices, they called Denton and we all gathered together in the living room to hear the good news.

"The Derg gave her permission, and she even got to take Amaha with her. Maybe we will get to visit him next time!"

"That's marvelous," I chimed in, and then we all began asking questions at once, "Was your father well? Was he able to talk freely to your aunt or were there prison guards listening to everything?"

Loly disappeared into the bedroom briefly and returned with several pieces of paper. She proudly showed us pictures her father had drawn and had sent with Tsige for each of the children. They were lovely drawings done in colored pencils. I knew these were precious treasures and, for the present, their only link with another time—that time when they had all been together, united as a family—a time that so much of us take for granted.

Later that evening during dinner, Loly's mind was still on her father.

"Daddy has been in prison for nearly two years," she reminisced. "He was on his way to Wollege where we used to live, when the soldiers stopped him and took him to prison. We never saw him again after that. He used to be governor of Wollege, and we used to live there. That was before Grandpa made him Minister of Agriculture."

I knew that "Grandpa" was Emperor Haile Selassie. Loly's pride in both her father and great-grandfather was undisguised and yet childlike. As she continued, her voice began to quiver, and her eyes filled with the inevitable tears. She looked down at her plate, embarrassed by the unexpected deluge streaming down her cheeks. Fumbling in the cuff of her sweater, she took a tissue and began dabbing the tears, trying to regain her composure.

Seeing her sister's discomfort, Kokeb came to her rescue. Drawing our attention away from Loly, Kokeb added, "Daddy was president of the university once, too." Not sure what else to say, Kokeb became silent, too.

Everyone was uncomfortable with the silence that followed, and no one knew what to say. I was happy when Denton intervened with a humorous story about how I was

almost arrested the first time I saw the Emperor in person.
"We didn't know that it was against the law to point
toward the Emperor. When Mom saw him for the first time,
she was so excited she pointed at him and said, 'Oh there he
is!' About four soldiers in the Emperor's personal bodyguard
grabbed her and scared her to death. We were both speechless as they told her never to point at him again. For a
moment I thought they might arrest her. I've never seen
Mom so quiet!"

Everyone laughed and the tension was broken.

The small monsoon rains of February and March subsided, and the warm weather returned. We began planning
weekend trips to our favorite picnic, camping, and swimming spots, Sodere and Lake Lagano. More often we went to
Sodere, because it was only a two-hour drive from Addis,
and we loved the large swimming pool filled by the lovely,
naturally warm springs. At Lake Langano we had to swim
in the lake, and it was a six-hour drive from Addis. We
usually saved Lake Langano trips for the summer holiday,
when we could camp for a week or more.

The girls began looking forward to these outings with our
family, and their weekends with Tsige became less frequent.

It was good to see the girls more relaxed. Menen was still
very quiet and spoke only when I spoke to her, and then in a
whisper that was barely audible. I usually had to ask her to
repeat her answer two or three times just in order to hear
her. My concern for Menen grew as the months passed and
she didn't seem to communicate any differently. One day I
expressed my concern to a Dutch lady who had known the
royal family for years and had worked with Princess Sebele
at the Ethiopian Women's Welfare Organization before the
princess was imprisoned. Miss van de Loo came frequently
to visit the children, and I knew she was concerned about
their well-being. I was relieved that she was also deeply
concerned. She explained that Menen had always been very
quiet, but that it had become more serious after Princess
Aida and Menen were separated and the princess was transferred to Akaki prison. I agreed to have Menen checked at a
local hospital to make sure there was nothing physically
wrong with her throat or possibly her hearing. As often as I

asked Menen why she didn't talk out loud, she said she was talking as loudly as anyone else.

The day I took her for her physical she was frightened. It was the first time she talked to me without my first addressing her. "Mommy," she said, almost squeezing my hand in two from fright, "are you going to leave me here?"

My heart went out to her. "Oh, no, Mini," I assured her. "You will just have a checkup, and we will go home. Maybe we'll stop and buy you something special on our way home."

She smiled as if the idea pleased her, but she didn't murmur another word during her examination.

I was very happy that the children remained so healthy. Menen, short for her age, was stockier than Loly, Kokeb, and Shellie. I was pleased when Loly and Kokeb began to put on a little weight.

The only other time we had to go to the hospital was when Menen fell off a swing. I thought her arm was broken, and rushed her to the emergency room at the Seventh Day Adventist Hospital. It was another one of those rare times when Menen spoke in the presence of an adult without being spoken to. Her eyes as big as two caramel apples, she watched as the x-ray technician focused the x-ray equipment over her arm. Finally she looked at me and, nearly in tears, asked, "Mommy, what are they going to do with that machine?"

"They are only going to take a picture of your arm, Mini. It is like a big camera. It won't hurt you, dear." I sat beside her until the man had adjusted everything, and then he asked me to leave while he took the x-ray. Menen squeezed my hand and whispered, "Please, Mommy, don't go."

"I must, dear. Be brave. Remember, you get a special treat on the way home."

That was how I had always bribed Shellie and Brent when they had vaccinations, x-rays, or their physicals. Menen was the envy of the household when she walked in with a big box of Smarties, a chocolate-covered candy like American M & M's. She had long forgotten her fears of the x-ray equipment and the doctor. Her arm had not been broken, just badly sprained. She wore it in a sling for two weeks and then was as good as new. Only her voice never improved.

I was certain she could talk. I had heard her in the bedroom with the other children, talking as normally as any of them. I was only concerned that she never talked to adults. Her teachers at the English School began expressing their concern. The best I could do was to ask them not to press her and add more stress. I hoped that given time the problem would resolve itself.

One Friday as we came out of school, Ruth, Menen's nanny, was waiting to take the children to Tsige's. It had been several weeks since they had visited. Tsige not only liked to have them home occasionally to visit with them herself, but she wanted them to come for Amaha's sake. Tsige didn't want Loly and Kokeb's little brother to forget his sisters and cousin. Amaha had come with Tsige on several occasions when she had visited the girls at our house. He was adorable, and I always wished she would let him come and stay with us, too.

I offered, as usual, to drive Ruth and the girls to Tsige's, and Ruth just bobbed up and down, obviously pleased with my offer. During our ride Ruth began talking about Menen's father, Ras Mengesha. Ruth had been one of Menen's five brothers' nanny many years before Menen's birth, so I knew she had been with the family a long time. Ruth looked over her shoulder from time to time to make sure the girls were still engrossed in their own conversation and not listening to us.

Lowering her voice she said, "He escaped from the palace at Mekele just hours before the soldiers came to arrest him."

Besides being married to the Emperor's granddaughter, Princess Aida, Ras Mengesha was governor of Tigre Province, one of the largest provinces in northern Ethiopia, and was one of the Emperor's closest advisors. Before the Emperor had come to power and united the thirteen provinces, each province had been a small, independent feudal kingdom. Ras Mengesha's great-grandfather had ruled Tigre.

As governor of Tigre, Ras Mengesha had gained a great deal of respect from the people. He worked hard to establish cottage industries and to stave off the threatening famine that loomed over most of northern Ethiopia.

Ruth talked as though Ras Mengesha were the coming

messiah. Having heard many others talk about him, I knew she wasn't alone in her belief that Ras Mengesha and his recently formed Ethiopian Democratic Union would sweep down from the mountains surrounding the capital city and restore peace and tranquillity to this once sleepy mountain kingdom.

I always thought of how it would help Menen to see her father again. Even a message from him would help. If she could just hear from him, perhaps some of her confidence and hope would be restored. At this point she didn't even know for certain he was alive, although his picture was posted all over the capital city and countryside as one of the Most Wanted Men in Ethiopia. The present government feared him and wanted him dead or behind bars. We had never heard a word from him, and in some ways I was glad. As it was, we suspected that our phone was tapped and our mail censored just because we had Ras Mengesha's daughter living with us, not to mention the fact that the girls were all the great-grandchildren of the deposed Emperor.

C H A P T E R F I V E
The Tension Builds

One morning as the three girls and I arrived at the English School, the parking lot was teeming with army jeeps and soldiers. My first instinct was to turn my car around and leave. Instead, I pulled into my parking spot, turned off the motor, and listened. Everything appeared quiet; however, my fears ran rampant as I wondered if the soldiers were looking for the girls.

"Loly, you stay in the car with Menen and Kokeb. I want to see what is happening before you go to your classes."

As I neared the teachers' lounge, I saw two soldiers leading Ababa, a young Ethiopian lady, out of her classroom. Other armed soldiers were positioned all over the courtyard. I could hardly believe that they had come in such force to arrest only one woman.

Ababa was a teaching assistant, and she had worked at the school since her own graduation four years ago. We had talked many times during our morning break. Just last week she had confided in me that her husband had been arrested.

The soldiers were walking toward me. They were unusually abrupt and rough as they pushed Ababa in the direction of the parking lot. Her hands were handcuffed behind her back, and her head was lowered. All I could think of was returning to the girls before that horde of roughnecks got there. I turned and walked hastily back to the car.

"Come on, girls, quickly! Get out of the car and come with me! Leave your things here for now. I will get them later. Come on, come with me!" I nearly pulled them around the corner of the building. I didn't want them to see Ababa as the soldiers put her into the military jeep and drove away. They had experienced enough of that kind of thing first-hand when they were arrested two years ago.

I was relieved when we cleared the end of the building before the soldiers and Ababa came into sight from the opposite direction.

"They were arresting Ababa," I whispered, as we neared their wing of the building. "It is better if you don't talk about this kind of thing with your friends. If anyone asks you about it, just say you didn't see anything and try to change the subject. It's best if you don't become involved in any political discussions," I reminded them. It wasn't the first time I had admonished them to avoid political discussions. It was too easy for things we said to be misconstrued and used against us. The children's political situation was volatile enough without their being led innocently into some political discussion that could later backfire. They were very loyal to their family. Their feelings could easily be aroused when teachers with communist leanings led in heated talks against the Emperor and his family. Loly had come home on more than one occasion depressed and near tears after her outspoken, highly political history teacher, Hailu, had spent the whole period denouncing the Emperor's entire fifty-year reign. I encouraged Loly to keep her composure, remain quiet, and not try to contradict her teacher. He knew who Loly was, and I was quite certain he was determined to ridicule and torment her.

"I know how difficult it is for you, sweetheart, but if you let him get you upset in the classroom, there is no telling where it might lead. Try to be patient. There are only two months of school left before our summer holiday, and I will try and make sure you don't have him again next year."

I encouraged the children to talk at home and express their frustrations, but I always reminded them of the dangers involved if they did it at school.

When the school bell rang, I sent them off to their classrooms and I returned to the car for their things. I knew Elizabeth, my teaching assistant, would take roll in my classroom and handle things until I got there.

That evening as I tucked the children into bed, Loly asked, "Mom, did you hear that Mr. Adams was arrested last night?"

"Mr. Adams, the missionary?"

"Yes, his children go to our school. Do you know them?"

"No, I don't, Loly. Why was he arrested?"

"The kids said it was for hiding barrels of gasoline. The government calls it 'hoarding.' "

Brent heard us talking and came into the girls' bedroom, curling up beside me on Loly's bed.

"Mom," he asked quietly, almost as if someone would hear him ask, "what if they arrest Daddy like they did that man? Daddy is a missionary too."

I thought quietly for a few seconds before I tried to answer Brent's question.

By this time Shellie had slipped down from her bunk and was curled up beside Loly. Menen and Kokeb had sat up in their beds.

"Come over here, Mini and Kokeb," I said, patting the bed beside me. I lifted Kokeb's tiny frame onto my lap. She was still so petite. I loved to cuddle her and make her giggle. I hugged her tight as Menen found an open spot on the crowded bed.

"We have to remember that Jesus loves us very much. He holds each one of us in His arms just like I'm holding Kokeb. He loves us even more than I love each one of you. He will watch over us day by day. That doesn't mean that we won't ever go to prison. But if we do, He will be with us there, too. He has promised never to leave us. Do you understand?"

"Is He watching over Mummy and Daddy in prison?" Kokeb asked.

"Yes, of course He is, Kokeb. We must believe that and trust God. He makes no mistakes."

"Mom," Loly interjected, "when they came to arrest Ababa, I was afraid."

"Me, too," Kokeb added.

Menen nodded her head affirmatively.

I gathered them all toward me. "I was afraid, too. When I tell you to trust God it doesn't mean that we won't be afraid. Trusting him is just knowing He loves us and cares about us even when things don't seem to be going the way we want them to go. Brent, you asked me what we would do if Daddy was arrested. We will pray that that doesn't happen. If it does, we must still trust God to be with Daddy, to take care of him and protect him. God will give Daddy courage just as He is giving Loly, Kokeb, and Menen's parents courage."

They were all very quiet and listening intently. I continued. "If soldiers ever do come here for any reason, we must all try our best to be very quiet and calm. I know how hard that seems, but we must be brave. If we act afraid of them or try to run away, they will be angry, and they might hurt us. If you are in bed, you must be very still. Listen to the soldiers and do what they tell you. Don't jump up suddenly. We all remember what happened to that young boy who went to the English School last semester when the soldiers came to his house to search. He was afraid and jumped out of bed quickly to turn on the lights. A soldier shot and killed him. So you see it is very important that we stay quiet and calm even if your heart is beating very fast and you feel like running away. Do you all understand?"

They all nodded their heads. I kissed them all good night and tucked them into bed.

Later as we lay in bed, I told Denton about the talk I had had with the children.

"These are such difficult things to explain. I feel so inadequate to answer all their questions. There are no easy answers, are there?"

"No, there aren't," he agreed. He was unusually quiet and withdrawn.

"Denton? Are you OK? What's wrong?"

"I'm just fed up! Fed up!"

Denton rarely expressed feelings like this. I was shocked, and sat up on the bed beside him. "What is it, Denton? What's wrong? Did something happen?"

He lay there almost lethargic with his hands behind his head. "The soldiers . . . it's like anarchy. No one seems to be in control. Coming to your school like that and taking a young woman off with such force. Don't you see? They can go into any home, any place of business, even a school, and take anyone they want off to prison."

"Honey, this is nothing new. They have been arresting people on a whim ever since they deposed the Emperor two years ago."

"They came to the printing press across the street from the Headquarters today." His voice trailed off, and I could barely hear him. "I watched them from my office window. They marched a group of people into the field beside our building. They just shot them. Right there in cold blood. They shot them—and one of the women was pregnant. I watched the soldiers throw their bodies into a truck, and they left. I've never seen anything like it, and I hope I never have to see it again. I just kept thinking how horrible it would have been if the children had been there and had seen it all happen. Then you came home and told me about Ababa. Who will be next? One of us?"

Neither one of us talked for several minutes, and then Denton continued. "It is at this point where you really have to trust God, isn't it? When you are all out of answers and all you have left is lots of questions."

On the verge of tears, I nodded my head in agreement. I didn't trust my voice. He sat up and put his arm around me.

"I wonder how much time we have left here in Ethiopia, Denton? Do you think our time is running out?"

"I just don't know, Jodie. It's hard to tell if they are going to ask us to leave or just make it too uncomfortable for missionaries to stay. Did you get a chance to read the *Addis Zemen* today? It said agents of the imperialist spy organizations dress in the role of preachers carrying Bibles. The article suggested that certain religious organizations are the leaders of this imperialism and that they should be completely destroyed and replaced with scientific proletarian ideology. The whole thing tells me that our days here are numbered. I'm just not certain how the end will come."

"But Denton, what will happen to the children if we have to leave? You know this government will never let us take them out of the country legally."

"I've thought a lot about that, Jodie."

"Do you think we could ever escape with them?"

"It seems remote. At this point I can't even imagine where we would begin."

As the days unfolded, it became increasingly apparent that our work in Ethiopia was coming to an end.

One Saturday after choir practice, Denton came home too upset to talk. It wasn't until we were alone, much later that evening, that he broke the news to me.

"The leaders of the commune office came to the church today. They put government seals on seven of our classrooms and informed me that the rooms are no longer ours. They belong to the masses."

"They can't do that!" I raged.

"When I said to them that mission property had not yet been nationalized, one was belligerent and yelled, 'The law and the revolution have taken separate paths, and we will do as we please!' I will have to take my appeal to a higher office."

"Will we get the rooms back? Where am I supposed to put four hundred children on Sunday morning? Where will the night school students meet?"

"I don't know," he sighed. "I'm to meet with them again tomorrow, but I will contact the American embassy before I do."

The whole city of Addis Ababa had been divided into small areas and each area had its own commune office. These were called *kebeles,* and if a person had a complaint against someone else, he would take it to his *kebele* leaders.

The *kebele* that the Mission was assigned to had always been hostile toward the Mission and the leaders were particularly antagonistic in their dealings with Denton or his assistant, Joseph.

Not only did the *kebele* keep the seven rooms during the weeks that followed, but they also appropriated our enclosed parking lot, opened it to the public, and began showing films on the life of Lenin and other Marxist themes. As the tension grew at the Headquarters, the missionaries who usually came from their mission stations in the countryside and stayed in the apartments at the Headquarters while they did their shopping and visited their children in boarding school, found it increasingly difficult to stay there. Their cars were vandalized, and they and their children threatened and insulted.

It didn't take a genius to realize that the street boys who flooded the city streets from the countryside, as well as the hordes of thieves and beggars, recognized the lack of civil order. The government seemed to use them to intimidate the upper class. Their belligerence was a constant source of frustration whenever I went grocery shopping or had to run errands for my family. When I parked the car, they threatened to break all the windows or slit the tires if I didn't give them money to watch my car until I returned. They were splitting their profits with the police, so we could expect no help from the occasional patrolman who wandered by while we were being harassed.

The daily newspapers, both in English and Amharic, continued their barrage of insults against missionaries in general, implying that missions in Ethiopia were only a front for CIA activities. When Americans walked on the streets, the children would yell, "CIA, go home!"

The week following the confiscation of our classrooms, Denton telephoned me from his office, warning me not to come to the Headquarters. He said he would discuss everything when he got home that evening.

"I was in my office at the building," he explained at the dinner table. "A group of thugs, about eight of them, pushed and shoved their way into my office right past the guard and Joseph. They were screaming, 'Imperialist pigs, imperialist pigs, go home!' They stood in front of my desk, accusing me of being a spy for the American government. I thought they were going to drag me out of my office."

I knew better than to ask him if he had called the police. The police were as hostile as the people on the streets. If they sided with the "foreign devils," they would be accused of standing in the way of the revolution.

"What happened, Dad?" Brent asked, his eyes as big as saucers.

"Just as they were standing there making all of these wild accusations against me, against missionaries and all Americans in general, a lady from the American embassy called me to tell me about a meeting they are having with mission representatives tomorrow afternoon. I said to her, 'I can't talk right now,' and she asked me if there was something wrong. I said, 'Yes, definitely!' and she asked if she should send help. I told her to call me back in five minutes, since the people in my office would be gone by then. I knew the fellows standing there could understand me. When I hung up, I told them that it was the American embassy and that they were phoning back in five minutes. They all left in a hurry, and by the time Mrs. Lindsey called back, they were gone. I explained to her what they had done. She said the embassy would file a complaint with the Ethiopian government."

"File a complaint," I screamed. "A lot of good that is going to do. Just who are they planning to complain to, the local *kebele* officials? They probably ordered the thugs to harass you!" I was furious.

Denton laughed. "You're probably right, Jodie, but if we allow them to see how frustrated and upset we are, they won't let up for a minute. If we keep our equanimity and go about our business, we might be able to continue our work here."

"Yes, and when they come into your office and drag you out into that field beside your office before Mrs. what's-her-name from the American embassy thinks to call you and see if you're OK, what will you do then? Or what will *we* do? Denton, do you really believe things are going to get better?"

His voice was strained and tired now. "I don't know, honey, but I sure hope so." I could tell he didn't want to say anything more in front of the children. They had been listening intently, without interruption, to our whole conversation.

When they sensed we were not going to continue, they asked to be excused from the table, and they all went into Shellie's room, where I imagine they continued their own discussion of our future in Ethiopia.

Unfortunately the pressure did not let up. All the various mission boards represented in Ethiopia began calling their missionaries into Addis Ababa from their remote outposts. Considering the unrest and uncertainty in the capital, I could not imagine that anyone would be safer there than in the countryside. Each night after the midnight curfew we could hear rifle fire all over the city. It was not uncommon to see bodies lying on the city streets as I drove to school with the children. Fortunately the neighborhood *kebele* near our home was peaceful and quiet, although the officials kept close tabs on our comings and goings.

Our concern grew when Ethiopian church leaders began disappearing from their homes without a trace. Because of the long-time alliance between the United States and the deposed Emperor's government, many Ethiopians associating with Americans were suspect.

Denton kept busier than ever as our missionaries began to make application to close their mission stations and apply for exit visas. As mission director for our Baptist mission board, Denton was the official liaison between our missionaries and the Ethiopian government. Even though the government was making it nearly impossible for missionaries to remain in Ethiopia, they made it, even more difficult to leave. They imposed years of back taxes on every mission. They insisted the missionaries include Marxist teachings in their school curriculum, which most mission boards staunchly refused to do. Denton, like other mission directors, became responsible for paying the back taxes, which amounted to thousands of dollars for our mission alone, as well as for the implementation of the other requirements they had begun enforcing.

Denton could apply for exit visas for our missionaries; however, he became guarantor for each family that left, assuring the Ethiopian government that that particular family would return or Denton would become accountable to the government. Missionaries had established schools and clinics all over the country, and the government lacked the manpower to provide adequate numbers of teachers, nurses, and doctors to fill in if the missionaries did not return.

The simplest clerical task took weeks to complete, and many evenings Denton would come home exasperated, having spent the entire day in one or two offices just sitting and waiting for a single signature.

"The old government worked slowly, and it might even

have taken them months to approve something, but at least there was a chain of command. If you followed that chain, it was possible finally to get something accomplished. Now there is no chain of command. No one knows what he is doing. What's more, no one wants to accept responsibility for making a decision, because government policy is so vague, and the cost of making a mistake is so high," Denton explained.

During the weeks that followed, Denton prepared more sermons while waiting in government offices than he did in his own office. He just learned to take his attaché case full of his books and his Bible and sit in the offices, waiting to see the officials or to get a certain paper signed while he studied and prepared his sermon and Sunday school lessons.

CHAPTER SIX
The Farewell Party

By June several couples were packed and ready to leave Ethiopia. Most of them were not planning to return. We had still made no decision about leaving.

Our good friends Shara and Jerry Piercey had made their final plans for furlough. Another family, Jim and Barbara Singleton and their children, were coming from their mission station in northern Ethiopia to take the Pierceys' place at the Bole Road Deaf School.

Denton and I had planned a farewell party at our home for all of the families who were leaving. Although they weren't missionaries, our good friends Hagop and Hrip were coming. We had adopted them into our mission family, and no party was complete without them.

I loved to give parties, and I woke up excited about the day. I lay in bed listening to the sounds outside our bedroom window. The rain fell softly on our tin roof. I was eager to begin my day. I jumped up and snuggled into my warm robe and slippers. The rains always brought the cold, and our home was heated only by a fireplace in the living room. None of the homes in Ethiopia had central heating.

Denton must be having coffee, I thought as I ran a brush through my hair. A few more gray hairs seemed to have appeared since yesterday morning. It didn't worry me. I considered them hard-earned medals! "No wrinkles anyway," I said aloud to my reflection in the mirror. "Not bad for thirty-five," I encouraged myself.

I smelled the freshly brewed coffee as I walked down the hall. The house was quiet, and the children's bedroom doors were still closed. I hoped I'd get a cup of coffee before the household awakened. After pouring myself a cup of steaming coffee, I joined Denton in the living room. He looked relaxed and was enjoying the beautiful view out our front window. "Good morning, honey," he greeted me cheerfully. "Isn't it beautiful? Everything is so green from the rains."

"It is beautiful," I agreed. "I often wonder if we could ever live anywhere else that was this beautiful and have such a lovely home besides." We both sat sipping our coffee, enjoying our few quiet moments together.

"What more could I ask for?" Denton interrupted the silence. "Coffee, nice fire in the fireplace, all the kids fast asleep. I wish it could last forever!"

He didn't have to explain. I knew he didn't mean the moment at hand. We both understood a way of life was coming to an end for us.

I could still remember the lights glittering along the African coast like brightly colored jewels as our ship lay anchored in the Gulf of Aden. Darkness shrouded the deck of the Norwegian freighter, *The Hoegh Cliff*, as it rocked quietly in the black water. It was midnight, and I had just left our comfortable, air-conditioned quarters below and wandered up onto the deck, too restless to sleep. I was sure it was the excitement. Within the next twenty-four hours we would be there. Addis Ababa, Ethiopia! It was a dream come true! It would be the culmination of our years of planning and preparing for our life's work. There it was, right off the starboard bow of the ship: Africa, the Dark Continent.

Ever since Denton and I had met in Bible college, this had been our goal: Africa. Even before I had met him, I wanted to be a missionary to Africa. Not only had Denton been the song leader for Mission Prayerband in the Baptist Bible college where we met, but he was the prayer leader for the African group. We had begun dating almost the first week of my freshman year. He was a senior. Every Friday night we attended Mission Prayerband, where we read letters from the missionaries in Africa and prayed for them. It was comforting to think that now that Denton and I were missionaries there would be a group at home faithfully praying for us.

Tomorrow morning we would catch a flight from Djibouti, French Somaliland, and fly to Addis Ababa, the capital city of Ethiopia, that ancient African kingdom—three times the size of California—perched proudly on the Horn of Africa.

"You couldn't sleep, Mrs. Collins?" The captain's voice startled me.

"No, I'm much too excited! It seems impossible that that could be the continent of Africa just a few miles away."

"It's Africa, all right! I just came from the bridge, where I checked the temperature. It is 120 degrees, and it is past midnight. Is that hot enough for you?"

"Quite," I replied. "But I don't think it will be like this in Ethiopia. Addis Ababa, the capital, is in the mountains, more than eight thousand feet high. I understand that the climate is more like my home in San Francisco, California, than the climate here in the Gulf of Aden."

The heat and humidity hung in the air like a wet blanket. I was thankful for our comfortable suite. It had been hot since we entered the Mediterranean Sea and had gotten hotter yet as we neared the Suez Canal and traveled southward toward Djibouti.

I chatted briefly with the captain about tomorrow's arrival in Djibouti. He explained that a pilot would come aboard our ship early in the morning to guide *The Hoegh Cliff* into the congested port where we would disembark. Everything except our hand luggage would be loaded onto the train and transported overland to Addis Ababa. I was thankful we were flying.

"It might take several weeks before your personal effects arrive in Addis," the captain explained. "Things move very slowly in Africa. It will be quite different from your fast-moving American lifestyle, I'm afraid."

"I just hope everything arrives safely and that we don't have to pay an arm and a leg for customs." My voice was hopeful.

"Mrs. Collins, would you mind if I ask you a rather personal question?"

He really gave me no time to answer before he continued. "Just what brings a young couple like you and Mr. Collins to such a god-forsaken place as Africa to live? You both look as if you are in your twenties. Your little daughter, Shellie— did you say she was nine months old?"

I barely had time to nod my head before he continued. "You could have such a comfortable life in America. Why are you doing this? Why live in Africa?"

I thought momentarily about his questions. It wasn't the first time I had heard them. During our year of traveling to raise financial support to come to Ethiopia, I had faced this question again and again.

"Captain, Denton and I have been married three years. Since we began dating, a year before our marriage, we talked about our future, and what we both wanted more than anything else was to be missionaries in Africa. Don't you see? For us, this is a dream come true! We want more than anything else to share our excitement and faith in Jesus Christ with the Ethiopian people. Did you know that only 2 percent of the Ethiopian people can read and write?

"The Emperor, Haile Selassie himself, has invited our mission board to send one hundred missionaries to Ethiopia during the next ten years, not only to teach the Bible, but to teach the Ethiopian people to read and write their own language, Amharic. The Emperor believes the future of his country is dependent upon the education of his people. He wants elementary schools, clinics, and hospitals established on all of our mission stations throughout northern Ethiopia. He has given us a large piece of property only two blocks from the university in Addis Ababa, where we have already begun to build our Mission Headquarters, a church, school, library, apartments where the missionaries who work in Addis will live, and small efficiency apartments where missionaries can stay when they come to the city from the countryside to do their shopping and visit their children who will have to go to boarding school. The work has already begun, and we are joining other missionaries who share the same excitement and vision as we do."

"How long do you plan to stay in Ethiopia?"

"We plan to live there the rest of our lives. We hope to

build a home of our own and raise our children there. No, I'm not afraid."

He stood quietly for a few minutes. From time to time he shook his head as if he still found it difficult to comprehend what I had said to him.

The ship rocked gently, creaking and groaning, making eerie sounds in the night. As he turned to take his leave, he put his hand out to shake my hand. "Well, I don't understand it, but I do wish you and your husband the very best."

We shook hands, and he disappeared into the thick darkness.

Still I wasn't sleepy. I made my way below to the air-conditioned sitting room just down the hall from our quarters. For thirty days this had been our home. The captain had permitted Denton to go into the ship's hold our first day aboard, where Denton opened the end of our large crate of household items. He had assembled Shellie's crib, playpen, and high chair in our suite. Along with Shellie's things, he also unpacked his accordian and my typewriter.

I settled behind my typewriter to make my final entry in my journal from aboard *The Hoegh Cliff.*

June 30, 1964: *This must be one of the most exciting days of my life! Since leaving California to go to Bible college in Springfield, Missouri, four years ago, I have been anticipating this day. I must admit I was reluctant when Denton first suggested that we travel to Ethiopia by ship rather than by airplane, but he had felt the experience of visiting other foreign countries en route to Ethiopia might be easier on us than boarding a jet in New York and arriving in Ethiopia two or three days later. I have to admit he was right. I am learning that we can survive a lot more than I had thought possible! Like our experience in Alexandria, Egypt! Denton decided that we must see the pyramids and sphinx in Cairo while our ship was docked to unload its cargo of railroad ties. The captain estimated it would take at least three days, since Egyptian longshoremen unloaded them one at a time.*

Denton tried his best to get us first-class train tickets to Cairo. Unfortunately, he could only get third-class tickets, and no one warned us that foreigners should not travel third class in Africa, particularly with a nine-month-old baby! When we boarded the rickety old coach, the first thing I noticed was that there was no glass in the windows. It didn't take me long to realize that the hot wind, sandy grit, and hard wooden planks we were sitting on would make our trip very uncomfortable. Shellie obviously objected to the whole idea. She screamed from the minute we boarded the train until we arrived at the Cairo train station nearly four hours later. Denton and I both paced up and down the aisle of the train trying to quiet her, but nothing helped. My nerves were in shreds. The beggars, thieves, and street vendors eyed us suspiciously as we made our way into the depot in Cairo to try and find a telephone.

While Denton tried to make hotel reservations, I continued to pace up and down in the waiting room, still trying to quiet Shellie's shrill cries. I had fed her and then searched her from head to toe in case something was poking or cutting her. I found nothing. Back and forth I paced, patting her on my shoulder. I hoped she would fall asleep from sheer exhaustion if nothing else! I was beginning to feel desperate, wondering if she was sick.

Suddenly she stopped crying. It was so abrupt that I was afraid to lift her from my shoulder, thinking she had fallen asleep or passed out. Cautiously I lifted her up so I could see her face. I surely didn't want to awaken her if she had finally fallen asleep. Someone standing just behind me caught my eye. I turned to face a shriveled old leper woman, her hand outstretched toward Shellie. I glanced at Shellie's hand and noticed she was clutching a crumbled piece of dry bread. The little woman behind me had obviously just handed it to her. Before I could do or say anything, Shellie stuck the piece of bread into her mouth and contentedly began chewing on it. I took a step back from the leper woman, her face deformed and distorted from years of disease and obvious pain. I tried to smile and I nodded my head, trying to act grateful. Inside I whispered a prayer, "O God, please protect Shellie from sickness, particularly leprosy, Lord!" The

*woman smiled back at me, her tiny face contorted and
misshapen. It was the first time I had seen leprosy, but it
probably won't be the last. Rather than risk Shellie's sobs
again I didn't try to coax the piece of bread away from
her until we were in the taxi on the way to our hotel.*

*By the time we returned to the ship three days later I
had had my first initiation into missionary life!*

I pulled the page from the typewriter and read over the
words. I could smile now, but there was no doubt in my mind
that the last thirty days had been an adventure I would
never forget.

Now, sitting in the comfortable living room of my own
home thirteen years later, I had many more adventures I
could add to that one, each one a precious memory stored up
for just such a rainy day.

My thoughts were interrupted when Denton asked, "Jodie, what time is everyone supposed to arrive today?"

"One o'clock."

"What would you like me to do to help you get ready?" he
asked thoughtfully.

"Well, let's see. The table is all arranged for the buffet. Let
me get my list."

I had lists for everything. I didn't think I could survive
without lists: lists for groceries, chores, people I wanted to
have over, books I had read, books to read, things to buy on
furlough in the States, things to take camping. I loved lists.
They kept me organized, and I loved to be organized.

My list in hand, I settled back into my chair. One reason I
enjoyed entertaining so much was that Denton was always
so willing to help me. He was talented in so many ways. The
table always looked beautiful when he set it. He could make
the most beautiful flower arrangements. When we were
first married he was always embarrassed when I told people he had fixed the centerpiece. But so often my friends
came to me with arms full of flowers, telling me how they
admired my floral arrangements and asking me please to
make an arrangement for them, that I finally had to confess
who did it. Our beautiful yard was a testimony of Denton's
green thumb as were all our lovely house plants. I refused to

let him learn to cook, because it was the only thing I felt I did better than he.

"We finished most everything last night," I said, checking over my list. "Feyesa will be in soon, and then I will put the final touches on lunch."

"If the rain clears, I'd like to do some work in the yard," he added.

"That would be nice. I hope you don't have to go to the Headquarters today." It was more a statement than a question.

"No, I don't. With everyone in from his mission station, the apartments are all full. There are five families staying there."

I knew they were all there, because in a few hours they were all coming for lunch. We were like a big family, and we enjoyed getting together like this. We had all raised our children in Ethiopia, and they were like cousins getting together at a big family reunion. Like many of his peers, Brent had been born in Ethiopia. This was like home to all of us. That was the saddest part about today; it was really a farewell party, and some would not be back again. I guess if we were honest with ourselves, we'd have to admit no one was coming back once they left this time. I wasn't going to spoil my day by thinking such morbid thoughts.

"Well, let's get to work!" I said cheerfully, resolved to make it a good day filled with more happy memories.

By noon the house was a beehive of activity. Each time a car horn sounded outside, Assefa would run and open the big gate and another family would pull into the driveway. Children would pile out of the car and join the others already playing in the compound. I loved the excitement and the sound of the children's laughter outside the kitchen windows. The women gathered in my large kitchen, all talking at once. When we all got together like this, there always seemed so much to catch up on. The men sat in the living room. Feyesa had just carried a tray of cold drinks and potato chips in to them, when the telephone rang. "Go ahead, Feyesa, I will answer it," I said, as I saw him look toward the telephone.

I wondered who could be telephoning, since everyone who usually called was already there.

"Hello."

"Hello, Mrs. Collins. This is Joseph. I am sorry to bother you, but may I please speak to Mr. Collins?"

I sensed immediately that something was wrong.

"Yes, of course, Joseph. Just one moment."

I called to Denton and stood beside him while he talked to Joseph. I heard him say, "When did it happen? All right, I'll be there in a few minutes."

Denton's face registered the alarm I had sensed in Joseph's voice. "What is it, Denton?"

"The government has just impounded our entire Headquarters building! Everything—the church, offices, apartments!"

"They what?" I gasped. "What does that mean?"

"Shh," he said, covering his lips with his finger and looking across the room. "It is better if we don't say anything right now. I'm not certain just what it means. I will try to slip out quietly. Go in and tell Jim to come outside. Tell him that I need him to help me for a few minutes. Don't say anything to anyone else. There is no point in getting everyone upset until I find out what is going on. I'll take Jim with me. I will contact the American embassy if things are as serious as Joseph implies."

"It's Saturday afternoon. Who will be at the embassy?"

"There are always marine guards on duty. They will know whom to contact."

Within minutes, Denton and Jim had left. My heart was pounding, but I knew it was important that no one find out just what was going on. It only stood to reason that if the Headquarters had been seized, everything the five families had in the apartments had also been impounded. I wondered where Phyllis and Don Sidebottom's airline tickets, passports, and traveler's checks were. They were to leave the first of the week. What if they couldn't get their things out of the building? Don't borrow trouble, Jodie, I reminded myself. Just as I returned to my work at the kitchen sink, Jerry came into the kitchen. "Jodie, where's Denton?"

"He had to go up to the building for a minute," I answered as calmly as I could. "He should be right back."

"Anything wrong?"

"We don't know yet, Jerry," I answered nonchalantly.

"Denton should be back in a few minutes. He said to wait lunch for him. If something were seriously wrong, he wouldn't ask us to wait, would he?"

"No, I guess he wouldn't," Jerry reasoned.

When the telephone rang an hour later, I knew I would have to make some further explanation about Denton's sudden disappearance. Jerry heard the phone and came back into the kitchen, and all the women got very quiet.

"All right, Denton. Yes, I'll tell them."

Turning directly to Jerry, I said, "There does seem to be a problem at the Headquarters. Denton and Jim are on their way home right now, and he said he would explain everything when he got here."

I was surprised how calm everyone remained as Denton explained the sketchy details of how a group of demonstrators carrying sticks and stones had led the *kebele* officials to our building, shouting insults against the missionaries and Americans in general. They threatened Joseph and the guard, threatening to break down the gate if they didn't let them past. The rabble-rousers were accusing the Mission of hoarding grain.

"That's a serious crime nowadays, you know," Denton explained. "The *kebele* officials pushed right past Joseph and Berhanu to search the building. They found only one sack of grain and that belonged to the Bible Institute for their boarding school students. From their accusations you would have thought we had turned the Headquarters into a grain silo!"

We all laughed, and it helped to relieve some of the tension we were all feeling.

"They must be crazy," Frank Auterson concluded angrily.

"We went to the local police at first, but all they said was that they had no authority. They insisted that the commune leaders are the authority now. Then we went to the American embassy."

"They usually take no responsibility for missionaries or mission property," I interjected.

"But wait until you hear their response," Jim added. "I was really happy with their reaction. The political advisor began calling other embassy officials right away."

Loly, Shellie, and Lisa, the Pierceys' oldest daughter, came into the living room where we were talking and sat quietly listening as Denton continued to explain what had happened.

"The political advisor told us to come home, explain to all of you what is going on, and return to his office at four o'clock this afternoon. By then he hopes to have some word for us on what we can do."

Brent came running into the living room. "Mom, when are we going to eat? We're getting hungry."

"Maybe we should go ahead and eat now, so you can get back to the Headquarters," I suggested.

"That's a good idea," Denton concluded.

"Should we make some plans in case we don't get the Headquarters back tonight?" Barbara suggested.

"It is probably a good idea to have an alternate plan," Denton agreed.

"This party might last longer than any of us could have guessed," I said jokingly.

We all laughed.

After dinner, Denton and Jim returned to the embassy. The rest of us gathered in the living room to discuss our alternate plans. By this time the children understood there was a problem, and they were gathered together on the floor at one end of the living room, listening to our discussion. There was still a party atmosphere. I was pleased that we were all taking such a serious situation so good-naturedly.

The Pierceys' home was less than a mile from ours. We decided which missionaries would stay where. The Singletons, Barbara and Jim, would stay with us. Frank and Karen Auterson and their two preschool-age boys would also stay with us. Barbara and I taught together at the English School, so we knew we could use one car to go to school. This would leave the other for Denton and Jim to handle the Mission's business. Frank and Karen Auterson volunteered to hold things together at home. Frank would shop and run errands; Karen would work with Feyesa to prepare meals.

"With sixteen people living here, Feyesa might need some help," Karen projected.

We were still discussing our new living arrangements

and laughing about how Jim and Frank, both much smaller than Denton, were going to look in Denton's clothes if they weren't able to get their clothes out of the Headquarters building, when Denton called, telling all the men to come to the building with the keys to their apartments.

It was nearly eight o'clock when the men returned. It didn't take an experienced psychologist to detect their frustration and anger. The commune leaders had refused to return any portion of the building. Because of Phyllis and Don's imminent departure date, they were the only ones allowed to remove anything from the apartments. Phyllis looked relieved to know their plans would not have to be postponed.

Hagop and Hrip offered to let someone stay with them in their home; however, we felt we had it fairly well arranged.

It was getting late, and we all had a lot of settling in to do before anyone would get to sleep. Pierceys loaded up their four children. The Sidebottoms followed them.

Feyesa brought our camping mattresses into the living room, where Barbara and Jim's two children, James and Julie, and our five would all sleep together. Barbara and Jim would sleep in the girls' bedroom, and Frank and Karen and their two little ones would sleep in Brent's bedroom.

It was well after the midnight curfew when everyone finally settled down. I thought about how the day had begun, so tranquil and relaxed. The events of the day had nearly shattered any remaining illusions I had that we might weather the revolution.

Two weeks later there were only three couples left in our Mission in Ethiopia.

CHAPTER SEVEN
First Step to Freedom

I was happy that my trip to the States was planned for July.
It was only a forty-five-day excursion ticket, and I planned
to take Shellie and Brent with me. Since April I had been
making plans to visit my mother and stepfather, Ben, in
California during July and August. Mom and I had planned
a special return trip to the Shakespeare Festival in Ashland,
Oregon, which we had attended just prior to my returning
to Ethiopia a year ago. I was excited about the trip, and the
preparations took my mind off the Pierceys' departure and
the increased political tension in Addis.

The Autersons had left Ethiopia, and Jim and Barbara
moved from our house into the Piercey's house at the Deaf
School. Another missionary couple, Bob and Mary Jo Morrow, were expected back from furlough while I was in the
States. I suggested to Denton that he ask them to stay with
him rather than in a hotel or the Headquarters.

We had finally managed to get our apartments and church
returned to us, but there was always the uncertainty of
whether or not the same type of thing would happen again.

Of course, the Shakespeare Festival was not my only purpose for going to the States. I had arranged to return to
Ethiopia through London, England, where I hoped to make a
contact regarding the royal children.

One evening not long after the children had first come to

stay with us, Menen had given me a small piece of paper. "This is my brother Michael's phone number. He lives in England."

She hadn't said a great deal more than that, but I had tucked the paper into my wallet, and I had every intention of trying to contact him before I came back.

I knew that Michael, as well as other members of the royal family, had resided in England even prior to the revolution. During Mussolini's occupation of Ethiopia during the 1930s, the Emperor had fled to England. From Bath, where he had lived, he had petitioned for Allied help in his struggle against the Italian forces occupying his country. Loly's mother, Princess Sebele, as well as Menen's mother, Princess Aida, had been educated in England. Most of the relatives had congregated in and around London since the revolution. I hoped to enlist their help in arranging an escape for the children. Surely they have enough friends and various contacts that we can pull something together to save the children's lives, I thought hopefully.

Weeks before I planned to leave, the children were busy looking through a Sears catalog, making lists of the clothes they wanted me to bring for them. I took measurements of Loly, Kokeb, Menen, Tolessa, and Feyesa and carefully recorded them in my notebook. During a visit with Tsige I took Amaha's measurements. I had all the children stand on a piece of paper while I traced their foot size. I didn't think we would find a piece large enough for Tolessa's foot. We had a good time teasing him.

Arrangements were made for Loly, Kokeb, and Menen to stay with Tsige while I was in the States. Miss van de Loo had made arrangements for them to take sewing classes at Singer.

Denton applied for our exit visas, and they were issued with no problems. The children's shopping list was getting longer every day. I finally told them it would be easier just to take the catalog and bring one of everything!

The week prior to our departure it became very clear to me how much a part of my life the three children had become. It was obvious now that I no longer felt we were just taking care of the girls "for a short time." I loved them! I cared about their future, and what could their future be if they remained in Ethiopia? I had never let myself ask the question before, but I asked myself now: What if their parents were never released from prison? I thought of little Amaha. Ruth had told me that he was only three months old when the Marxists had arrested his father, Dejazematch Kassa, and he was only ten months old when they arrested his mother, Princess Sebele. Tsige had brought Amaha to our home on many occasions, and I had grown very fond of him, too.

The day before we were to leave, I drove to the American embassy to say goodbye to Carol. Another goodbye, I thought drearily. Does it ever end? At least this one is just for forty-five days. Carol and her husband, Bill, had at least another year in Ethiopia before he was transferred.

Carol was surprised when she saw me. "Jodie! I didn't think I would get to see you before you left. I knew you were busy getting the children settled and all. Where will they stay while you're gone?"

"With their Aunt Tsige," I said, collapsing into a chair beside her in her office.

"You look tired, Jodie. I'll bet it's kind of hard leaving them behind, isn't it? I'm glad you're coming back."

"I guess I'm trying not to think about it."

"I've seen it coming, Jodie. You've become so attached to them. Not just you. I've seen them with Shellie and Brent when you've brought them all up here."

Oh, no, I thought, as tears rolled down my cheek and my glasses began to fog up. To Carol I said, "I've been crying over everything the last few days. I can't seem to stop! Especially when someone mentions those kids! What am I going to do with myself?"

"For one thing, Jodie, don't be so hard on yourself. It's only natural. You're a mother first and foremost, and this is how a lot of mothers would react. You feel protective, and you don't want to see them hurt any more than they have been. Come on, Jodie, have a Coke," she said walking over to the snack bar fountain. "You will be all right. You can't stand being normal, that's all!"

I didn't sleep much that night, and the next morning at the

airport, tears overwhelmed me again as I hugged the children goodbye. I was torn between anticipating a lovely holiday with my mom, Ben and other friends, and feeling like a deserter. My head was pounding by the time we said our final goodbyes and Shellie, Brent, and I made our way through the security check and out toward the plane. I was surprised when the security officers took us through a third security check before we were finally permitted to board the plane. They ushered us into separate compartments. When we came out, Brent was furious. "They are so rude, Mom. They search you everywhere!"

"Yes, I know, Brent." What else could I say? They had embarrassed me, too, by their search. I had wanted to slap the soldiers' impertinent faces as they ran their hands up and down my body. I couldn't blame Brent for being angry. I was seething!

Our plane landed in Jedda, where most of the passengers disembarked. Nearly half the Ethiopian population is Moslem, and each year thousands of Ethiopian Moslems made a pilgrimage to the holy city of Mecca. Women who were not Moslem were not allowed to get off the plane during our layover. The heat inside the cabin of the plane was stifling. It was a relief when the doors were closed and we were on our way again. Our next layover was in Djibouti. I had not been here since June 30, 1964, when we came ashore from *The Hoegh Cliff*, the Norwegian freighter that first brought us to Ethiopia just about this time of year twelve years ago. Shellie, Brent, and I went into the airport lounge during our brief layover. It looked as if nothing had changed in twelve years. I reminisced with Shellie and Brent about the first time Denton and I had traveled through this part of the world. We took the last sip of our warm Coke just as we heard them calling for our flight to board.

It was a great relief when we arrived at our hotel in Paris. The first thing I wanted to do was take a bath. I left Shellie and Brent watching television, filled the bathtub with steaming hot water, and settled my tired, aching body into the soothing water. Just as I began to relax and feel the tiredness seep from my body, I heard something like a gunshot in our hotel room. Just as I jumped out of the water I heard Shellie and Brent laughing. Nothing made sense. I grabbed a bath towel and wrapped it around me as I ran out of the bathroom. Shellie and Brent stood there looking sheepish, but still giggling.

"Look what we found in the refrigerator, Mom." Brent was holding up a bottle of French champagne and a can of smoked almonds. I sank down on the bed, greatly relieved that they were all right. The longer I sat there thinking about it, the funnier it got. Shellie and Brent continued to snicker until I joined in the laughter.

"Do you know what that is you have opened, Brent?"

"It looks like Seven-Up."

"Well, it isn't Seven-Up. It is French champagne. And it isn't free. We will have to pay for the things you take out of that little refrigerator."

"This was the only thing to drink. I didn't know it was champagne until after I opened it. When that cork blew out of there it scared me to death. I thought I had been shot to death!"

With this we were all reduced to laughter again, and I couldn't really find it within me to be angry.

"Just put the cork back in the bottle and leave it in the refrigerator. After I dress we will go out and find a place to eat and get something to drink—not champagne!"

The remainder of our trip was uneventful until we reached the States. We visited Ethiopian friends, Guenet and Assamenetch, in Oklahoma City, and from there Shellie and Brent caught a plane to Kansas City, where Grandma and Grandpa Collins met them. They spent two weeks with the Collinses on their ranch in Sun City, Kansas. The next day I flew to California, where Mom and Ben met me at the San Francisco airport.

Mom threw her arms around me and gave me a big hug. "Oh, it's so good to see you. We've been reading such horrible things in the newspapers about Ethiopia. Are Shellie and Brent all right, too? How is Denton?"

"We're all just fine, Mom. It's so good to see you both. It seems so much longer than a year since I last saw you. I guess a lot has happened. I've got so much to tell you."

I gave Ben a hug and kiss as he took my hand luggage and

we headed downstairs to pick up my other luggage. I hadn't brought much home with me in the way of clothes. My suitcases were full of our Ethiopian artifacts since I planned to do shopping for everyone, and I hoped to fill my suitcases with all the special things I wanted to take back. We talked nonstop all the way home. Everything looks so good when you've been away from it for awhile.

Two days after I arrived home Ben and I packed the last few items into the car as Mom checked over her list to make sure we had everything together for our trip to the Shakespeare Festival in Oregon.

"We'll call you tonight when we get into our motel, Ben," Mom called as I started the car and pulled out of the driveway. Ben was such a wonderful man. I loved him dearly. He always encouraged Mom and me to do special things together.

Our whole week was delightful. We saw five plays in five days and enjoyed every minute of it. We talked as if I had been away five years instead of one. I told her all about Shellie, Brent, and Denton, and just as much about our four Ethiopian children: Tolessa, Loly, Kokeb, and Menen.

"On my way back to Ethiopia," I explained, "I want to spend a few days in England and try to contact some of Menen's relatives. Several months ago she gave me a phone number for one of her brothers, Michael. I want them to understand the danger that the children are in, and see if there is anything that might be done about getting the children out of there."

"How would you do that, Jodie? Would the present government ever allow them to leave?"

"No, they wouldn't. I'm not thinking of anything legal, Mom. We would have to escape."

She got very quiet then, and I understood her apprehension, and tried to put her mind at ease.

"Mom, you know how remote the idea of an escape is, but I at least want to discuss the alternatives with their family. We know that we won't be there much longer. Conditions are making it impossible for our work to go on."

"Why can't they go back and live with their aunt again, Jodie?"

"They probably will have to do that, Mom. Now please don't think anything else about it. I will let you know what happens in England, at least whether I meet with anyone or not. Remember, all I have is one phone number. I might not be able to find anyone to talk to."

When we returned from Ashland, I telephoned Jean and Moe Hernandez. During the next three weeks Jean and I shopped nearly every day. She was the right person. Jean loved to shop and knew where to go for the best bargains.

Guenet, my friend from Oklahoma City, flew to California with Shellie and Brent during the third week. The children stayed at Jean's with Michelle, Jean and Moe's daughter. Guenet joined Jean and me in our shopping sprees. Each of us took a list and a tape measure and set out for a different department in the store. We would set a time to meet for lunch. As I checked out with mountains of clothes day after day, the salesladies in a few of the stores were curious enough to ask me for whom I was buying all the clothes. When I explained I lived in Africa and had six children, they were usually so stunned they couldn't think of any more questions.

The days passed all too quickly. Each evening I would wrap several boxes and the next day I would ship them off to Addis.

I wrote Denton, telling him about my trip to Ashland, the shopping trips, and my visits with everyone at home. I asked him to save the boxes to open until we were all back together again. It would be like Christmas when I got home. I could hardly wait to see the children's faces when they opened all their boxes.

Our visit was refreshing. It was wonderful to sleep nights without hearing rifles being fired. With only one week left on our forty-five-day excursion ticket and suitcases stuffed full of new clothes for Shellie, Brent, and me, we said our final goodbyes in San Francisco and boarded our plane for the flight to London.

The telephone number Menen had given to me for Michael was his office number. I only had to mention my name and that I was caring for his younger sister in Addis, and I was overwhelmed by his warmth. He seemed to know who I was. I assumed that Tsige had somehow written and informed him about the children's new living arrangements. We arranged to meet in the lobby of my hotel.

Michael brought a young woman whom he introduced as his cousin Wynam.

I wasn't disappointed by the warm and kind welcome I received from them. Their gratitude was unconcealed. We were no sooner seated in the restaurant where we were having lunch, when they began asking questions about the children.

"How are they? Is their health all right? What grades are they in at school?"

During our meal two other young ladies joined us. Michael introduced them, "This is Jote, Loly and Kokeb's sister. And this is Hanna, their cousin." We shook hands as Michael pulled up two more chairs for the girls to join us. I answered many of the same questions for them.

Brent and Shellie were growing restless, and Hanna offered to take them for a walk in Hyde Park. Jote had to return to work. When Wynam, Michael, and I were alone, I decided to express some of my deeper concerns for the children. We discussed at length the continual emotional stress the children were under as a result of their parents' imprisonment and the harassment they had experienced from certain teachers in the English School. I stressed what I considered to be their most serious problems, particularly Menen's unwillingness or inability to communicate with adults.

"This isn't something we should take lightly, Michael."

His directness surprised me. His questions were pertinent and he talked with the finesse of a diplomat. He certainly registered no disapproval of anything I said, only the deepest concern. Wynam was very quiet, but I knew she was listening carefully to all we said.

I described the uncertainty that filled each day, the horrors we witnessed on the streets as we drove to school, the bodies stacked on street corners—young people who had been shot during the night.

"And the government refuses to release the bodies of

those who have been killed, until relatives come and pay a 'bullet fee' for the bullets used to kill the person," I concluded.

I heard Wynam gasp. Michael shook his head in disgust and said, "You must be kidding!"

"I wish I were, Michael, but it is true. You cannot imagine the things the children are subjected to under this government." I described the massacre of the college students that I had watched from my car near the Tobacco Monopoly. Michael and Wynam were both stunned as they listened in revulsion.

"My concerns go much deeper than just our dangerous surroundings. It is true, the children could be in danger of kidnapping or even assassination by radical groups who opposed the Emperor so violently, but I am particularly concerned about their psychological welfare at this point. What is all of this stress and strain doing to them emotionally? The girls have been with us for six months, Michael, and Menen has never spoken audibly to an adult. That worries me. At the dinner table she won't ask for anything she wants. She will nudge one of the other children under the table, and when she has her attention, she will point to what she wants, but never once utter a sound. I have taken her to the Seventh Day Adventist Hospital, where doctors did a series of tests. They could find no physical problem. As a last resort, I took her to the U. S. Navy clinic in Addis, but the doctor there found nothing physically wrong."

We all sat quietly for a few minutes before I made my final point, "Michael, isn't there anything we can do to get them out of Ethiopia?"

"Mrs. Collins, I too am very concerned by everything you have told me. I had no idea how serious things were. I have not been back to Ethiopia for six years. It is difficult for me to imagine these atrocities happening in my country, much less to my own family. We do care very much."

He fell quiet. I didn't interrupt his thoughts. Wynam was silently watching him, too.

"I don't know what we can do at this point. I will need time. I cannot tell you how grateful the family is to you and Mr. Collins for all you are doing."

Another long pause.

"I am going to contact several people. Perhaps some of them will want to talk to you and hear these things directly from you about the children. Do you mind?"

"No, not at all. I am happy to do whatever needs to be done to help the children. I just feel we must do something!"

The next two days were a whirlwind of activity. I visited with many people who were immensely sympathetic and interested in both the children's and their parents' welfare. I was encouraged by the sensitivity and concern of each person I talked to regarding the children. I became even more hopeful that I would find help.

On my third day in London, I had lunch with Michael. After the waiter brought our sandwiches, I asked, "What do you think, Michael? Are we going to be able to get the children out of Ethiopia?"

"Mrs. Collins," he began slowly. "At our first meeting I suggested that we would need time. Let me repeat how much we appreciate the fact that you and Mr. Collins have taken my sister and two young nieces into your home. We are overwhelmed by your kindness. You didn't even know us prior to all of this trouble, in the days when we could have been some help to you," he said a little sadly. "There were many people who were indebted to the royal family, but now that we need them, where are they? You owed us nothing, and yet you have helped us immeasurably. What can I say?"

I felt flushed and embarrassed by his praise and gratitude; however, I was eager to hear something more about the children's future.

"Michael, I want to be as candid as possible at this point. I want to know if we can get a small plane to airlift them out of Ethiopia. Can we raise money? What I want to know is, can we plan an escape? I've made it as clear as possible to you that I think it is only a matter of time until the children's lives are in danger, either from the present government or other radical groups. What are we going to do?"

"Mrs. Collins, if you can only take care of the girls until summer—give me until July, and then come back. We will talk again then. Maybe by then we can arrange something."

My heart soared with excitement. He had given me the answer I had longed to hear. He had given me hope. It wasn't a "no." His next statement took an edge off my momentary excitement.

"Mrs. Collins, we are hoping things will change in Ethiopia. We hope it will be soon. If the political situation reverses and there is a change, perhaps we won't have to risk escaping with the children. For now they are safe. They are with you and Mr. Collins. They go to school with you each morning and come home with you every afternoon. They don't appear to be in any particular danger. But if the situations changes, if things get worse, then come back and see me, and perhaps we will find the help we need."

What could I say? I was grateful. On the other hand, I was terribly troubled that he thought things might change for the better. I wished I shared his optimism.

That evening nearly all the family members we had met during our brief stay in London came to our hotel to say goodbye. The next morning we left for Addis Ababa.

My lengthy meetings with Michael and thoughts of an escape were eclipsed by my excitement and anticipation of seeing Denton and the children again.

Shellie and Brent squealed with delight as the plane circled above Addis. Rain washed across the window of the airplane as we landed. The kids both strained to see through the window.

"There they are! I can see them on the observation deck!" Shellie shouted. As they waved frantically, I laughed and said, "You guys are silly. They can't see you!"

"Well, we are waving just in case they can," Brent argued, determined to have the last word.

It was a marvelous reunion. When we emerged from customs, we were smothered in hugs and kisses. Everyone was there: Denton, Loly, Kokeb, Menen, Barbara and Jim, Hagop and Hrip. Everyone seemed to be talking at once. As we piled onto the church bus, Loly, Kokeb, and Menen quickly slid into the seat beside me. I gathered them into my arms once again and began asking them all about their summer holiday. Their answers were brief and then they asked at once, "When do we get to open all the boxes at home?" Their excitement was contagious.

We went to Barbara and Jim's home where Barbara and

Hrip had prepared a lovely brunch. James and Julie, the Singletons' children, were at school. In the excitement, I had not realized that Tolessa was not there. I looked around the room again to make sure he wasn't sitting out of the way somewhere.

"Denton," I asked. "Where is Tolessa?"

Denton walked over and put his arm around me. "I'm not sure, Jodie. I wasn't going to mention it until later if you hadn't noticed he wasn't here. He hasn't been home for the last week. I'm not certain just where he is. It isn't like him just to go off with friends and not let me know. I have had Joseph ask around at several of the police stations. You know how it is when they arrest people. You may never hear where they are being held. I just don't know what to do next."

I sat there stunned. I was certain that Denton had done all he could to find him. One other time Tolessa had run away. Denton had caught him sneaking out of his room at night and going to a bar with his friends. He was very young then, and Denton had taken his bicycle away from him. He left and was gone a year. He finally came back repentant and in tears, begging us to take him back into our home.

Thinking of this, I asked Denton if they had had an argument.

"We didn't have an argument at all, but I did tell him that I didn't like some of the friends he was running around with. I was afraid he might be arrested just being with those boys. He didn't say anything to me, and after dinner he went to his room. He was around for a few days after that, and then he disappeared."

"Well, I guess all we can do is hope that he is safe," I said solemnly. It was depressing news. Tolessa was like a son. He had lived with us nearly ten years.

It was good to be home again. We had lived in Ethiopia so long, I was never sure if I was happier when I arrived back in the States or when we returned to Ethiopia!

While we ate, Denton began telling me of the trip everyone was planning to Sodere.

"We were hoping to leave early Monday morning and spend the week there, returning Friday afternoon. I want to be back for choir practice Saturday afternoon. I'm teaching the choir a new song that I hope they will be ready to sing Sunday morning. There are several things I want to do Saturday to get ready for service Sunday. It would be great to get out of Addis for a few days before the kids go back to school."

"Monday sounds good to me. That gives me five days to get over my jet lag and to get our camping things together. After the trip we will have a week to get the kids ready for school. Oh, nuts! I just remembered! I have my first teachers' meeting on Thursday next week."

Everyone sort of groaned.

"Well, I know what we can do!" I suggested enthusiastically. "Denton, you'll probably be driving the church bus, won't you?"

"Yes, then we can all go together," he agreed.

"Well, I'll drive our car, and that way I can drive home Wednesday afternoon and be here for the teachers' meeting on Thursday morning."

"That sounds good," Barbara agreed. "I'd be happy to drive back with you if you don't want to come alone," she offered.

"Oh, I don't mind coming back alone, but we can work that out later. Right now I think I'd better excuse myself and get home. I'm getting a bit weary, and I know the kids are excited about opening the boxes of things I've been sending home. Barb, Hrip, thank you so much for the lovely brunch. Everything was delicious—as always. I'll call you tomorrow so we can begin planning what food to take to Sodere. Right now I'm so full, I don't feel as if I could eat another bite until we get back from Sodere."

We called the kids, got onto the bus, and made our way home. Brent was rather subdued, but the girls were beside themselves with excitement when we got home. Brent wrestled with the dogs, ran to the corral with Shellie to see how Golden, Shellie's horse, was doing, and then into his bedroom to make sure everything was still in place.

"Hey!" we heard him yell as ran into his bedroom. "What happened to my room? Dad!"

We all came into the room. Denton had already explained

to us while Brent was checking on the animals, that termites had weakened the supports under the floor of the girls' room. Denton thought that with the four girls in one room, it would be better if he traded their room with Brent's. That wasn't our only surprise.

Hagop and Hrip had sewn new curtains for all the bedrooms in our house. They were beautiful. "What special friends," I commented to the children as we toured the house. They all nodded their heads in agreement.

Their patience was short-lived.

"Come on, Mom. It's time to open the packages."

I laughed and said teasingly, "Oh, no, we can't open them now. I thought we were going to save them for Christmas!"

I nearly had five kids attack me. "All right, all right. Let's all go into our bedroom and see what we have."

We opened the boxes one at a time, and one at a time the children modeled their clothes. Even Feyesa joined the festivities and modeled his new clothes. Loly had asked for all clothes, but Kokeb and Menen had each asked for a doll. I saved their dolls until last, and when I took them from their boxes, I heard Kokeb squeal with delight. I think she thought I had forgotten about them. Within minutes after I handed the dolls to them, they disappeared into their bedroom to play. I wasn't sure, but I thought I saw tears in Menen's eyes, she was so excited.

After dinner, as Denton and I sat in our bedroom in the upheaval of opened boxes and tissue paper, I said, "That was fun. I'm glad you waited until I was here to enjoy it. It's like Christmas in August. What will we do for an encore in December?"

We laughed together, and then he said, "Yes, it was nice. I only wish Tolessa were here to enjoy it all."

I had set Tolessa's box of clothes to one side.

"Perhaps he will show up again in a day or two. It's happened before, you know."

Just then Feyesa knocked on the bedroom door. It wasn't closed, but he wanted our permission before he came in to carry away all the empty boxes and paper.

"Come in, Feyesa. It is all yours!" I said jokingly.

"Madame, thank you for the nice things you brought for me."

"You are welcome, Feyesa. Thank you for taking good care of Mr. Collins while I was gone. The house looks lovely, too." He grinned and looked pleased that I had noticed. Gathering all the loose papers and boxes into his arms, he turned to Denton and said, "Mr. Collins, Tolessa has just come home. He is in his room."

"Tolessa's home!" I screamed. Jumping up from the bed, I was about to bound out of the room.

"Wait, Jodie, maybe it is best if I talk to him first. I want to hear what he has to say about where he has been. It's best if I talk to him alone."

I stopped in my tracks. Denton was right, of course.

An hour later when Tolessa and Denton came into the house, Tolessa's eyes were downcast and he looked embarrassed when he approached me. I was so relieved to see him, I threw my arms around him and hugged him.

"Sorry I wasn't here when you got home this morning, Mom," he said, his voice heavy with regret.

"It's all right, Tolessa. I'm glad you are home. I brought some things for you. Do you want to see them?"

Denton interrupted. "I think it's better if he sees them tomorrow. It is late now. We should all be getting to bed."

All of the kids came running into the room, screaming, "Tolessa, Tolessa, you're home. Where were you? Did you see what Mom brought us?" They were all still wearing their new clothes.

Tolessa grabbed Brent and lifted him off the ground. "Oh, my goodness, Brent," he groaned. "You have grown in six weeks! You are getting to be such a big boy!"

Brent grinned sheepishly as he reveled in Tolessa's compliments. He hugged Tolessa tightly, obviously relieved to see him back home.

After we had settled all the children into their beds, Denton and I sat in the living room, sipping our favorite tea. Tolessa and Feyesa had gone to their rooms, and we were all alone.

"Denton, what did Tolessa say when you went out to talk to him?"

"He didn't have much to say. He was evasive about where he has been. He just said he was with his friends. When I asked him what friends, he said I didn't know them. I'm afraid I do know who they are, and I don't approve of them at all. They are worse than street boys, rabble-rousers, and he is sure to get into trouble if he continues to associate with them. I'm not certain just how to handle it, but I feel I must do something. I told him how it scared me when he didn't come home and how I had had Joseph look for him at several of the police stations, thinking he might have been arrested. He did act embarrassed, and he apologized to me."

"Do you think he was sincere?"

"Yes, I do. But I think peer pressure is strong, and I'm not certain at this point if he will choose what's sensible and safe or if he'll yield to the pressure of those roughnecks. The government is so hard on young people once they pick them up. I doubt that I could do much to get him released if he is ever arrested. I will be lucky to know where he is taken. Last week Guenet's brother-in-law came to see me. He was nearly in shock with fear. His daughter—I think she is only eleven or twelve—was spending the night at a friend's house. It seems her little girl friend had several older brothers, and the police came and arrested everyone in the house, Tariku's daughter included. He had no idea where they had taken them. Neighbors had seen the police and soldiers come and when Tariku came to pick up his daughter, they told him what had happened. He was scared to death to tell his wife, and he came asking me to help. I had no idea where to begin, but I had been looking for Tolessa all week, too. It is so frightening."

"Did he find his daughter?"

"Not to my knowledge. He hasn't been back to see me."

"Oh, my goodness! It is so frightening. Just think of sitting in your home and suddenly police and soldiers come and arrest everyone in the house—men, women, and children. It's terrible!"

"Yes, it is. Jodie, not to change the subject, but I was thinking it might be better to wait and give Tolessa his clothes when school starts. I want him to think about what he has done, and to shower him with gifts right now seems a little inconsistent."

I was disappointed, but I understood what Denton was saying. "You know, Denton, maybe it would help if we put

Tolessa in the English School. We've talked about transferring Shellie and Brent from Bingham Academy this year. What if all the kids go to the same school? I worry about their being so spread out all over town. If something happened and trouble or shooting broke out, I would go crazy worrying about them. It seems much safer to have them all with me at the English School. And you are only a few blocks away when you are in your office. What do you think?"

"I think it might be a good idea. That might be particularly good in Tolessa's case. I think the fellows he is running around with go to his school. A change of scene may be just what he needs."

"Yes, maybe he'll meet some new friends in the English School. I can look into registering all of them when I am there for the teachers' meeting next week."

It had been a long day. I was exhausted. As we walked toward the bedroom, I heard the girls still chattering. I wasn't worried. I knew they could sleep late in the morning. They had plenty of time to catch up on their sleep.

CHAPTER EIGHT
A Family Outing

It was good to see all our Ethiopian friends at church on Sunday. Even though we had been away only six weeks, everyone welcomed us back warmly, greeting us in the traditional Ethiopian manner, a kiss on each cheek. It had been several years since I taught in the Ethiopian Sunday school. Demoz, the Sunday school superintendent, greeted me enthusiastically.

"Good morning, Mrs. Collins; welcome home!"

"Thank you, Demoz. It's wonderful to be home. How are you, and how is the Sunday school going?"

"I'm well, thank you. Mrs. Collins, we just thank God for His blessing. We have so many children we don't know where to put them all. Since the *kebele* took our Sunday school classrooms it has been difficult to find enough space, but it hasn't dampened the spirit of the children or the teachers."

"I'm happy to hear that, Demoz. You are doing a fine job. You have good teachers to help you, too. I'm thankful for all of you. Have a good morning, Demoz. It is good to see you again."

"God bless you, Mrs. Collins," he said shaking my hand again.

As I walked toward my office where I taught an English Sunday school class for the English-speaking children, my five among them, I thought of the earlier years when we first thought of starting the Sunday school. Mrs. Cain and I had walked through the villages behind the Headquarters, inviting children to come to the Mission to learn about Jesus. Many had just laughed, some had come out of curiosity, and a few had come to learn about the Bible. In the early days Mrs. Cain and I taught the Ethiopian children in Amharic. My Amharic was simple, but that was adequate for the younger children I taught. Mrs. Cain taught the older ones. We awarded the children a New Testament for six months' perfect attendance, and a complete Bible for the second six months. There were other awards for learning Bible verses. The children's enthusiasm grew, and so did the Sunday school. Within three years there were more than 450 children in attendance. I began teaching Ethiopian high school students how to teach the children, and it was exciting to me to see young people who had grown up in the Sunday school become teachers themselves.

During the three-month school holiday in the winter months, we held a two-week Bible class for children who had had perfect attendance during the school year. We usually had well over a hundred children in attendance. By the time I stopped teaching in the Amharic Sunday school, we had nineteen Ethiopian teachers, and Demoz became Sunday school superintendent. For ten years I worked, organizing and translating Sunday school material from English into Amharic. I loved my work, and couldn't really imagine how I would feel if I had to leave it.

After church and Sunday school all the missionaries planned to meet at our favorite Italian restaurant, Villa Verde. We couldn't cook food at home for the price of a meal at Villa Verde. Of course, I never told Feyesa that for fear he would suggest we eat at Villa Verde instead of at home!

Denton and I spent Sunday afternoon gathering our camping gear and getting organized for our trip to Sodere early Monday morning. Denton wanted to get our things all together so he could pack them first thing in the morning. He couldn't load the bus on Sunday, because Sunday evening after church he took everyone home from church who did not have a car. He usually had quite a busload. I could drive our car to church, bringing all the kids with me. After church they were the first ones onto the bus. They didn't want to miss going with Dad to take everyone home. They always stopped by a little bakery after everyone loaded up, and they bought a huge bag of crispy French rolls for everyone on the bus. There was singing until the last person was safely delivered.

It was usually after nine o'clock by the time the weary travelers got home, but I always had a big pot of hot soup and freshly popped corn ready for them, which they quickly devoured before going to bed. I was sure tonight would be no exception, and the children would go with Denton. I knew we would feel like getting all our gear together after Denton got home. Feyesa and I had spent Friday and Saturday preparing spaghetti, chili, and Ethiopian *watt*, a hot, spicy stew we ate with a large pancake-like bread called *injera*. We froze everything but the *injera*, which we would buy fresh the morning we left. It lasted only three days and then would begin to mold. The last two days of the trip we would have to eat *watt* with the crisp French bread we bought at the bakery and took with us in large plastic bags. It seemed to last much better than the *injera*.

While we were putting all the things together, I saw Denton look around to see if we were alone.

"You know, Jodie, ever since you told me about your visit with Michael, I have been thinking about the escape. It has crossed my mind to build a false bottom in the bus, tell everyone we are going to Sodere or Lake Langano, and drive out of Ethiopia over the Kenyan border."

"Do you think it is possible, Denton?" I asked enthusiastically.

"I'm not certain, but I have given it some thought. I think the difficult part would be the heat. I don't think the children could take the intense desert heat for as long as they might have to stay under there. It might be an hour or it might be several hours. I don't know how you could know for sure."

Just then Feyesa came into the storeroom where we were working, to help Denton carry some of the heavier things outside. We didn't continue our conversation after that.

Early Monday morning Denton loaded the bus, and all the kids climbed aboard. They were all eager to get to Sodere.

"I will pick up the other missionaries and Hagop and Hrip. Why don't you meet us at the Mobil service station on the road out of town in about an hour," Denton said as he climbed into the driver's seat of the bus. "Feyesa will ride with you."

"That's fine. We have a few more food items to get together, and then we'll leave. We have to pick up the *injera*."

Feyesa and I met Denton and his busload at the Mobil station as planned.

Denton leaned out the driver's window and called to me as I pulled alongside the bus. "Jodie, why don't you follow me through the army checkpoint, at least? Then you and Feyesa might want to go on ahead."

"All right," I called back. "Lead the way."

I always dreaded the checkpoint as we left Addis. Since the revolution, everyone leaving the city or returning to the city was subjected to a thorough search. It was left to the discretion of the military guard whether or not they inspected. I hoped they wouldn't make Denton unload the entire bus. On several occasions I had seen them make the public busses unload every passenger and all the luggage and subject everyone to a long, arduous search. I remembered one time I watched the soldiers make a driver take off all four of his car's tires so they could check inside them.

Denton stopped the bus beside the inspection post, and I watched as two soldiers climbed aboard. Oh no, I thought, I hope that doesn't mean a long, tedious delay. I was relieved when I saw the soldiers step off the bus and wave Denton on. The two soldiers lumbered over to my car. Their rifles were slung across their backs. I wonder if they sleep with their rifles, I thought irritably as one of the men motioned for me to roll down my window.

"Open!" he shouted rudely as he pounded on the front of the car. I pulled the latch and he lifted the hood of our little Volkswagen. Feyesa stepped out to watch him just as the other soldier walked up to my side of the car and said, "Get out!"

I began to open my door when the first soldier closed the

trunk, held up his hand signaling for me to stay in the car. I remained seated, but left my door open in case they changed their minds again. The first soldier walked to Feyesa's side of the car and peered into the back seat.

"What's in there?" he asked Feyesa, pointing to the ice chest sitting on the back seat.

Feyesa leaned over to open the ice chest. The soldier checked it and motioned his hand for Feyesa to close it. Satisfied we were not gun smugglers or antirevolutionaries, they waved us on our way.

Denton had stopped down the road from the checkpoint to wait for us. He had gotten off the bus and was a little concerned when we were delayed.

"Did they give you a hard time?" he asked as I pulled up beside him.

"Oh, they were just their usual pleasant selves," I sneered, angry because of their crude and unpleasant manner. "Let's get going before they walk down here thinking we are collaborating to overthrow their inspection post," I said sarcastically.

"We planned to stop in Nazareth for lunch at the usual place. Do you want to go on ahead and meet us there?" Denton asked in his typical calm manner.

By midafternoon I had forgotten about the incident at the checkpoint. As we wound down the mountain into Sodere, the thorn and acacia trees stretched their straggly limbs outward, forming a low ceiling across the valley. The terrain was dry. The Awash River curved lazily around the low-lying hills like a brown snake stretching as far as I could see. Crocodiles slept along the banks of the river, camouflaged in the high grass. Hippos rose to the surface of the brown river, snorting and gulping the warm dry air, then disappearing into the murky waters to continue eating from the river bottom's rich vegetation. At night the hippopotamuses would lumber up the muddy banks to continue their search for food. It wasn't unusual to see their tracks through our camp. Only the river bank and a flimsy barbed wire fence stood between us and the wilds of the river.

The spider monkeys knew no boundaries, and they raided our camp as often as we failed to keep a watchful eye or forgot to zip the doorway of our tent. We considered the monkeys a bigger nuisance than the flies, mosquitoes, and other wild animals. I had never seen a snake at Sodere. I was certain they were around, and I kept a watchful eye, but I was grateful I had never come across one. During one of our many trips to Sodere, Feyesa had caught a five-foot-long lizard. I thought he had caught a crocodile at first, but he quickly assured me it wasn't and that the lizard was harmless.

The children loved to fish in the river, although they caught only small, bony fish. Only Feyesa had the patience to fry or eat them. I was always amazed that the crocodiles never harmed the Ethiopians who forded the river day after day to get to their villages. There was no bridge, and all the workers in the hotel and restaurant at Sodere lived in villages scattered in the forest across the river from the hotel. I always reminded the children to keep a careful eye out for them, even though they appeared harmless.

I recalled one summer holiday when we had come to Sodere. Brent, Guenet, and I, with Coffee, our little poodle, were walking along the pathway between the restaurant and the river. Brent and Coffee were walking between Guenet and me. The rains had been particularly heavy that year, and the river was unusually high. Suddenly, a crocodile lunged right at my ankle. Guenet screamed and started running as fast as she could. Coffee ran right behind her. I grabbed Brent, lifting him right off his feet, and ran twenty or thirty feet down the path. When I finally stopped, I noticed Brent's feet were still going as fast as mine and I was still holding him off the ground! As I set him down, he kept right on running until he reached the camp, where he climbed right into Denton's lap and recounted the whole story.

Later a worker explained that the mother crocodile had swum over the fence during the flooding and found a spot to lay her eggs. When the river receded, she was trapped on the wrong side of the fence with her newly hatched babies. Unfortunately we had happened along the path near her nest, and feeling her babies were threatened, she had tried to attack me. I felt grateful to still have my leg. Afterwards we were all able to laugh about it. Since then, however, I had to watch more carefully, and often reminded the children of the incident.

That evening after dinner we all decided to go to the pool for a midnight swim. It was a warm, beautiful, moonlit night. The lights were not working at the pool. Barbara and I decided to give each of the kids a number, and when we yelled "Sound off," they were to call their numbers in the proper order. That way we could make sure everyone was safe and accounted for.

The first time we yelled, "Sound off!" the kids called out their numbers until it got to six. Then there was silence. "Five," I heard Julie call a second time. Silence.

"Hey, who is six?" I called from the side of the pool.

"Oh, Mom," Shellie called, "it's Menen. She is whispering her number, and you can't hear her. She's fine. Come on, Menen, yell louder so Mom can hear you!" Shellie coaxed. It was no use! She wasn't going to say it louder. As soon as number six had been accounted for, I heard James call, "Seven," then Brent, "Eight," and I knew they were all safe.

Sitting under the flow where the hot springs filled the pool I reminded Denton of my talk with Michael concerning Menen. "I do hope we will have a chance to see Menen overcome this muteness."

"Yes," he agreed. "Today when we were leaving Addis, I tried to imagine how it would have been if we were planning to escape."

"That's funny, the same thing crossed my mind. Especially when those soldiers checked my car so thoroughly."

"At that point it wouldn't matter if they checked the bus," Denton explained. "The children wouldn't even have to be hidden. We would just be leaving town for a camping trip or picnic, like today. The problem would come when we got near the Kenyan border, or if we came across a military patrol. The heat on the desert there is so intense that I'm not sure the children could survive if they were hidden under a false floor board. And imagine how horrible it would be if they were discovered. We would all be executed on the spot, no questions asked!" he emphasized.

"That's true," I concluded gloomily.

Neither of us mentioned an escape again for several weeks, but it was never off my mind completely.

Tuesday was a relaxing day. The children fished and swam, while the adults chatted together near the pool. Feyesa fixed a lovely lunch and we all gathered around a big table. At Sodere it was difficult to believe the country was in the grip of a violent revolution.

Wednesday arrived all too quickly. Sodere was like another world, so peaceful and quiet—no rush of appointments or calendars. I regretted having to leave before everyone else, but I felt I needed to be at the first teachers' meeting of the new school year at the English School.

Tolessa had agreed to drive back to Addis with me so I would not have to go alone. It was only a two-hour drive. The monsoon rains had blessed the countryside with a rich, thick cover of emerald green grass. Shepherds were herding their small flocks of sheep and goats to the rivers and pastures for the day. Huge herds of cattle sauntered slowly across the road in front of my car. One of the most exasperating things about driving in Ethiopia was all of the domestic animals that crowded the roadways. Animals usurped the right of way on all the roads, even in the capital city. The herdsmen never hurried to move the animals. They just meandered along behind their herds, carelessly ignoring the irate drivers waiting impatiently for the animals to cross the road.

"In America," I explained impatiently to Tolessa, "the animals like sheep, goats, and cattle don't just walk on the roads and streets like this. They are all kept in fenced pasturelands."

"How do they get them to the marketplace?" he asked.

"They transport them on trains or by trucks."

"You mean animals ride trains and trucks in America?" he asked incredulously.

"They sure do," I answered proudly.

Our trip back to Addis passed quickly in spite of all the delays because of animals. I left Tolessa at the house and went directly to school for my meeting.

"I'll meet you here at six o'clock, and we will go to the Chinese restaurant for dinner," I called to Tolessa as I left the house.

The day passed quickly. It was good to see everyone at school again and to catch up on the news of the summer holiday. Many of my friends were English; in fact, I was the only American teaching in the school. Many had been to England for the summer, and I told them about my trip to the States without mentioning to anyone that I had been to London as well.

I was happy that I had planned to meet Tolessa for dinner. The Chinese restaurant was one of my favorites. As Tolessa and I walked into the restaurant, the old Chinese couple who had run the restaurant since we first came to Addis twelve years ago bowed again and again as they shook my hand and greeted us like old friends. The old man seated us near the large window at the front of the restaurant. We knew the menu by heart so we ordered almost immediately. I felt famished as the waiter set the big bowl of wonton soup on the table between us and began ladling it into smaller bowls for us. The tasty hot soup only whetted my appetite for the sweet and sour pork, spring rolls, and fried rice that followed. Our waiter had just refilled our small teacups and set our fortune cookies on our table when I heard yelling outside the window beside me. The curtain kept me from seeing whatever was causing the confusion. Suddenly there was a violent explosion that shook the entire building. I felt intuitively that the window beside me would shatter at any moment, and I dived for the table across the aisle. The lady who had been eating at the table across from us jumped under the same table. We met face to face on the floor. When the window did not shatter, I uncovered my face and looked around for Tolessa, who I assumed had gotten beneath another table. I was shocked to see him still sitting at the table. He looked frozen in his chair. "Tolessa!" I screamed. I crawled toward him, grabbing his arm. I shook him, calling out, "Tolessa, get down. Listen to me!" He responded as if he were coming out of a trance. I thought he must have been shell shocked. "Get down here, quickly," I said, pushing him under the table beside me. There wasn't a second explosion, but the shooting had not stopped.

"What do you suppose is happening?" I asked the lady under the table with us.

She shook her head as if too frightened to talk.

We listened.

The shooting stopped. Silence followed. No one moved from his protected position for several minutes, and then one by one we climbed out from under our tables, brushing dust from our clothes.

As soon as the shooting had started, the waiters had run to pull down the metal shutters that covered the outside of the windows. Every business had them. Now the waiters were emerging one by one from the kitchen, where they had run for protection.

"Tolessa, let's try to get home," I said, pulling him toward the counter, where I paid the bill.

The old Chinese lady who usually sat so prim and proper behind the counter was dusting off her beautiful silk dress as she emerged from underneath the counter to take my money. Her porcelain-like face registered little surprise.

People were beginning to stir throughout the whole restaurant now. A waiter went to the door and pulled up the metal guard. Opening the door, he peered out cautiously. We could immediately smell the smoke from the explosion and gunfire. The waiter stepped back, allowing me to look outside. The street was empty.

"Tolessa, we are parked right here in front of the restaurant. I'm going to run to the car and unlock the doors. You come as soon as you see me open the door. Do you hear me?" I asked, shaking his arm. I wanted to make sure he was all right.

"Yes, Mom, I hear you. I'm fine. Go ahead."

I unlocked the car doors and jumped in. As Tolessa ran to join me, I started the engine. As soon as he closed his door, I spun around in the middle of the street and drove toward home as quickly as I dared. We didn't pass another car. As unusual as it was, we saw no cars or people until we pulled up to our house and Assefa opened the gate. He looked as stunned as Tolessa had in the restaurant. Obviously he had heard the explosion and shooting.

"Are you all right, Madame?" he asked respectfully. I could tell he was concerned.

"Yes, we are fine, Assefa, but it frightened us nearly to death."

I hurried into the house. Tolessa followed on my heels. We turned on the radio, hoping to hear a report of what had taken place. We listened for several hours before we gave up, realizing we would probably never hear an explanation of what had happened.

In the days that followed, only rumors trickled throughout the city relating an attempted assassination of Major Mengistu, the second vice-chairman of the Derg, one of their more conspicuous spokesmen. According to the rumored reports, the explosion was a hand grenade that was thrown at his Land Rover as he was returning to the barracks after a meeting. Most of the gunfire came from his body guard trying to capture the assassins. No one was found or arrested.

I was happy when Denton and the other missionaries arrived home on Friday. It seemed nearly impossible that so much could have happened in such a short time. Everyone was speechless as I recounted Tolessa's and my adventure at the Chinese restaurant.

CHAPTER NINE
Amaha Joins the Family

September and October passed quickly. Shellie and Brent had settled easily into the English School. Tolessa, on the other hand, remained restless, and I grew increasingly alarmed by his attitude, which appeared to be sullen and depressed. I tried on several occasions to talk to him, but it was obvious he did not want to talk. I could only hope that he would come to Denton or me before his attitude caused him trouble at school.

We had a new headmaster at the English School, Mr. Cole-Baker. The Casbones had moved to Cairo, Egypt, to open a new school. When Mr. Cole-Baker called me into his office one day in November, I had a premonition that it concerned Tolessa.

"Mrs. Collins," he began in his very typical English manner, "I regret to tell you this, but we are having some difficulty with your son, Tolessa. It seems he has been skipping some of his classes. Are you aware of this?"

"No, Mr. Cole-Baker. I am sorry to hear this, and I will talk to my husband about it this evening. We will discuss it with Tolessa immediately," I assured him.

"That will be fine, Mrs. Collins. I just wanted you to be aware of the problem before I had to speak to him."

"Thank you, Mr. Cole-Baker. I appreciate your concern."

That evening before dinner, Denton and I were sitting in

the living room, discussing my talk with Mr. Cole-Baker, when Feyesa came rushing into the room.

Simultaneously I heard Tolessa screaming at the top of his lungs, "Let me go! Let me go!"

Before we could reach his room I heard glass shatter. Denton got to his door before I did. The door to his room was open. His lamp lay on the floor, smashed to pieces. Assefa was trying to hold Tolessa, but Tolessa had broken away and grabbed a chair and smashed it against his dresser. Denton grabbed Tolessa's arms and held him.

"Let me go, Dad! Don't hold me," he screamed at Denton.

His speech was slurred, and it was obvious from his rage that he was drunk. Feyesa and Assefa moved into the room to help Denton control him.

"Tolessa, calm down," Denton's voice was firm, but quiet and controlled. "Get control of yourself, Tolessa, and calm down!"

"Never!" he screamed. "You imperialist! Why did you come to Ethiopia anyway? You just came to make slaves of us!"

"Denton," I said over Tolessa's screams. "It's no use trying to talk to him when he is like this."

Turning to Assefa and Feyesa, Denton said, "Just get him off the compound, and don't let him back in until he is sober!"

Together Feyesa and Assefa were able to drag Tolessa to the gate. He continued screaming, "I'll report you to the commune officials. You'll see; they will listen to me. I'll have you arrested!"

We could hear him shrieking insults as he staggered down the road toward the *kebele* office.

As Denton and I turned to go back into the house, the children were huddled together at the back door.

"What's wrong with Tolessa?" Brent asked. The children were obviously shaken by the incident. Both Denton and I tried to reassure them that Tolessa would be all right.

At the dinner table a few minutes later, Denton explained. "He has been drinking. He has probably been with his friends. When they started drinking they probably started telling him how abused he is, living here with us. He can't stay out all night and he can't do this and he can't do that.

What they didn't tell him was how fortunate he was and how much we care about him. It looks to me as if Tolessa is going to have to do some serious thinking and make some choices if he wants to remain here with us!" Denton said firmly.

"Do you think he will come back again?" Brent asked sadly.

"We just don't know yet, Brent. At this point, the very best thing we can do for Tolessa is pray for him," I said, trying my best to sound reassuring.

Before we had finished our dinner, there was a knock on our gate. Assefa hurried to open it. It was the *kebele* officials. They had come to talk to Denton about accusations that Tolessa had made to them. While Denton went outside to talk with the two officers, the children and I sat silently at the kitchen table, afraid to move. I couldn't imagine what I would do if they arrested Denton. Feyesa went outside and stood beside Denton. We could just barely hear their voices, only enough to recognize which one was speaking. I heard Feyesa talking, and then Assefa. I was happy they had been with Denton when Tolessa came home. It was always best to have several witnesses.

Denton's anger was undisguised when he returned to the kitchen. "I must go to the *kebele* office tomorrow for a hearing. Tolessa is supposed to be there to make his formal accusations against me."

The Ethiopian children looked embarrassed by the whole incident. Shellie spoke up angrily, "That's not fair at all. What's wrong with Tolessa? He has never acted like this before."

"He has just been listening to too much of the propaganda against Americans. He is caught in the middle," I explained, trying desperately to make some sense out of the whole affair. "He wants to be accepted by his friends, yet he is living with an American family, and I'm certain his friends are anti-American at this point."

I wasn't certain the children understood a word I was saying, and I wasn't certain what I was saying was intended just for them. I was trying to sort my thoughts, and I was doing it out loud.

"May I be excused?" Loly asked, when it appeared I had said all that I had to say.

"Yes, dear, you may all be excused. If you have homework to do, please work on it so you'll be ready for bed by ten o'clock."

During school the next day I worried about Denton's hearing at the *kebele* office. I was relieved that it was being held in the *kebele* where our home was located rather than the Arat Kilo *kebele* where the Headquarters building was located. The Arat Kilo *kebele* was much more hostile toward missionaries and foreigners in general. I felt Denton's chances for justice were better at the Bole *kebele*.

Overwhelming relief swept over me that evening at dinner when Denton told me that Tolessa had not appeared for the hearing and that all the charges were dismissed. The children cheered, and Feyesa beamed his approval as he served dinner.

A week after Tolessa's sudden departure, Tsige telephoned me, asking if she could come to see me. We planned to meet on Friday afternoon after school at the house.

When she arrived, I was pleased that she had brought Amaha. He was wearing some of the clothes that I had brought back for him from America. He climbed into my lap after I bribed him with a cookie! He chattered endlessly in flawless Amharic. I was amazed by his vocabulary. He was going to be three years old the following week.

When Tsige asked Loly to take Amaha outside to play, I knew this was more than just an informal visit. I waited for her to speak after the children left the room.

"Mrs. Collins," she paused and looked down at her hands folded on her lap. I waited.

"Mrs. Collins," she began again. "I have scheduled my eye surgery, and I am to go into the hospital next week."

I leaned forward in my chair. Whatever it was she was going to say, it appeared to be very difficult for her.

"You have been very generous, you and Mr. Collins. You have taken such wonderful care of Loly, Kokeb, and Menen for the past ten months."

"We have been delighted to have them. They are precious

children. I love them very much," I assured her, trying to
give her time to recover her composure.

"I understand that I am asking a great deal, Mrs. Collins.
However, I was hoping that Amaha could come and stay
with you while I am in the hospital. It would be much easier
for me to know that he was with you and his sisters while I
am away."

A smile broke across my face. She could not have said
anything that would have made me happier. Since the first
time I had seen little Amaha, I had wanted him to come and
stay with us.

"Oh, I'd be very happy to have him," I assured her enthusiastically.

She smiled and looked greatly relieved.

"When do you want to leave him with us? I know that
Loly and Kokeb are going to be very excited when they hear
this. Isn't his birthday next week?"

"Yes, it is," she said, answering my last question first.

Before she could continue I suggested, "Maybe he could
come the day of his birthday. We could have a party for
him."

"That is a lovely idea," she said, smiling and looking much
more relaxed than when we first began talking.

"His birthday is November 15. I believe that is Monday,"
she continued.

We made arrangements for her to bring Amaha on Monday afternoon after we returned home from school.

When we called the children into the living room and told
them our plans, their joy was overwhelming. They all
hugged me at one time, jumping up and down until I suggested that they go and tell Feyesa about it. It was more an act
of self-defense than anything else! Besides, Tsige and I had a
few final arrangements to discuss.

When the living room was quiet again, Tsige asked, "Mrs.
Collins, do you think Mr. Collins will have any objections?"

"No, not at all. We have discussed how much I would like
Amaha to come here and stay, and he has expressed interest
himself. I think it will be good for Brent, too. I remember
when I first told him that three little girls might come and
live with us, he looked at me and said, 'Why don't you get

some boys? Why all girls?' He and Amaha will share a bed-room. I know he will be excited. I will talk to Mr. Collins this evening, and I will discuss with Brent the idea of Amaha's staying in his room. If there are any major objections, I will telephone you tomorrow, but I don't anticipate any prob-lems."

"My mind is at rest. It will not be nearly so difficult to face my surgery now that Amaha will be with you."

She rose to leave, and we walked together to her car. I had a great deal of respect for her. She was a woman of great fortitude and strength. She had certainly exhibited that since I met her.

After she left, I went back into the kitchen to talk with Feyesa. He, too, was beaming. I could tell he was pleased that little Amaha was coming to join the family. Feyesa loved children as much as I did. It was a good thing. He had six wives! I always assumed that was why he wanted to live on our compound. He could visit home, less than two blocks away, whenever it suited him and for as long as he could endure. Polygamy was neither illegal nor frowned upon in the Galla tribe. Most of Feyesa's wives lived in the country-side. Only his most recent wife and child lived nearby. He usually spent his day off there, but rarely more than that. I couldn't say I blamed him. Living with us he had a lovely room, hot and cold running water, a shower and toilet, wall-to-wall carpeting. His wife lived in a small village in a thatched-roof hut. It was very primitive, with no indoor plumbing. She had to walk several blocks each day carrying a waterpot on her back to buy water at the spring. She lived as nearly all of the twenty-six million people of Ethiopia lived.

That evening when Denton came in from his office, I greeted him excitedly and told him about Tsige's request.

"I'm not certain how long he will stay with us, but it could be several weeks. I didn't even ask Tsige how long she would be in the hospital. Isn't that horrible? I was just so excited about Amaha."

His excitement matched mine. Hagop and Hrip were com-ing over for dinner and to spend the evening playing Rook and Love Your Neighbor. I could hardly wait to tell them.

On Saturday Denton and I shopped for a crib for Amaha. He still seemed too young to sleep in a twin-sized bed. When we brought the bed home and put it in Brent's room, you would have thought we had just brought a new baby home from the hospital. Everyone, Feyesa included, gathered in Brent's room to inspect the new crib. Everyone approved. Now all we needed was Amaha.

On Sunday afternoon Loly asked if she could help me make Amaha's birthday cake. I was always pleased when one of the girls wanted to spend time with me in the kitchen. The other children were outside riding Shellie's horse, Golden. I enjoyed cooking, and I usually spent Sunday afternoons in the kitchen making cookies, pies, and other special desserts for the week. Loly was usually the one who wandered in and spent the afternoon with me. I was happy to have the time alone with her.

"Mom, you know what I like about you?" she said, after we had been measuring out the ingredients for the cake.

"No, Loly, what's that?"

"Well, I like how you like to do everything. You like to cook, but you also like to swim, play tennis, and teach school. You seem to enjoy so many different things."

"Well, you are right. I do enjoy doing all of those things. Don't you like to do a variety of different things, too?"

"Yes, I guess I do, but it doesn't seem to me a lot of women do, especially Ethiopian women. Mummy didn't like to cook, but she was President of Ethiopian Women's Welfare, you know."

"Yes, I heard from Miss van de Loo what a wonderful job she did at that. You must be very proud of her."

She was quiet for a time. I knew it was very difficult for her to talk about her mother and father, and I didn't want to push her.

When we put the cake into the oven, Loly asked, "Mommy, can I make you a cup of tea?"

"Yes, that would be nice, Loly. Are you going to have one, too?"

"Yes, I thought I would."

I sensed that she wanted to talk, and after she had fixed our fresh lemon tea, we sat at the kitchen table. I was glad that Feyesa was gone for the afternoon and we were alone in the kitchen. Wanting to give her a chance to talk, I sipped my tea in silence.

"You know, Mommy, when Kokeb and I were visiting Menen during our summer holiday two years ago, Amaha was just a baby. He and Mummy were alone in Addis Ababa that summer. Daddy had already been put in prison, and Mummy had sent us to the palace at Mekele to stay with her sister, Princess Aida. We used to have so much fun at Mekele. We had a lot of fun that summer, too, until it was almost time to return to Addis. Then everything seemed to go wrong, and I was really afraid."

"What made you afraid, Loly?" I asked curiously.

"I can remember Princess Aida telling us that she had talked to Mummy, and they had decided that we were not going back to Addis. I knew it was time for school to begin, but we had also heard from the servants that there was a lot of trouble in Addis. I wasn't sure what kind of trouble, and I didn't like it that no one told us what was really going on. I really got scared when Princess Aida told the servants not to let us listen to the radio. I know she was trying to protect us from hearing all the bad things about Grandpa, but I felt it would have been easier to know than just to guess what was happening. Do you know what I mean?"

"I guess I can understand both sides, Loly. As a mom I would want to protect you, too. I'm sure Princess Aida did what she thought was best for you, but I truly do understand your feelings, too."

Loly continued, "One morning we were all eating breakfast. It was Menen, Kokeb, and me. Someone had turned a radio on in the dining room. When I heard the military anthem, I knew there was going to be a government announcement. Then they announced that Grandpa had been removed from his office. I couldn't believe it. Kokeb, Menen, and I couldn't even talk. We just looked at one another, and then the servant and Princess Aida came into the room and saw that we were listening."

"What did Princess Aida say when she saw that you were listening to the radio?"

"She didn't say anything right then. She just asked us to

come with her. We followed her to her bedroom, and she told us we were going for a short holiday to a hotel that belonged to one of Menen's brothers."

"Did you go?"

"Yes, she sent us with one of the chauffeurs and Emama Ruth, Menen's nanny. But we didn't go to the hotel.

"They took us into the countryside to a village. We had to stay in the back room of the village chief and hide there. It was terrible, Mom. There were fleas, and we had to sit on the floor in a corner. It was so boring, I thought I would die from boredom. Emama Ruth kept giving us candy and gum and she kept telling us stories to try and entertain us. The only time we saw anyone else was when they brought us food. I didn't think they would ever come back from Mekele and get us. Each night Emama Ruth made us all kneel beside the bed together and we would pray. We stayed there three days. Boy! When I saw the chauffeur again, I was never so happy in my whole life."

"Did he take you back to Mekele?"

"Yes, and it was so good to be back there, but a few days later it was horrible."

Loly's mind seemed to trail off as she recalled those final hours in Mekele. I was reluctant to prod her. I knew she would continue if she wanted to, so I sat and waited.

"I remember we were in the bedroom with Princess Aida. Emama Ruth came rushing into the room, telling us that soldiers were coming. Before we could do anything else the soldiers came into the bedroom. Mommy, I don't think I was ever so scared in my whole life. They grabbed Princess Aida and took her into the other room. We all started to cry, and Emama Ruth tried to quiet us. She was afraid the soldiers might harm us. They put Princess Aida into an ambulance, and all the windows were painted. I couldn't believe all the soldiers that came to the palace. Then they put us into a jeep and took us to the airport. We saw them take Menen's mom up the stairs of the airplane. At the top they stopped her and made her take off her shoes. Maybe they thought she had a bomb or gun in her shoe. A soldier broke the heel off her shoe searching it, and when he handed it back to her she hit him over the head with it."

We both laughed, and it helped to relieve some of the tension. Loly had never opened up like this, and the words continued to tumble out.

"Then they put us on the plane, too, with Emama Ruth and several others from the palace. Princess Aida refused to be seated. She kept insulting the soldiers, asking them if they had to send all those soldiers just to capture one woman and three little girls. I was afraid they might harm her. One soldier kept asking her to sit down, but she refused. Finally, when the plane took off, she sat down. Then she made us start singing hymns. We had to sing one after another. I didn't want to sing. I just wanted to turn my face away and cry, but she kept telling us to sing, and I felt like I had to do it. She sang, too. When the plane landed in Addis, they drove us to my grandmother's villa."

A little confused by the identify of all her aunts, and her grandmother and grandfather, I asked her who her grandmother was.

"Grandmother is the daughter of Emperor Haile Selassie," she explained, "—Princess Tegneworke," she added for clarity.

"Well, when you speak of your grandpa, do you mean her husband or the Emperor, your great-grandfather?"

I was a little embarrassed to admit I had never sorted out the sequence of the royal family. I could only have identified the Emperor.

Loly went on to explain, "No, my grandmother is Princess Tegneworke. She is the daughter of Haile Selassie. Her husband is in England. His name is Ras Andargachew. I heard that he got out of Ethiopia just a few days before they arrested Grandpa. When I speak of Grandpa, I mean the Emperor. We call my grandmother's husband Apapa Andargachew."

I wasn't certain that I had it all straight, but I nodded as if I understood.

"What did they do to you once they took you to your grandmother's villa?"

"Well, it seemed like everyone was there. My grandmother was there, and my aunts. The only one of the women who wasn't there was Mummy. I wasn't sure where she was, and no one would talk about it. They brought her several days later. You know, Mommy, it is kind of funny, but my grandmother raised me. It is sort of an Ethiopian custom for the daughter to give one of her children to her mother to raise. I lived with my grandmother. I love her dearly, but I always kind of missed being at home. There at the villa before they took everyone away to the real prison, I had my mother *and* my grandmother. It was just wonderful to be with both of them at one time. I slept between them each night. It wasn't even like being under house arrest to me because I was so happy. All the women were there together. The men were all imprisoned at the Menelik Palace, in the wine cellar.

"The thing I hated most was that no one ever told us what was going on. The adults didn't explain anything to us. They thought we were just kids, and they didn't explain anything!" she emphasized a second time. It was obvious that this exasperated her more than anything else.

"We were kept there only a few days. Aunt Tsige came one day and took us home. They didn't let Menen go at first, because she was older than us. Kokeb and I went with Aunt Tsige, and Menen was released a few days later and she came to our home. We stayed with Aunt Tsige until we came to live with you."

It was the first time Loly had told me the story of their arrest at Mekele. It may have been the first time she had told anyone. She looked tired, and we had long since finished drinking our tea.

It was getting dark outside, and I said to Loly, "I'm glad you shared these things with me. We must continue to pray for your mother, aunts, and grandmother that they will be released from prison quickly."

Loly got up and put her arms around me. "Thank you, Mommy," she said softly. I could sense she was on the verge of tears.

"Why don't you call the other kids and we will get some dinner. It is almost time for church," I said cheerfully, trying to cheer her up. It had been an emotional afternoon for her, reliving those weeks of uncertainty. I couldn't help but wonder how much longer the uncertainty would envelop our lives.

As we drove home from school Monday afternoon, we talked excitedly about Amaha's arrival.

"Finally I'm going to have someone share my bedroom," Brent commented. "And I won't be the little brother; I'll be the big brother."

When we arrived home, Feyesa had everything looking spic and span for the birthday party. The kitchen sparkled, and Amaha's birthday cake sat on the kitchen counter, decorated with three red candles.

"Mommy, do you have any wrapping paper? We want to wrap Amaha's birthday present from us," Shellie asked as she came into the kitchen.

"Yes, there is some in my desk. Shellie," I called after her, "please put back the scissors and tape when you finish!"

"Oh, I will, Mom," she called back lightly.

If she does, it will be a first! I thought.

The birthday party was a success. Amaha beamed when he saw his new red wagon, coloring book and crayons, and a large ABC picture book. The girls were all like doting mothers. Shellie sat with him on her lap, showing him the pictures and telling him the English word after he told her the Amharic word.

As we finished our cake and ice cream, Amaha slipped down out of his chair and came and stood beside me. In Amharic he said, "Do I have to go to bed now?"

A little shocked by what I mistook for his eagerness to get into his new bed, I said, "No, Amaha dear, you don't have to go to bed yet." I lifted him onto my lap.

"When do I have to go to bed?" he prodded.

I was certain then that I saw tears filling his big brown eyes. Eager to dispel any fears he might have, I held him tight and said, "Ami, it's your birthday. You don't have to go to bed now. Don't cry! We haven't sung 'Happy Birthday' yet, everyone. Let's all sing 'Happy Birthday' to Ami!"

Everyone joined in, and I was relieved to see his bright smile return to his face and his eyes dance with laughter. After our singing, he wiggled to get down, and I set him down. He ran over to Loly and asked her, "Do I have to go to bed now, Loly?"

I was troubled by his great concern about having to go to

bed. I got up from the table and began to clear some of the dishes off the table.

"Brent, why don't you take Ami outside for a little ride in his wagon?" I suggested, hoping I would get a minute alone with Loly.

Brent lifted Amaha into the wagon as Feyesa followed them to the back door, where he helped lift the loaded wagon over the threshold and onto the patio at the back door.

"Loly, why is Ami so afraid of going to bed?" I asked, eager to resolve the mystery.

Frowning, Loly got up and came to me as I worked to cover the remaining birthday cake. "I think I know what is wrong with him," she began. "His nanny at home is a young girl. She has been fooling around with her boyfriend. Whenever they want to go to bed together, she puts Amaha into his bed. Since my aunt isn't there to know what's happening, he spends most of every day in his crib. It has become like a prison to him, and now he hates to go to bed. He was never like that before."

Suddenly, his preoccupation with bedtime became quite clear. Less than a half hour later he was back in the house, tears in his eyes, asking if it was bedtime.

"Yes, Ami, it is almost bedtime. Let's put your new pajamas on, and I will read your new book to you, and then it will be bedtime."

Everything went smoothly until I lifted him into his crib. He began sobbing, and I picked him up again and tried to comfort him. By this time Brent had gotten into his bed, and I said, "See, Ami, even Brent is in bed. He will be here with you. Tomorrow you will get to play with your new wagon."

Nothing distracted him. I finally decided I must let him cry, so I put him into his bed, kissed him lightly on the cheek, and covered him. He turned his small face into his pillow and sobbed, deep, heartbroken sobs. I couldn't stand it, so I picked him up again and carried him to the living room. I tried to rock him to sleep in the rocking chair Denton had given me when Brent was born. He continued to lie there in my arms, watching me carefully, knowing he would have to return to his bed. An hour passed, and he hadn't gone to sleep. I carried him back to the bedroom and put him into his crib. He began crying again, much more loudly this time. "Brent is here, Ami, please don't cry, sweetheart. Everything is going to be all right."

His little body shook with sobs. Suddenly he vomited. I quickly lifted him from the crib and carried him to the bathroom. I bathed him, changed his pajamas and sheets, and sat down with him on Brent's bed, perplexed about what to do next. He crawled over beside Brent. Brent lifted the covers and Ami crawled in beside him. Such a contrast, I thought, listening to them giggle as I snuggled the blankets up under their chins.

"Brent, let Ami stay here with you until I get ready for bed. I will come back in a few minutes."

Both Brent and Ami were delighted.

When I returned to their bedroom fifteen minutes later, I found two slumbering boys. I carefully lifted Ami from Brent's bed and tucked him gently into his own new bed. We had cleared the first hurdle, but it certainly wasn't the last. This ordeal lasted nearly two weeks. Hours before bedtime Amaha would begin asking, "Do I have to go to bed now?"

One evening I decided we were going to have to resolve the situation. Everytime I put him to bed, he vomited his dinner and would delay bedtime for at least an hour while I bathed him, and changed his pajamas and sheets. I was becoming exasperated. As I lifted him into his crib, I said sternly, "Amaha, you mustn't cry. Mommy is right here, and I won't leave you." I felt wretched as I pulled the covers over his little body. I saw the huge tears rolling down his cheeks.

"Amaha, you must not make yourself sick. I want you to be a big boy. Mommy is not going anywhere except into the other room with Daddy." I was reluctant to leave him crying.

I said firmly, "If you vomit all over your bed and pajamas, Ami, I will swat your bottom. You must stop this crying!" My voice was firm, but my heart felt like jello! Poor Brent, I thought as I turned off the bedroom light. He has been so patient. We've been going through this for nearly two weeks. I hadn't gotten to my bedroom door when I heard Brent calling, "Mom, you better come!"

I hurried back into the room. Ami was standing in his

crib, vomit all over the floor and his bed. I lifted him up, wiped his tear-stained face, and swatted his bottom three times. He was so shocked that he stopped crying, though he was gasping for deep breaths from his long, hard crying. He didn't say a word during his bath. I put him into his crib all freshly changed, covered him, and he didn't make a sound. There wasn't even a tear. It was the last night he ever cried when I put him to bed. Another hurdle!

Unfortunately, the political situation remained tense. Rumors of disappearances, house searches, and killings ran rampant. I began to worry about Amaha being left home alone with the servants while all the other children and I were at school. I inquired about preschool for Amaha, and decided to put him into one of the classes. He loved it, and each morning he was the first one in the car ready to go to school. On the way to school each morning Amaha received an English lesson. Everything he saw he would ask in his first English phrase, "What's that?"

Within weeks his vocabulary grew immensely, and he began forming sentences. He was a remarkable child. I was happy that he enjoyed school; each evening he entertained us with the new things he had learned at school during the day.

It wasn't unusual to see bodies of men and young boys lying beside the road or stacked on street corners as we drove to school. We could only assume that they had been slain by soldiers during the night. What appalled me most was that the family of anyone who was killed for what was considered antirevolutionary activity, was required to pay a two-hundred-fifty-dollar bullet fee before they were allowed to take the body of their loved one home to bury. I knew this had to have an unsettling effect on the children, but after we discussed it several times, we unconsciously took it in stride just as we did all the other inconveniences of the revolution. Such sights just became part of our everyday experience. It was strange, but it was how we coped.

Regularly I warned the children about what to do if trouble were to erupt while we were at school.

"Listen to me, kids. It is important for you to know this. If there is shooting or any kind of trouble at school, please, just stay in your classroom. Don't go looking for the shooting or trouble. Just stay put so I can come and find you. Do you all understand?" I asked, trying to sound firm. They tended to take my warnings lightly, and I was intent upon making them realize that the situation in Addis was precarious. After all, including the Emperor's overthrow, we had had three major shifts in the government, and each one had ended in a bloody massacre of the previous government's officials. We never knew when another government uprising would occur.

CHAPTER   TEN

"Get Those Children Out of Town!"

By February 1977, a year after the girls came to live with us, we were well settled into our routine. We were looking forward to the Easter holiday and another vacation to Sodere. On Monday morning as we drove to school, there seemed to be more military activity than normal. I didn't mention it to the children; however, I kept a watchful eye out for any sign of trouble. I was relieved that the children didn't seem to notice. I watched nervously as military jeeps sped by me in the direction of the old Menelik Palace. Passing just below the main gate, I saw tanks poised along the embankment in front of the palace. No one would be crazy enough to try to get through those gates, I thought to myself.

Just after the morning break I was busy with one reading group while my assistant Elizabeth worked with the other children. Suddenly I heard rifle fire. I watched the children to see if they were aware of what it was. There was a violent explosion that sounded like a tank firing. I stood up. Some of the children covered their ears. Fear registered on their tiny faces.

"Children," I began. My voice was muffled by another round of machine-gun blasts and the explosion of hand grenades—then another respite. "Children, let's play house. I want everyone to pretend his desk is a little house. Everyone crawl into his house. Get down," I called as I moved along the aisles helping them get under their desks. Elizabeth caught on quickly and began helping the children on her side of the classroom.

Just as I had tucked the last child safely under his desk, my classroom door burst open and in ran all six of my own children.

Shocked by their sudden arrival, I yelled, "What are you doing here? I told you if there was trouble you were to stay in your classrooms. You might have been shot! We have no idea where this shooting is!"

They were nearly in shock with fear, and I realized my motherly lecture was inappropriate. Another explosion!

"Get down!" I shouted. "Those windows might break! Elizabeth, get under my desk," I yelled across the room. My classroom door opened again. It was Denton. "What are you doing here? How did you get through all of that?" I asked pointing toward the shooting.

His face was pale. "Jodie, there is trouble at the palace. I'm sure the school will be evacuated soon. Parents are pouring in here in droves! As soon as the school is evacuated, you come home the back way, over the river. You might have to park the car on this side and wade across if it's too deep to drive. Don't try to come the regular way. It's chaos! I'm going to take the kids and head home!"

Within five minutes Denton had come and gone. I was relieved not to have to worry about my own children. I waited as each child's parent arrived and whisked him away. Within the hour the entire school was empty.

It was hard to believe the uproar of the past hour as I drove home. The streets were quiet.

When I arrived home, everyone was gathered around the shortwave radio, trying to find some news about what had happened. "I'm sure it is too early to learn anything, but maybe the British Broadcasting Company will have something to report later today. Why don't we just keep the radio on?" Denton suggested. There was no news until the next day. Denton was the only one who ventured out of the house. He returned with a copy of the *Ethiopian Herald*. The headlines explained yesterday's uprising. "Counter-Revolutionary Coup Foiled," the article was entitled. "The Provisional

Military Administration Council announced that it had yesterday foiled an attempted counterrevolutionary coup d'etat against it." The article implied there had been a subtle plot from within the Derg and described the revolution as impotent and unable to march forward as fast as it should have, due to the ring leaders' subversive activities with other groups working against the revolution. A list of the dead included the chairman of the Derg, Brig. Gen. Teferi Bante. The article did not mention who had usurped the power from Teferi Bante.

Two days after the coup, the *Ethiopian Herald* carried pictures of the First Vice-Chairman, Lt. Col. Mengistu Haile-Mariam, receiving ambassadors from German Democratic Republic, People's Republic of China, and Hungary, expressing their countries' wholehearted support of the Ethiopian Socialist Revolution. Other headlines described the grand rallies and massive demonstrations of an unprecedented scale and enthusiasm being held throughout the country, congratulating Col. Mengistu and reiterating unequivocal support of the revolution. One article stated, "The death of genuine revolutionaries will lay the cornerstone of the proletariat dictatorship."

By the following week the political situation appeared stabilized, and life in Addis Ababa took on its normal appearance.

Two weeks after the coup, I went to the American embassy for lunch. I hadn't seen Carol since the trouble, and I was happy when I saw her taking the telephone orders. I signaled for her to join me when she had finished.

I had just settled into my chair when she came up beside me. She looked worried. "Jodie!" She leaned over as if to whisper something. "Have you heard the news?"

"What news, Carol? There seems to be so much lately." I smiled.

"Jodie, please, be serious." Her voice trembled and it was obvious that something was wrong. "We've got to talk, and we can't do it in here. Let's go for a walk." I followed her outside. We both knew the snack bar was a lair of Ethiopian secret service men in the guise of dishwashers, waiters, and cooks.

She barely cleared the snack bar door, when she began

again, "Jodie, haven't you heard the news? It's about your Ethiopian children!"

"What news, Carol? I haven't heard anything about them."

"Jodie, listen to me. There is talk that you are going to lose those kids. This new government is considering arresting the children, putting them back into prison with their parents, and then putting the royal family on trial. You know what that means, don't you? It means they will execute them."

I was dumbstruck. I couldn't find words to respond.

"Carol . . ." was all I could say.

We walked silently around the circular driveway in front of the ambassador's residence. Neither of us spoke for several minutes. A barrage of thoughts was going through my mind: An escape. Michael. England. Denton. The parents.

"Jodie, what are you going to do?"

"I don't know, Carol. I just don't know."

"You've talked for months about getting them out of Ethiopia. You are going to have to move and move quickly if you are to succeed at all. What about those people in England you visited last summer? Can you go back there?"

We began our second lap around the ambassador's driveway.

"Yes, I must go back. They said to come if things got worse. I don't see how things can get worse than this. Once the government puts the children back into prison, there will be no way to escape. It is now or never!" I concluded with resolve.

"What will Denton say?" she asked.

"I'm sure he is going to be as shocked as I am!"

"Will he let you return to England?"

"I can't imagine his saying no," I responded thoughtfully. I sighed deeply.

"Jodie, come back to the snack bar with me. There is someone there I want you to meet. I hope he's still there."

Reentering the snack bar, I walked back to my table. Carol disappeared across the room, leaving me deep in my own thoughts.

How will I get out of my contract at the English School?

What will we say to the children when I suddenly leave? How will Denton react to all of this? God, I thought, what will I do if soldiers come into our home and try to take these children? My thoughts raced until I heard Carol beside me again.

"Jodie, come over here."

I followed her across the room. We stopped beside a handsome man who seemed to be in his late thirties or early forties.

"Jodie, this is Brad. He flew helicopters in Vietnam. Why don't you sit down here?" she said, pulling the chair out for me.

Brad waited until I was seated and then gave Carol a knowing nod. Patting me on the shoulder, Carol continued, "Brad knows everything! Trust him." And she disappeared into her office, leaving us alone.

"Carol tells me you're interested in helicopters."

With Carol gone, I felt uneasy, embarrassed, and abandoned. Leaning toward me, he continued, "Carol has explained your situation. Maybe we should go for a walk."

"All right," I agreed.

Shall I trust him? I've never seen this man before, and Carol just dumps me into his lap. I trust Carol, so why not trust Brad? Who is he, anyway? Carol didn't say anything except that he had flown helicopters in Vietnam. He must be military. Is he the military attaché or with the secret service or CIA?

"How long have you had the royal children with you, Jodie?"

"One year this month." I hoped I wouldn't start crying. I wanted to keep my composure and try to resolve this terrible dilemma. It couldn't help if I dissolved into a mass of tears. I felt my throat constrict as I began talking about the children. I waited, giving myself time to calm down. Brad didn't rush me. We continued to walk up the hill toward the ambassador's residence. Before I began talking again, I knew I had decided I was going to confide in Brad. At this point there appeared to be no other alternative. Carol obviously trusted him.

"Brad, I just can't let the children go to prison. If soldiers come to our home and take them away, I think I will die. I would never just sit there and let them be carried off!"

I fumbled in my jacket pocket for a tissue. I couldn't stop the flood of tears. Stop, I chided myself. Why do you have to be so emotional?

"Carol mentioned you have talked to someone in England about planning an escape."

"Yes, last summer I made a few inquiries. They told me they were hopeful things would get better in Addis. They also said they needed time to consider the things I asked them about: getting an airplane, raising money for an escape—you know, technicalities like that."

"Did they sound hopeful?"

"The only hope I had was when they told me that if things got worse, I should come back and see them."

"Are you going?"

"I'm not certain at this point. Carol just told me about the rumor. Is it true, Brad?"

He put his hands into his pockets as we walked slowly around the driveway. His mood was contemplative.

"Jodie, I do know this. You need to get those children out of town this weekend."

"This weekend! I can't plan an escape by this weekend!"

"No, not the escape. You just need to be out of the city for this weekend. There is a huge military rally in support of this new leader, Mengistu. There is a possibility that the children will be arrested this weekend, a political maneuver to assure the people that Lt. Col. Mengistu is committed to the revolution and that there are no reversals planned in dealing with the old system."

"What am I going to do?"

"Talk to Carol. She and her family are going to Lake Langano this weekend to the American campground. We talked earlier today about your family going with them. Just get those kids out of Addis."

We rounded the corner near the rose garden. I had trusted Brad this far, so I decided to risk everything and ask for Brad's help.

"Brad, Carol said you flew helicopters in Vietnam. Is there any chance we could get the kids out of here in helicopters?"

"I do have a few contacts; unfortunately I'm not still connected with anyone flying helicopters. Over the weekend I will do some checking around. You'll be here on Monday, right?"

"Yes, I'll be here."

"All right. We'll talk again then."

As we approached the snack bar, we changed the subject completely and began talking about the weather and the lovely grounds surrounding the embassy. "I like the sod tennis courts they've just redone, don't you?" Brad asked nonchalantly.

"Yes," I smiled, trying to look more relaxed than I felt. "Do you play tennis?"

"Yes, do you?"

"Yes, in fact, last Christmas I bought a tennis membership at the Hilton Hotel for Denton and the family. There are so few places where we can go where the children aren't recognized. I thought the Hilton would be a nice place to swim and play tennis. Denton and I try to play tennis several times each week and swim daily. The kids and I go nearly every day after school."

"That's great. The Hilton has a lovely pool. I haven't played on their tennis courts. Are they good courts?"

"They're fine," I said as he held the door open for me. Carol was beaming as we walked into the snack bar. "Well, did you two have a good walk?" she asked knowingly.

"Yes, we did. It was nice meeting you, Brad," I said. "Thank you for everything. I will see you Monday. Carol, I need to get back to school, but Brad's suggestion about this weekend sounds great. I'll call you tonight, and we'll make plans."

Things didn't go well at home that evening. Denton was usually eager for a chance to leave Addis Ababa for a few days, but when I explained my lunch with Carol and the subsequent meeting with Brad, he became very quiet and withdrawn. I was reluctant to tell him what Brad had suggested for the weekend, but I continued, "Brad suggests that we get the children out of Addis for the weekend, Denton. He feels it is risky to stay in town. Carol and Bill are going to Lake Langano with their children. They are leaving Friday evening. Why don't you get someone to preach for you on Sunday so you can go?"

"No, I'm not going," he said quietly.

"Denton, be reasonable," I shouted. "Brad said there is a real chance the children will be arrested this weekend."

"Jodie, you can go and take the children if you like, but I'm not going."

"Fine then," I raged. "Stay in Addis. I'm taking the children to Langano. I don't understand you! You say you want to help them, and now when it is a matter of life and death, you won't even go with me to Langano. You make me sick!" I yelled, storming from the room.

We barely spoke throughout the rest of the week. When the children and I arrived home from school Friday afternoon, he was there. "I'll help you get the gear together and pack the car," he offered, much more like his usual self. He didn't seem to mind that I was going, but I was still upset. Did he doubt the validity of my story or Brad's? Obviously he wasn't taking the situation seriously.

I planned to meet Carol and Bill at the Mobil station on the Debre Zeit Road and follow them to Lake Langano. It would be a late night, I thought, filling the thermos with the hot coffee Feyesa had fixed for me to take. It usually took us six hours to drive to the lake. By the time we got the tents set up and got settled tonight, we would be ready for a good night's sleep!

I glanced around the kitchen, making sure I had packed everything into the big wooden box we used for our kitchen box when we camped. "Feyesa," I called through the kitchen window, "if you have finished helping Mr. Collins pack the car, would you carry the kitchen box out to the car for me?"

As he and Denton lifted the box into the back of the Kombie, I climbed into the driver's seat. "Is everything ready?" I asked, trying to sound more confident than I felt. I wondered if I could really set up a camp by myself. *Never mind, Brent and I will do it*, I thought. *I can always ask Bill to help me if I need it*, I reminded myself.

The kids piled into the back of the car. "Can I ride in front?" Loly asked through the window.

"Sure, hop in."

Denton came around to my window to say goodbye. "Have a good trip," he called to the kids in the back of the car. "And you, too," he said as a peace gesture.

I only nodded. I was still put out with him that he wasn't coming. I just couldn't figure it out. He had never been like this.

As I neared the Mobil station, I saw Carol and Bill's car. As I pulled up beside them, Bill called out the window, "Why don't you follow me out of town? We'll go through the army checkpoint together."

I waved, indicating I would follow.

We were several miles from the roadblock when I saw army jeeps and tanks along the roadside. The checkpoint had been here for three years, but I had never seen such heavy military equipment around. Traffic was backed up for miles. I saw Bill drive off the road and park under some trees. I followed. I pulled up beside Carol's side of the car just as she was rolling down her window. "What could be wrong?" I asked softly. There were thirty or forty other cars parked around us.

"I can't imagine," she said, obviously concerned.

I got out and walked over to their car. "Carol, do you think they are looking for the kids?" I felt panicked by the thought.

"Maybe we should go back to the American Club and see if we can find Brad," she said in a hushed voice.

"What do you think, Bill?" I asked.

"Well, we won't be getting through here for awhile. Let's go get something to eat and try again later."

"OK, I'll follow you out to the Club," I said, turning to get back into the car.

"What's wrong, Mom?" Brent asked.

I was deep in my own thoughts, and his voice startled me. When we had started seeing the tanks, soldiers, and jeeps, they had all been quiet, and I had been very intent on the whole situation.

"Oh, it's probably nothing. Some kind of a delay," I reassured them, sounding more confident than I felt at the moment. I wondered if the children sensed the seriousness of this weekend. I hoped not. They have been through so much,

I thought sadly. I wished I could spare them any more scares or threats of arrest. Being under house arrest was surely enough. But I knew that I couldn't predict what this government might do to prove to the people that they held firmly to the goals of the revolution. They might even arrest children to prove their resolve. Putting the royal family on trial and executing them might be all they would need to show their determination and confirm to the people that the revolution would move forward at any cost, including that of the children's lives.

"O God, help us," I uttered half to myself and half out loud.

"Mom, where are we going now?" Loly asked.

"We are going to the American Club and have dinner."

"Hurray," they all shouted. "Can we get ice cream?" Brent piped up.

"Oh, sure," I said. "What's the American Club without ice cream!"

We were not the only ones who had to change our plans. The American Club was buzzing with rumors of why we had all been turned back. "Maybe it's another coup," someone suggested.

As the children were ordering their hamburgers and milkshakes, I saw Brad across the room.

"Order me a hot dog and fries, Shellie. I'll be right back. Carol, do you want to come with me?" I asked.

"Sure, Jodie. Bill has gone to see if he can find out what is going on."

"Kids, you all stay right here until our order comes. We'll be right back."

I walked directly toward Brad. He saw me coming and nodded for me to follow him outside onto the patio.

"Do you think this roadblock has anything to do with us? Are they looking for the kids?" I asked as soon as he had closed the sliding glass door behind us.

"No, Jodie, there has been a bank robbery. Counterrevolutionaries robbed a branch bank. They are looking for them."

He smiled, and I felt better than I had in the last hour. He laughed aloud and asked, "Did you really think they were looking for you?"

"Yes, of course I did. I can't tell you how much better I feel now!"

"Is your husband here?" he asked.

"No, he didn't want to come. Maybe I'll call and ask him if he's changed his mind since we have been delayed. He could still join us."

"Good idea. There's the phone over there."

"Thanks, Brad. See you later."

"Yes, I'll see you Monday at the embassy snack bar. Don't forget," he reminded me as I headed for the telephone.

"Don't worry," I called back to him. "That's one appointment I won't forget!"

I felt so much better as I dialed home. I was happy when Denton answered the phone. I explained all that had happened, and then asked, "Denton, please, won't you go with us to Langano?"

"No, Jodie, I just don't want to go this weekend. That's all there is to it!"

I was mad at him all over again and sorry I had bothered to phone him. When I returned to the table, everyone was laughing and having such a good time, it was difficult to stay angry or depressed by Denton's refusal to come along. I decided to join in and make the best of the weekend. I ate my hot dog and fries and ordered ice cream for all of us.

"Shall we get on the road?" Bill suggested. "We still have a long drive ahead of us."

"Sounds good to me. Does anyone know if the road is open?"

"We just got word that it is open, and traffic is moving along again," Bill assured me.

"Are you ready, kids?" I called to them. They all sat at the table across the aisle from ours.

"Brent, why don't you wipe the ice cream off Amaha's face and take him to the bathroom and wash his hands and face? He is really sticky."

"Why doesn't one of the girls take him?" he argued.

"Just do it, Brent," I said, feeling some of the strain of the evening.

Soon we were back on the road. The soldiers at the checkpoint were edgy. They must have had a long night looking for the bank robbers. They examined Carol and Bill's car quite thoroughly and made them get out. I was happy when they only opened the back door of our car, looked in, slammed the door, and waved us through. Whew! I thought, you never know what they are going to do! Before an hour had passed, the children were curled up in their blankets, and the only noise was the hum of the car's engine and an occasional gurgle or deep breath as sleep overtook each child. I was thankful for the respite from their chattering. I settled back in my seat and concentrated on the road to Langano.

We arrived at the lake about two o'clock in the morning. I was surprised by how smoothly we were able to get the tents up and get settled with only our Coleman lanterns and flashlights. Brent was a great help to me and worked diligently until the last bit of work was completed. I was greatly relieved when all the children were tucked into their sleeping bags. I think they were asleep before I got my sleeping bag spread out. I was too tired to take off my clothes. I just crawled into my bag and fell sound asleep. I didn't stir until I smelled coffee brewing about mid-morning.

The weekend went smoothly. We enjoyed swimming and fishing, and Saturday afternoon we went waterskiing. It was great fun, and I was sorry that Denton was not there to enjoy it. He loved to waterski, and I knew he would be disappointed when he heard Bill had arranged for a boat and skiing.

We returned to Addis on Sunday afternoon, and our trip was uneventful. Although we had to stop at the checkpoint, the soldiers were more relaxed and not as thorough as they had been on Friday evening.

Denton appeared relaxed when we arrived home. Maybe he just needed a weekend to himself, I thought, as he hugged each of the kids and welcomed us all home. Feyesa greeted us warmly and began unloading the car.

"I couldn't even get out of here to go to my office on Saturday, not even for choir practice. Red Square was packed with a huge rally. All the roads were blocked. Working in the yard, I could hear the masses cheering and the loudspeakers, although I could not make out what they were saying. The radio said it was the largest rally ever held at Red Square. They reported that over 100,000 people attended the 'spontaneous gathering,' " Denton said a bit sarcastically. "Of course, you know what happens if you don't attend a political rally; you are shot. I'd hardly call them spontaneous."

Denton never mentioned why he hadn't wanted to go to Lake Langano. I didn't bother to bring up the subject again.

During lunchtime on Monday, I returned to the American embassy to meet Brad and Carol. I knew what I had to do as soon as I saw Carol walking toward me. Her face was tense and pale. It was like looking in a mirror, I was sure.

We only greeted each other in the snack bar. "Shall we go for a walk?" she asked solemnly. As we strolled toward the tennis courts, I saw Brad coming our way. A deep sense of foreboding enveloped me, and I knew the outcome of Brad's weekend encounter with his contact before he even reached us.

"Hi, Brad. Did you have a good weekend?" I asked.

He tried to smile. "It was eventful, let me put it that way."

Carol stood at my side quietly. I knew just by the expression on her face that she had already talked to Brad.

"What did you find out, Brad?"

"Shall we walk?" he said, leading the way up the driveway. Carol and I fell into an easy stride beside him. "I'm sorry, Jodie," he began haltingly. "I tried. I really did. I should never have risked meeting my contacts like I did on Saturday, but I wanted to help you.

"You won't believe this," he continued, "but I lay in the back of this lady's car, on the floor, while she sat in the driver's seat, staring out the window. We talked for nearly an hour, but she assured me there is nothing she can do to help at this time. She did say that they might be able to help at some future date, but Jodie, I told her that you didn't have that much time to wait. From what I understand, you are running out of time. You need to find a way to get those children out of Ethiopia."

I felt sick at my stomach, and I knew it was just nerves.

"It's OK, Brad. Please don't feel bad. I really do appreciate all you have done and the risks you took contacting that lady. What is the best thing for me to do at this point? Does either of you have any ideas?"

"Jodie, I think you should proceed with your previous plan. Return to England and see if your contacts there can help you out. Don't you agree, Carol?"

"Yes, that seems best. Thank you, Brad, for trying."

"I should get back to my office," he said, looking very troubled and apologetic.

"Brad," I repeated, "please don't feel bad. I know you tried."

"One other thing, Jodie. I mentioned an alternative plan to Carol earlier this morning. She will explain it to you, but I think it has possibilities. Talk it over with Carol and see what you think. She knows where to reach me."

I shook his hand firmly, wishing I could say more, but I didn't trust myself. I didn't want to cry again. Taking a deep breath, I hoped to stay my next deluge of tears until I was alone again.

"I'll see you later, Carol," he said as he turned and headed across the lawn toward his office.

I felt Carol's arm in mine as we passed the rose garden for the third time. Neither of us knew what to say. I sensed how much she wanted to help, but it seemed as if I would have to carry on from this point.

"Jodie," Carol interrupted my thoughts. "Brad suggested that you divide the children up and put each child in a home with diplomatic immunity. Then report to the Ethiopian officials that the children have been kidnapped from school. In the case of a mass evacuation of American personnel, the children could be shuffled to the airport and airlifted out of here."

We walked for some distance before I responded to the suggestion. "I don't know why, Carol, but I'm not comfortable with that plan. At that point, if anything went wrong, it would be too late to get them out. Too many people would have to be involved. Besides, I don't think it would be good for the children's emotional state to be separated from one another. Although they have never mentioned it and I doubt that they are even aware of it, I think they draw strength from one another. No, I just don't think it will work," I said intuitively.

Carol must have sensed that I was thinking, and she didn't interrupt my train of thought as we made another loop around the driveway.

"We must escape," I whispered. "I'm just not certain *how*."

We continued walking arm and arm.

"Yes, there is no turning back. I know we must try to escape." My mind was made up. I knew I had to try.

"What will you do, Jodie?"

"I must leave for England immediately."

"When?"

"There are many things to work out, a lot of details. They aren't all clear in my mind, but I know I must try to resign my job at the English School. I am under contract through this school year. I must find a way to convince the new Headmaster to release me from the contract. I wish the Casbones were still here. They would understand, I'm certain. I guess the most important thing I have to do is to try to explain the urgency of all of this to Denton. Brad repeated today that we don't seem to have much time before the children are picked up. I wish he could have been more specific. I will have to apply for an exit visa. If the Ethiopian government gets wind of my plan, I will never get out of here. What worries me the most right now is how to tell the children I'm leaving. I know I cannot tell them why I'm leaving. Carol, the fewer people who know about all of this, the better."

"What can I do to help you, Jodie?"

I began walking to my car. "I'm not certain just now. I feel as if you've done so much already."

"Oh, Jodie, I've done nothing."

"Don't be silly. No one has been more supportive and understanding than you, Carol. I wouldn't even know the children's lives are in danger if it weren't for you," I reminded her.

When we reached the car, I turned and gave her a hug. "If it were not for your encouragement, I can't imagine how I would face all this upheaval. I'll see you tomorrow. Maybe I'll have some answers for you then."

As I pulled out of the embassy grounds, I whispered to myself, *Escape, escape.* It sounded so ominous!

CHAPTER ELEVEN
The Secret Code

"Escape! England!" Denton sat in the living room shaking his head in disbelief.

"Denton, you sound as if we've never even discussed escaping with the children. This isn't a new idea, you know. Remember my trip last summer? Wasn't it for this very purpose? You know they told me to come back to England if things got worse. How can they get worse than this unless soldiers actually come and take the children away? I can't just sit around and wait for that to happen, Denton. Don't you understand? We are going to lose them if we don't do something and do it quick!"

We had been talking for nearly an hour. I was glad it was Feyesa's day off. I wouldn't have been able to talk as openly if he had been there. The children were outside playing with Amaha. I had gone over everything that Brad, Carol, and I had discussed.

"I don't like the alternative plan. Putting the children into separate homes and waiting for a major crisis so they can be evacuated sounds too risky to me."

"An airlift doesn't sound risky?" Denton emphasized.

"I'm not saying there are not risks involved. There are! And I don't underestimate what I'm asking you to do, Denton. But one of us must go to England and try to arrange something. It would be next to impossible for you to get an exit visa with all of the back taxes still pending against our Mission. You insist it is better for me to go than for you, since I made the initial contacts. It sounds to me as if we have decided what needs to be done."

"Jodie, listen to me. You and I can hardly believe all that is happening in Addis. How are you going to convince anyone in England how serious the situation here really is?

"Denton, I have no idea how I will convince them. To be perfectly honest, Denton, without God's help I don't think we are going to accomplish a single thing. You're the minister. I don't have to remind you of that. You know that wall plaque you have on the wall behind the pulpit in the church. It is a quotation by Jim Elliot, 'Ask great things of God; expect great things of God; attempt great things for God.' I think that is what we need to do in this case."

Denton leaned forward in his chair with his head in his hands.

"What are you thinking, Denton?" His silence annoyed me more than when he argued or brainstormed with me.

"I know you are going to do just what you want to do. What I say won't make any difference. If you have made up your mind to go to England, you'll go. I don't think you are being sensitive to the other missionaries and how all of this is going to affect them."

I was angry that he seemed so emotionally detached from what I was feeling. "How can you say that, Denton?"

"Jodie, all you are thinking about is the children. What about all the other lives you will be affecting? Can't you see that?"

"Denton," I pleaded. "Our time is limited! Anyone can see that it is just a matter of time until all missionaries will have to leave here, and I don't want to leave the children behind in prison!" My voice was irate, my patience exhausted from the emotional strain of the past week.

"What will you do in England?"

"I've already said, I don't know at this point. I will try to convince them to help me plan an escape, an airlift of some sort."

Our nerves were cracking. I was shouting, and my anger had replaced any objectivity I might have had. The angrier I got, the more Denton withdrew and said nothing. We had reached an impasse.

I got up and left the room. During dinner I could barely talk. I was certain the children could feel the tension between Denton and me. They carried most of the conversation. I was the first one to leave the table. I was dressing for bed when Denton came into the bedroom. He stood with his hands in his pockets. He closed the door and stood quietly for a few mintues before he spoke.

"Jodie, I will apply for your exit visas tomorrow. I want you to take Shellie and Brent with you to England. If you can arrange an escape, all right. If you cannot work anything out, it's best if you just go to the States and wait for me there. Don't try to come back here. That would be too dangerous."

I was shocked by his change of mind. I said nothing.

"How do you plan to tell the four kids you are leaving?" he asked.

"I don't know. I hadn't really thought about it yet. I know we shouldn't tell them the real reason I'm leaving. If word got out, they would disappear before we had time to do one thing. That would be their death warrant for sure!"

"Maybe you could tell them you are going to be with your mother during her surgery."

"That's a good idea!" In all the commotion I had forgotten that my mother was going into the hospital for surgery.

"It would make sense that I would take Shellie and Brent, too, I suppose. Mom's surgery isn't that serious, but they don't know that. I didn't mention what kind of surgery it was when I told them about it. I will just say that it is best that we are with her."

Yes, the longer I thought about that, the better it seemed. I was relieved that Denton had warmed a little to the idea of my going.

"Denton." I was leery about bringing the subject up again, but I continued, "Why are you so reluctant to go ahead with the escape when we have been talking about it for months? I just don't understand."

"Jodie, we are talking about life and death. If one thing goes wrong, many lives could be lost. Have you thought of the parents? If we escape, the military might kill them! And have you thought about how the kids will feel ten or fifteen years from now, if we do get them out safely? You know good and well it will probably turn out just like it has with Tolessa."

"What do you mean by that?"

"Well, they will probably walk away from us and never look back, once they are in America and settled."

I thought about what he said. It hadn't crossed my mind, but I knew there was probably some truth to what he said. It didn't seem possible now, but I knew it might happen in the years to come. We had helped Tolessa for nearly eleven years, and now we didn't even know where he was.

"Denton, do you remember what Emama Yilkukulish said to me before she died?" Emama Yilkukulish was a very wise old woman. Her daughter, Aklok, and I had been very good friends. Before our own house had been completed, our contract on our rented house had expired, and Aklok and her mother had invited us to live with them until our house was ready. One day, after we had lived with them for nearly a month, I had been upset by Tolessa's attitude. Emama Yilkukulish was ill, and she called me to her bedside. "My dear one," she began, taking my hand in hers, "you are a kind woman. You are helping this young boy, and he may never understand all you have given to him. It goes beyond the food and clothes you have given him. However, whatever you do in this life, you must do unto God. You must never expect to hear thank you from those you help. You must do all unto God, and you will never be disappointed." I had never forgotten her words, and I quoted them again to Denton.

"If there is any way that we can do this 'unto God,' as Emama Yilkukulish suggested, perhaps it will be less painful if that time ever comes."

I was under no illusions, however. Even though I had reminded myself of this saying many times since Tolessa had left, I still felt the pain deep within me at times. The pain would never go away; it would only abate from time to time.

"I will apply for your exit visas tomorrow," he repeated, unable to think of anything further to say.

He turned and left the room.

Maybe I had underestimated what I was asking him to do, I thought as I lay there in the darkness of my bedroom—asking him to stay behind and care for four children who were not even his own while I go off to England and try to plan his escape. There aren't too many husbands who would even apply for your exit visa, Jodie! I reminded myself. They would just say, "It's out of the question. You are not going, and that's that!"

I was so glad Denton hadn't done that. Next I would have to face the children with the news. I would do that tomorrow night.

The following evening after dinner, I went to the girls' room. Brent was sitting on Loly's bed doing his homework. Amaha was sitting on the top bunk with Shellie, looking at his picture book and saying the name of each picture in perfect English. I couldn't believe how his English had improved in four months. The children looked up from their homework as I came into the room. I sat down on a chair near the door.

"I've got something I need to tell you," I began. They all looked very serious as if they knew intuitively what I was going to say. Perhaps it was just my imagination.

"Remember I told you the other day when I got a letter from Grandma Pavone that she was going to have hip surgery?"

They all nodded.

"Well, I have decided that it is best if I take Shellie and Brent and fly home to be with her. It is quite a serious operation, and I think it is best."

"You mean we get to miss school?" Brent queried.

"If we are home for any length of time, you will go to school there."

"Oh, Mom, let us stay here. We don't want to leave school now. It's the middle of the school year," Shellie pleaded.

"I'm sorry, Shellie. Daddy and I have discussed it, and we think it is best if you and Brent go with me."

I felt the walls of misunderstanding going up. I sensed they were shutting me out. As I left their room, I tried to convince myself they were hurt. If they understood the real reason I was leaving they would be happy. *Perhaps they will feel better about it tomorrow,* I thought.

I lay in bed that night thinking about the last two days. It hadn't been easy. Denton felt I was just thinking of the children and being insensitive to the missionaries. Now the children were upset with me. I felt lonely and weary.

The following morning I had made another decision. I made an appointment to see Mr. Cole-Baker during our twenty-minute morning break. I knew it was dangerous, but I decided to tell him the reason I was submitting my resignation. I wanted an immediate answer, not a complicated process of submitting my resignation to the board of directors and waiting for their long-drawn-out consideration of my application. It was a brief meeting. I had not had many opportunities to discuss things with him since he came to the school in September, but I found him warm and sympathetic. He accepted my resignation without delay, and offered to write me a letter of recommendation besides. I thought him very kind, and left his office feeling my first tinge of affirmation. At least something has gone favorably, I thought to myself as I returned to my classroom after break time. I would miss my class. I had been happier since I had taught at the English School than any time since I had been in Ethiopia. I had met many wonderful, interesting people, and I enjoyed the children immensely.

Something had been on my mind for days. At lunch I decided to do something about it. I drove to Miss van de Loo's office, hoping I would catch her before she left for her lunch. Often she worked through her lunch break. I hoped today was one of those days. Miss van de Loo had been very close to the mothers of Loly, Amaha, Kokeb, and Menen. For years she had worked to develop the Ethiopian Women's Welfare Organization. The organization's headquarters were completed just a few months prior to the Princesses' arrest. A pity, I thought, that they were not able to continue their work when there was so much to be done on behalf of the women of Ethiopia. Miss van de Loo had carried on much of the work begun by Princess Sebele, president of the organization. Each week Miss van de Loo took food to the prison. If the Princesses requested something special, and there was a way to get it into the prison, Miss van de Loo did it. When small letters were permitted to come from the prison to the family members, she was the one who brought them to the children. She also encouraged the children to write their mothers on very small pieces of paper, and each week I tried to make sure they wrote, so Miss van de Loo could deliver the letters whenever she had an opportunity. I knew she was an important link between the mothers and the outside world. She had visited the Princesses in prison on one occasion, and there was a possibility that she would be seeing them again soon. That was what I was counting on.

She greeted me warmly as her secretary took me into her office. She was a very straightforward lady. I liked that. We spent little time on trivialities, and I got right to the point. We sat together on a couch in her office.

She motioned to me to talk very softly. Perhaps she thought her office was bugged. I nearly whispered, "Miss van de Loo, are you going to see the Princesses?"

She shrugged her shoulders indicating she was still uncertain. "I want you to take a message to them. Ask them what they think about getting the children out of Ethiopia."

She immediately put her fingers to her lips. I didn't continue.

Lowering her voice, she said, "If you have any such plans, please—I don't want to hear them. It is too dangerous for me to know anything. If I am arrested and interrogated, I don't want to know such information. Please!"

She was honest. It was a sincere appeal and not unrealistic. She had such close ties with the deposed royal family that her position in Ethiopia was tenuous. I had said what I came to say. The rest was up to her.

I took my leave and returned to school.

Miss van de Loo came to the house two days before I was ready to leave Ethiopia. We had just sat down in the living room when Feyesa came in and asked if he could bring us coffee.

"No, thank you," Miss van de Loo replied. "I cannot stay. I

have another appointment in forty-five minutes, and I must be going."

I nodded to Feyesa and said, "It's all right, Feyesa. We will have coffee together another day when Miss van de Loo has more time. She won't be staying long."

She made sure he had returned to the kitchen before she leaned near to me and said, "The Princesses have said they will pay any price for the freedom of their children."

I sat back in my chair. Relief swept over me. I had their answer. I understood it to mean that they were willing to die if it meant life and freedom for their children. I knew we were risking at least that much. I didn't know how Miss van de Loo had done it, but it didn't matter. What mattered was that the mothers knew and approved. I could continue with my plans with even more confidence than I had felt up to this point. Miss van de Loo was gone within minutes of delivering her message. I wondered if she really had another appointment.

When she had gone, I went to the kitchen and asked Feyesa to bring me a cup of hot tea. I returned to the living room.

Curling up on one end of the couch, sipping my tea, I thought about the days ahead. I had no idea of how Michael would feel when I arrived in England nearly five months early. "I need time," he had said. "Give me until July, and then come back again."

It was only February, but I couldn't wait until July. Brad said that would be too late. How much time do we have? *Why can't the voice of God just come right out of heaven and tell me what to do? Why do I have to make all of these decisions on my own? What if this whole things blows sky-high and I lose Denton and the kids? God, where are You? I don't feel any specific direction. I hear no still, small voice guiding me, and yet you've promised to direct the steps of your children. Come on, Jodie. Where is all that trust you've learned about, taught about? You believe in God—just move ahead. Make the decisions you have to make, believing that God is guiding you, giving you the wisdom to make the right choices. Faith doesn't require voices and signs, Jodie.*

It was getting dark outside. I walked across the room and

stood in front of the large picture window. "Treasures in darkness," I said out loud. Yes, Denton had preached a sermon on that a few weeks ago. Would all of this darkness that seemed to encompass me like a shroud ever seem light again? What would become of our home, our friends, our Ethiopian children?

Was I having second thoughts about the escape? I had to admit I was afraid, but I knew it wouldn't keep me from going to England. If I didn't go, I wouldn't be able to live with myself. I had to try, and with God's help, I would succeed.

I spent my last afternoon with Carol. She took me to exchange my Ethiopian money for U. S. currency. As we were returning to the American embassy, Carol looked at me and asked, "Jodie, if an escape plan does materialize, just how will you communicate with Denton?"

"I guess I hadn't thought that far ahead, Carol."

"One thing is for sure," she said emphatically. "You don't dare talk openly on the telephone. It is likely that your phone is tapped, since you have the children with you. Your mail might even be censored, so don't risk trying to explain to Denton in a letter."

"Do you think I need a code, Carol?"

She laughed, "Really, Jodie, that might not be a bad idea."

We drove for several miles before I had an idea. "We could talk about an operation or surgery, and if I give the time and date of the surgery, Denton would know the time and date of the escape."

"That's great, Jodie! How about Catherine's surgery? That's my sister's name."

"I'm hoping I can get someone to come back to Addis and explain the details of this 'surgery' to Denton. We can refer to that man as the 'doctor.' "

"This is getting better all the time, Jodie. The code will help you when you talk to Denton by phone, too."

"Yes, that's true. Oh, Carol, do you really think this will all come together? Tell me you do!"

"You'll do it, Jodie. You aren't doing it alone, remember?"

When we reached the embassy, the guard, recognizing us,

waved us through the gate without checking our identification. I parked beside the snack bar. I wasn't going in. We both knew it was time to say goodbye, but we were hesitant, since we had no idea when we would ever meet again.

"I wonder if our paths will ever cross again, Jodie?"

I tried to keep our conversation light. "Carol, we are both world travelers. Surely we will run into each other again!"

We sat there for several minutes, and then she said, "Well, Jodie, this is it for now. You are in my prayers." She gave me a big hug. "Jodie, remind Denton to bring me any boxes he wants me to mail for him, any of your personal, smaller things that you want to get out of the country. When he leaves, he won't be taking anything but the kids with him."

"Carol, I really appreciate all you are doing—all you *have* done."

She hugged me again, and through her tears she said, "Be strong, Jodie. Trust God to work things out."

She opened the car door and stepped out. Neither of us could say anything more. She waved as I turned the corner and drove home.

All evening friends came to the house to say goodbye to Shellie, Brent, and me. It was Ethiopian custom; people had been coming for days to wish us well. Brent and the girls were very subdued, quiet, and withdrawn. In fact, they hadn't said much to me all week. This evening they came out of their bedroom only when company arrived, and they were expected to greet them and say goodbye. I understood that they were trying to draw courage from one another. I couldn't blame Shellie and Brent for their reluctance to let go of all they had ever known. They had both been raised in Ethiopia. Although no one mentioned it, everyone seemed to sense we were not coming back.

During a brief lull between guests, I called Denton into the bedroom. "Denton, Carol and I were talking today, and we thought it might be helpful if you and I had a code so we could communicate safely if I am able to formulate a plan in England. What do you think?"

He looked doubtful. "A code?"

"Yes, like a secret code, you know."

I quickly explained to him about Catherine's operation or surgery and the doctor. He remained skeptical, but said nothing until I completed my explanation. "Should we write it down somewhere?" he asked dubiously.

"No, no! I think it is better if we just try and remember it, don't you?"

"Probably," he agreed, not entirely convinced of the code's value.

I took this moment alone to ask him something that had been bothering me for days. "Denton, for months we have talked together about the possibility of escaping with the children. You had some ideas about fixing up the bus, and at one time we talked about a possible airlift with Jerry's plane. But ever since this last string of events came up, and Brad has insisted that the children's lives are in danger, you have been skeptical and withdrawn. Why is it? Can you put your finger on what is wrong?"

"Maybe," he began thoughtfully. "Before, it was something in the future, just an idea. Now it has become very much a reality. I think you are taking it too lightly. I'm really worried about it."

"Denton, please believe me. I do know how much I'm asking of you. You are the one staying behind with the kids. I know there aren't many husbands who would take such a risk. I do appreciate it, honestly I do. But at this point I don't feel that I have another choice. It is a matter of life and death either way, but something inside me feels as if we have a much better chance if we try to get outside help."

We had been over all of this before. I just felt that I wanted to clarify my thoughts one more time. The tension was still there when we returned to the living room to meet with the guests who had just arrived.

The last guest left at ten-thirty. No one wanted to risk being out after the midnight curfew. I was eager to complete packing the children's suitcases. Most of my things were packed. I planned to leave most of my older clothes behind, so I could pack a few of our Ethiopian artifacts. Denton had spent two days at the Ministry of Antiquities, getting the necessary approval for me to take them home. We had a nice collection of Ethiopian crosses, baskets, carvings, and paintings. I knew that Denton would take Carol up on her offer to send out several small boxes of our personal things, but I wanted to pack as many as I could and take them with me.

I didn't finish packing until after midnight. I opened Brent's bedroom door, and he and Amaha were fast asleep. The girls' light was off, but I could still hear their voices. When I opened their door, they stopped talking. "Good night, girls. See you in the morning." I was greeted with silence. At length I heard Menen's soft whisper, "Good night, Mom," and then the others followed suit. I closed the door and walked into the kitchen.

It was dark. Feyesa had gone to bed hours ago. I was going to miss my lovely large kitchen. Denton had drawn the plans for our home, and he had designed the kitchen with me in mind. Lots of counter space where Feyesa and I could work without bumping into each other. A special counter for rolling out my pie crusts. I think I enjoyed all the cupboard space most of all. It was a comfortable, cozy room, and as a family, we spent a lot of time there. I walked into the living room. It was dark, too. Only a few hot coals were glowing in the big marble fireplace. What will become of our home, I pondered?

Our years in Ethiopia had been good. God had blessed our lives in many ways; this home was just one. We had many wonderful friends. I wondered how many of them we would see again. I thought of Hagop and Hrip, and I was happy that things had worked out for them to move to Canada. They had given their upholstery and drapery shop to their Ethiopian workers, applied for permission to leave Ethiopia, and were planning to settle in Canada. I wondered what all the missionaries would do? Would they go to other countries in Africa? The Sidebottoms had written that they were planning to go to the Caribbean. They weren't certain just where as yet. The Singletons and Pierceys had talked of transferring to Kenya.

And what would we do? That was my biggest question. I wasn't even certain how large our family would be. Would we have six children or two? Would Denton get out of Ethiopia alive? How would he ever pay all those back taxes on the mission? I had a lot of questions, but no answers at this point. I heard the cuckoo clock chirp one o'clock, and I knew I had better get to bed.

My last night in Ethiopia, I thought sadly, as I walked toward the bedroom.

CHAPTER TWELVE
Back to London

It was the quietest drive to the airport I could recall. Amaha sat on my lap, unusually subdued. The hustle and bustle of the airport contrasted sharply with the way we each felt. Many of our Ethiopian friends had arrived at the airport before us and were waiting to say their final goodbyes. They gathered around the bus to help Denton unload the suitcases and carry them into the terminal. The airport looked as if it were under siege, it was so highly guarded by the military. Just one more reminder of the revolution.

Goodbyes were rarely easy, and this one had to be one of the most difficult I would ever face. It was interwoven with so much finality. Most of these people I had grown to love I would never see again. Haregwyn was there, one of the first Ethiopian women who had come to my ladies' meetings. We had been good friends for nearly twelve years. She spoke no English. I smiled to myself when I remembered she used to call me "Mrs. College." Of course, she knew what a college was, but she had never heard of "Collins." Now it was quite a joke between us. She was a large woman, and as I stepped down from the church bus, she enveloped me in her arms, crying openly. I held her tight. We were too torn to talk. We both just sobbed.

There were so many others: Bekele and Almaz, our pastor and his wife. How we loved them! Shaking my hand, Bekele said, "May God go with you, Mrs. Jodie. We love you. Be strong in the Lord." Almaz couldn't say that much, she just hugged and kissed me and said, "We love you." Shellie and Brent were enveloped in hugs and kisses as everyone told them goodbye. After I checked my luggage, I walked over to stand by Denton. Amaha held his arms up to me, and I picked him up. There were tears in his eyes, and I knew he understood that the time was close. Wrapping his chubby little arms around my neck, he squeezed me and said, "Bye-bye, Mommy." I didn't think I could stand it. I was too overwhelmed to respond. I handed him to Denton. I dreaded facing the girls, but I walked toward them. Shellie seemed to have her arms around all three of them. Brent had his arms through Kokeb's and Loly's. I stood behind Loly, almost afraid to touch her. I put my hands on her shoulders and she turned around to face me. Her eyes were swollen from crying. She looked at me accusingly.

"Loly, aren't you going to say goodbye?" I asked tearfully. She looked at me for several seconds, but she couldn't speak.

"Loly, why? Why are you so upset with me?"

Finally she spoke. "Mommy . . . my mother is in prison. Menen's mother is in prison. You are the only mom we have and you are leaving us!" Her words stung. I didn't know how to respond to her accusation. I held her arms and looked into her angry eyes. "Loly, sweetheart, listen to me. I love you, Kokeb, Amaha, and Mini so much. Please, Loly, please, just believe that," I pleaded, wanting to shake her. "Just trust me, Loly!" I let go of her arms and kissed her on the cheek. She kissed me coldly on each cheek and stepped back. I moved to each of the girls and kissed her goodbye. There was no more I could say, except, "Come, Shellie, Brent, it is time to go."

I walked back to where Denton was standing with several of our friends. Amaha held his arms out to me. "No, sweetheart, stay with Daddy. Mommy, Shellie, and Brent have to go now." Shellie and Brent kissed Amaha and Denton goodbye. There were more tears.

For the first time I was thankful for the seclusion of the small compartment where we were searched before going to the airplane. I blew my nose and wiped my eyes before I emerged. Shellie and Brent came out of their compartments just as I did. They were still sobbing. I put an arm around each of them, and we walked slowly to the next inspection booth. There were three inspections before we were finally cleared to board the bus that drove us to the runway where we would get on the airplane. As we settled onto the bus, I could not bring myself to look up at the observation deck. Shellie and Brent stood beside me, scanning the crowd for a last glimpse of our loved ones. "There they are; I see them!" Brent waved wildly. They had stopped crying now and were waving the last goodbye.

I took a deep breath as I felt the Boeing jet lift off.

The flight to London was uneventful. It was nearly nine o'clock at night when we finally checked into our hotel. I didn't want to waste any time before letting Michael know I had returned to London. As soon as I tucked Shellie and Brent into their beds and heard their gentle breathing, I knew they were already sound asleep. I envied them. My body ached, I was so tired. I sat on my bed for a few minutes before I took Michael's home telephone number from my wallet and dialed the number.

"Hello." I heard his familiar voice.

"Hello, Michael, this is Mrs. Collins."

"Mrs. Collins?" He paused. "Mrs. Collins?" he repeated. "Oh, Mrs. Collins!" he said, finally recognizing who I was. "Where are you?"

"I'm here, Michael, in London. I must see you immediately."

"Yes, of course." He sounded a bit confused.

"Can you come to the hotel, Michael?"

"Yes, Mrs. Collins. I will come. I have guests right now, but as soon as they leave, Wynam and I will come right over. I will telephone you just before we leave."

I must have fallen asleep. When Michael called me again it was two o'clock in the morning. "I'm terribly sorry it is so late, Mrs. Collins. Do you still want us to come?"

"Yes, Michael, it is quite urgent. I will meet you in the lobby. Shellie and Brent are with me, and they are asleep. Just give me a ring when you arrive."

It was a relief to see their friendly faces. They welcomed me like an old friend. Michael apologized again for not recognizing my voice and for being unable to get away from his guests any earlier.

"It's perfectly all right, Michael. I was happy to have a little catnap. I was extremely tired from our flight. I cannot sleep on airplanes. I'm just happy you are both here now."

"The hotel coffee shop is closed, Mrs. Collins, but as we were coming in, I saw a small coffee shop just down the street. Would you like to go there so we can talk? Will Shellie and Brent be all right?"

"That would be fine, Michael. I could use some coffee."

I wasted little time with formalities. I knew why I had come, and the sooner they knew, the more quickly we could get down to business. I talked steadily for nearly two hours, making my case. They interrupted me only to clarify a point, otherwise I continued uninterrupted until I had thoroughly described the situation in Addis and told them of Brad's warning about the children's safety and possible imprisonment.

"Brad has gone so far as to say that the Ethiopian government has discussed putting the royal family on trial and executing them," I emphasized.

Michael snorted sarcastically. "Why bother to put people on trial if you intend to execute them?" I knew his sarcasm was not directed at me, but at the military government that held his mother hostage.

"I'm sure it is only a formality as far as they are concerned, Michael, but I don't want those children put in prison."

Wynam listened intently, her eyes bright and attentive.

When I concluded and fell silent, no one said anything for several minutes. It was Michael who broke the silence.

"Mrs. Collins, you couldn't have come at a better time. My father is here. It is peculiar, because he is never here in March, but surprisingly enough, he came from the Sudan for a short visit, and he plans to leave in a few days. Your arrival couldn't have been better timed."

My heart soared with new hope. "Oh, Michael, that's wonderful. Do you think he will help us arrange something? Surely he has connections in Sudan or somewhere. When can I see him?"

"I will call you tomorrow. Let me talk to him first and explain everything that you have told us tonight—rather, this morning," he said looking at his watch.

"That's fine!" I felt more encouraged than I had in weeks.

"Mrs. Collins, this is not a good area for you to stay in. Tomorrow, we should change your hotel. I will take care of that in the morning, too. There is a place nearer our home and my office where other family members have stayed while they were in England. It is quite nice, and you will be comfortable there."

As we left the coffee shop, it was dawn. Twenty minutes later I was in bed asleep.

The next afternoon Michael came to the hotel and helped us move to a small, comfortable hotel across London called Queensbury Court. He arranged to meet us after he got off work at five-thirty. He had planned a meeting at his sister's home in West Croydon. His father would be there.

Shellie, Brent, and I were waiting in the television room of our hotel when Michael came to get us after work. The hotel did not have televisions in each room, but the television room had a comfortable living room type of atmosphere, and I felt at ease letting Shellie and Brent go there alone when I didn't feel like watching television. It was quite nice, actually, because I had a reprieve from the constant din of the television when I wanted to read or rest.

We took the Underground to the West Croydon station and walked from there to his sister's house. Michael rang the doorbell.

A very short man answered. He was dressed simply: a sportshirt, a pullover sweater, and dark slacks. He bowed graciously, and taking my hand, he kissed it; at the same time he uttered his name. Unfortunately I could not make out what he said, and I was too embarrassed to ask him to repeat it. He led the way into a small sitting room, crowded with overstuffed furniture. The pieces were lovely, but too large for the room. I sat beside the man who had kissed my hand, still unclear about who he was. He spoke English very well and chatted easily with Shellie and Brent, making them feel quite at ease. Two children came into the living room to join us. Michael introduced them as his nephew and niece, Abraham and Asede.

"These are Rebecca's children. Rebecca is my sister," Michael said to Shellie and Brent. Perhaps he thought I had already figured out how they were all related.

I kept wondering when Ras Mengesha, Michael's father, would join us. I was anxious to meet him. I had been thinking all day about meeting him, and I wondered how I would greet such an important man. Would I call him Your Highness or Your Excellency? After all, he was one of the Emperor's most important advisors, his grandson-in-law. I was eager to do everything right.

A very attractive lady came into the room. I stood when she entered the room. It was Ethiopian custom that when anyone came into the room and you were to be introduced, you stood for the introductions. I was pleased to see that Shellie and Brent followed my example. Michael introduced Rebecca. I nodded my head politely and shook hands with her.

The short man helped Rebecca turn the large mahogany table around and set it for a buffet. He carried dishes from the lovely china cabinet and arranged the table. He certainly knew his way around the house, I thought, as I watched him open cupboards and drawers. Shellie and Brent went off to play with Abraham and Asede. While Michael and the little man helped Rebecca, I sat nervously waiting for Ras Mengesha's arrival.

I was very disappointed when we started dinner and he hadn't arrived. Rebecca served a lovely Ethiopian meal. I was surprised at how many things she had been able to prepare, since Ethiopian food requires so many special spices.

"Yes, I am fortunate," she explained when I marveled over the lovely meal. "I can get nearly all the spices locally. Some of the spices are sent from Ethiopia by friends of mine, but I, too, am surprised by how many different ingredients I can purchase here."

Her English was perfect, and she had a delightful British accent. I enjoyed listening to her talk.

After dinner I helped to clear away the dishes. Since it was against Ethiopian culture for men even to go into the kitchen, I was surprised when the little man donned one of Rebecca's aprons and began rinsing the dishes. Is he just a live-in servant, English style? I pondered. Rebecca appeared to have read my thoughts. "Mrs. Collins, you look surprised to see my father washing dishes."

Her father! Ras Mengesha! Surprised? I could hardly speak. I was certain my face was beginning to color, I felt so embarrassed. Could it be that all evening I had been talking with Ras Mengesha, and I hadn't even realized it! Trying not to register the shock and embarrassment I felt, I said, "Well, it is strange to see an Ethiopian man in the kitchen. That is one custom that my husband, Denton, had no trouble adjusting to when we first went to Ethiopia," I said. We all laughed, and I hoped I had covered my shock.

I couldn't believe that this short, gentle, kind, soft-spoken man who had kissed my hand when I came into the house was the famous Ras Mengesha. As one of Ethiopia's most wanted men, his picture had appeared on "wanted" posters all over the captial city before we left Ethiopia, but it had been a cartoon drawing, which only vaguely resembled this charming man sitting beside me drinking coffee.

Ras Mengesha laughed softly at my dismay. He might have been hysterical if he had known the whole story of how I had mistaken him for a possible live-in servant.

After our second cup of coffee, Rebecca found a reason to excuse herself. Michael, Ras Mengesha, and I were left alone in the living room.

What I assumed was the conclusion of a lovely evening was just the beginning. Michael had obviously already informed his father why I had come to London so unexpectedly. Ras Mengesha was probably more aware of the situation in Addis than any of us. It was no secret that he headed the Ethiopian Democratic Union, an organization which aspired to overthrow the Marxist government now in power in Ethiopia, but there was no mention of his political involvement during the entire evening. He did, however, express an overwhelming concern for the four children. Menen, of course, was his daughter. Loly, Kokeb, and Amaha were his nieces and nephew. His tenderness and sensitivity amazed me. Earlier in the evening I had watched him talk and play with Abraham, Brent, Shellie, and Asede.

He had hidden candy bars for them to find, and he enjoyed watching the children find them as much as they enjoyed the treat. His sincerity gave me confidence.

He led me into a serious discussion of my ideas for an escape plan and probed my mind for ideas and details. It wasn't as though I had to convince him. He seemed aware of the children's peril.

"Where are the children now?" he asked.

"They are with my husband, Denton, staying in our home. At least they were still there when I left home yesterday morning. Since the rumor of their possible arrest, I don't know from day to day what is going to happen to them."

The front door opened, and I heard Rebecca greet someone in the hallway. She came into the living room with a man.

"Mrs. Collins, this is my husband, Assefa. Assefa, Mrs. Collins."

"Come, Assefa, join us. You will be helpful in this conversation," Ras Mengesha said, summoning Assefa into the living room. "Assefa is a seasoned military man," he added.

Assefa was not the last one to join us. Another man came about a half hour after Assefa, and Ras Mengesha encouraged him to join in our planning session as well. "Mrs. Collins, please meet Zetaos Gebre-Michael." I stood and we nodded to each other as we shook hands. "I'm happy to meet you, Mrs. Collins," Zetaos said, taking a seat beside Assefa.

We talked until the early hours of the morning. Shellie and Brent had found comfortable positions on the couch beside me and gone to sleep. Midway into our discussions, Ras Mengesha had produced maps of Ethiopia, enabling us to discuss different areas where an airlift might be possible. I suggested that we find someone who could return to Addis Ababa and meet with Denton to outline clearly the details of our plan. They thought it was a good idea and saw no difficulty in finding the person who would pose as the "doctor."

"Zetaos, you might be the person for this?" Michael suggested.

He looked more Italian than Ethiopian, which I thought would be helpful if he went back into Ethiopia to meet with Denton.

They all had a good laugh when I told them the code that I had given to Denton before leaving Addis.

"That was a very clever idea, Mrs. Collins, and it might prove very helpful. I particularly like the part about the doctor," Ras Mengesha said. The others agreed with him. As a reasonable plan began to form, Michael brought up the subject of finances for the airplane. I had been thinking about that, too, and I recalled a lady who had contacted me during my visit to London in July.

"I believe her name was Lady Bromley," I said, trying to recall the details of our brief conversation nearly eight months ago.

"She mentioned there were some funds for the children if we needed them or if we were able to get the children out of Ethiopia. I did not have time to meet with her last summer, but perhaps if we visit her now, she could be of some help."

"Of course. They are very good friends of the family— Sir Thomas and Lady Bromley. Wonderful couple," Ras Mengesha said approvingly. "Sir Thomas was the British ambassador to Ethiopia at the time the Emperor was deposed. Perhaps you and Michael should make an appointment to visit with the Bromleys."

"I will call Lady Bromley tomorrow morning," Michael volunteered. "Perhaps you, Shellie, Brent, and I can take the train to Oxford and have a visit with them. They have a lovely cottage in the countryside near Oxford."

CHAPTER THIRTEEN
Laying the Groundwork

The day following my initial meeting with Ras Mengesha, I wrote my first letter to Denton, using Carol's APO address. Even though the letter would circumvent censorship, I used as much of our code as possible.

Denton, I met with Michael's father regarding Catherine's surgery. It was something of a miracle finding him here in London. He is rarely here. He feels Catherine's prognosis looks good. I have had considerable affirmation regarding the surgery, and I'm more certain now than ever before that this is the right time to go through with it. It looks as if Dr. Morris will be getting in touch with you one day soon to explain all the details relating to the operation. I don't have a specific date, and we have not decided on what hospital, but I will get the information to you as soon as everything is arranged. I'm certain you already know that you are to be there with Catherine for the surgery. She would never make it without you at her side. Take care of yourself. I will be writing again soon. If for any reason you need me, call me here at the Queensbury Court Hotel.

Late in the morning Michael telephoned me. "The Bromleys are going out of town for nine days. They will be back on March 11. Lady Bromley has invited us for lunch at their home in Oxford on Saturday, March 12. It is a bit of a delay, but I told them we would be delighted to come. How does that sound to you, Mrs. Collins?"

"It sounds lovely, Michael. I'm certain the delay could not be helped," I answered trying to keep the disappointment out of my voice.

"We will take the train to Oxford, and Sir Thomas has offered to pick us up at the train station."

"Yes, I will get all the details about time and where to go to catch the train when I see you next."

"I would like you to meet Mimi, my fiancée. Perhaps you and the children would join us for dinner tonight. We will come to the hotel after I get off work at six o'clock.

"Of course. That would be nice. We'll see you about seven o'clock then?"

With the day free, the children and I visited the Tower of London and took a boat ride on the river Thames. Most days were free, because Michael had to work. He was a geologist and worked for an American oil company with headquarters in London.

On Saturday we had arranged to meet the two older sisters of Loly, Kokeb, and Amaha. Jote and Yeshi had been studying in England at the time of the revolution. They had never seen their baby brother, Amaha, and were delighted that I had pictures of him. After lunch together, we all went to Hyde Park for the afternoon.

Sunday I met another cousin, Hanna. Michael invited everyone to a movie, *The Pink Panther Strikes Again.* After the movie we all gathered around a table in a small Italian restaurant and had pizza.

Monday and Tuesday the children and I spent visiting Westminster Abbey, the changing of the Horse Guard, Buckingham Palace, London Zoo, and the Royal Mews. A week had passed since we arrived in London.

Each evening Michael, Ras Mengesha, and I met to discuss the escape. When we met on Tuesday evening for dinner, Michael said, "Mrs. Collins, we have just received word that the military government in Ethiopia has sent eight assassins to England to look for members of the Ethiopian royal family."

Alarmed, I asked, "What does this mean? How will any of you remain safe?"

"There are hundreds of Ethiopians in London. We will have to keep a low profile for a time and be more alert when we go places, but this is not the first time we've been threatened. We have learned to live with such threats."

It frightened me to think of all the implications involved in having assassins looking for Ras Mengesha and other family members in London. There was, of course, little I could do other than watch to see if we were being followed and to keep a lookout for suspicious-looking people. Until Michael's warning, I had felt relaxed and safe in London. After that, however, my business felt more clandestine than before.

Wednesday morning before we woke up, the telephone rang. A soft-spoken woman introduced herself as Princess Mary, daughter of the Crown Prince Asfa Wossen. I knew the Crown Prince had had a stroke and left Ethiopia prior to his father's overthrow. He had been hospitalized in Switzerland and recently moved to London. He had declined the Derg's offer to succeed his father, Emperor Haile Selassie, as a figurehead king after his father was imprisoned. Personally, I thought it was just a trick offer to get the Crown Prince back to Ethiopia and put him in prison, too. I was glad that he had declined the offer.

Princess Mary invited me to have lunch with her and her husband, Seyfou. We met at one o'clock at our hotel, and after a lovely lunch, a tour of the new Globe Theater on the River Thames, and St. Paul's Cathedral, we drove to St. James Park to let Shellie and Brent play on the swings and slide. The weather was sunny, but the air brisk. Seyfou, Mary, and I sat in the car to talk.

I did not know that Seyfou or Mary knew anything about my talks with Ras Mengesha and Michael regarding the escape plan. I thought this was a social visit, and I was shocked when Seyfou brought up the subject of the escape. I wasn't certain just how much he knew, and I was reluctant to volunteer any additional information. I merely listened. He asked me seriously to consider helping the children of his sister-in-law, Mary's sister, Princess Ejigeyehu.

"I'm sure you heard of Princess Ejigeyehu's untimely

death in prison even before you left Addis, Mrs. Collins?"
Seyfou asked.

"Yes, I did hear, and I'm extremely sorry. How many children did she have?"

"She has six children, but we are particularly concerned about the two youngest at this point—Bekere and Issac."

"Actually, Seyfou, we have no definite plans for an escape. At this time, we know nothing certain about how we can get the children out of Ethiopia. I felt it was important that the family be alerted to the potential dangers to the children in our care. I was unaware that the Crown Prince had six grandchildren still in Addis. I thought they were studying abroad."

"The four oldest were out of Ethiopia, and when they heard of all the trouble going on in Addis, they returned. We are asking only that you keep these children in mind. If you are able to plan an escape for the four children staying with your husband, we ask that you consider the risk to these six if they are left behind."

"Yes, of course," was all I could say. This discussion was unsettling to me.

I was relieved when I saw Shellie and Brent running toward the car. "We must get back to our hotel," I said. "I am meeting Michael for an early dinner."

When we returned to the hotel, Shellie and Brent went into the television room. I was thankful for a few minutes' respite and time to consider this new development.

When I met with Michael and Ras Mengesha later in the evening, I told them about my unexpected visit with Seyfou and Mary.

Ras Mengesha said nothing. Michael just shook his head and said, "Escape with ten children? Or even just six? How would Mr. Collins feel about that?"

"I can't imagine, Michael. Remember, he is reluctant about escaping with four, and rightly so!"

Changing the subject, Ras Mengesha said, "There is some important information we need immediately, Mrs. Collins. Perhaps with your contacts in Addis you can get this information for us. We have already discussed the rendezvous point. We must know the distance between the buildings and

His Imperial Majesty, Haile Selassie.

Jodie Collins.

Please forget us, say Ethiopian royals

By R. BARRY O'BRIEN in Stockholm

TEN frightened young members of the Ethiopian royal family who escaped from Addis Ababa to Kenya three weeks ago have been hidden by friends of their rescuers in a remote Swedish fjord.

Their secret refuge, where I visited them at the weekend, is a white painted timber house with a red roof half-hidden by fir on a wooded slope near 's edge, facing a with a ruined

The Daily Telegraph

LONDON, MONDAY, AUGUST 15, 1977

Printed in LONDON

...arnbarnsbarn till Haile Selassie på "hemlig ort" utanför Norrkö...

Vi är mycket lyckliga över att få vara Så säger den äldsta av de barn ur ka kejserliga familjen, som nyligen Sverige, då NT träffar dem på ort" utanför Norrköping. Hit har nit för att få vila ut och förbereda

minsta barnen, totalt är det sex prinsessor, sitter i kol storebror och lägger p och på golvet li minsta barn leksaker så

Selassie hålls sitter i husar Hur b Beta De d

Missionaries planned Ethiopia children's escape

By R. BARRY O'BRIEN in Stockholm

...ren and youths but was not
allowed to talk to them.
...ner did not give the exact

The ten royal children who his have escaped to Sweden were ere among a large number of n members of the late emperor's family who were placed under the detention in Ethiopia after the who 1974 coup, the emperor. die was deposed in the coup. in 1975.

The disclosure that a Swe ish mission body organised escape follows denials thiopian exiles in London anything to do

Safe in Kenya!
Standing, left to right:
Denton, Bekere, Jodie,
Aster, Menen, Samson,
Rahel, Meheret. Kneeling,
left to right: Loly, Amaha,
Issac, Kokeb.

Jigsaw puzzles were a
favorite diversion.
Clockwise: Denton,
Menen, Samson, Bekere,
Issac, and Meheret.

Denton with Kokeb,
Menen, Issac, and Amaha.

Denton and Amaha.

The four who have made
their home with us. Left to
right: Kokeb, Amaha, Loly,
Menen.

Kokeb, Aster, and Loly.

Issac.

Amaha, Loly, Menen, Issac, and Samson with Denton.

Bekere.   Issac and Loly.

Samson, holding Amaha.   Shellie Collins—1985.   Brent Collins—1985.

the runway, security at the landing strip that could present problems, a picture of a mission plane, preferably in color so the plane can be imitated. It will help if Mr. Collins can draw us a map of the area or a portion of a map showing landmarks, coordinates, degrees and minutes, and the best approach coming from the northwest from northern Yemen in order to avoid Dessie."

He paused to let me catch up with him. I was writing the things he wanted so I could relay them to Denton.

When I looked up he continued, "We need to know the possible air traffic in that area, commercial and otherwise. Have him find out what he can about possible patrols in that area, ground and air, and the day mission planes land at the airstrip. Ask him if other planes use the airfield, and the quietest time of the day, that is, when workers and people are least likely to be milling around. We thought lunch time, one-thirty to two o'clock. He should give us the direction of the prevailing wind in April if he can, landmarks seen from the air, and any other information that he thinks will be helpful."

Returning to the hotel after our meeting, I found Shellie and Brent in the sitting room, watching television. I went directly to the room and wrote to Carol and Denton.

"Carol," I wrote, "please try to encourage Catherine's husband to get the information we need regarding the surgery just as soon as possible. The information is pertinent to the surgery and necessary if Catherine's operation is to be successful. You know the doctor feels the sooner she has this surgery, the better. Remind Catherine's husband that he has an appointment with the same doctor as Catherine, so he should settle all of his business matters immediately. The doctor has mentioned the second week of April as a possible date for the surgery. We just hope Catherine's condition doesn't deteriorate before that time. I know you will do all you can to help us get this operation behind us. It has been a great strain on all of us. Let me emphasize once more the urgency of getting the information I have asked for from Catherine's husband. Take care of yourself, Carol, and I can't thank you enough for all of your help."

I wrote Denton a letter with no salutation and no signature, just a list of the information we needed. I concluded: "Please acknowledge these things one by one. Everything is pending until we receive this information. Please work quickly. Delay could mean cancellation. Send film to me; don't wait to have it developed."

Thursday morning I photocopied the letters and mailed them in care of Carol's address. We were now on hold until we heard from Denton or Carol and Sir Thomas Bromley.

The train ride to Oxford on Saturday was an adventure. Michael had called me early the morning after our first meeting with Ras Mengesha and asked me to meet him at the train station with Shellie and Brent Saturday morning at eleven o'clock. "I telephoned Lady Bromley and arranged for us to meet with her and Sir Thomas. Sir Thomas will fetch us from the train station. Lady Bromley is expecting us for lunch," he confirmed.

At five minutes before eleven Michael still had not arrived at the train station. I was uncertain about whether or not we should board the train, but I thought of Sir Thomas expecting us at the train station and Lady Bromley preparing lunch for us, and I thought it would be very inconsiderate not to go. When the train pulled away from the station, I was certain Michael had missed the train.

Shellie, Brent and I had just settled into our compartment when the door slid open and there stood Michael and his fiancée, Mimi.

"My goodness! We nearly missed the train," he said, gasping for breath. "We boarded after it was moving, and I thought I'd never convince Mimi to jump aboard," he laughed, collapsing onto the seat beside me.

We had a nice visit during our ride. The day was lovely, and the English countryside charming with its open spaces, picturesque cottages, and tiny farms. Sir Thomas was on time to meet us, and Michael made all the introductions.

The Bromleys were gracious and made us feel at home in their comfortable two-story cottage. Lady Bromley explained that the place used to be a stagecoach stop and the cottage had been an inn. After lunch they took us on a walk around the grounds. Shellie and Brent romped through the fields, enjoying the wide open space and exercise. Except for our few walks to museums and tour of the Tower of London, they had had very little exercise.

In the drawing room after our walk, Lady Bromley served us tea as I explained the reason we had come. Sir Thomas was a rather large, pleasant man. I found him very easy to talk to. He listened carefully and with great interest as I described my fears for the children and the apparent need to get them out of Ethiopia before any harm came to them.

I am not certain what I expected when Michael told me that Sir Thomas was an ambassador, but unlike the impression I had of diplomats, Sir Thomas got right to the point when I concluded my appeal to him for help.

"Mrs. Collins, I think we can help you, but it may take a little time. We were given several pieces of jewelry by a member of the royal family, and were told that they were to be used for Loly, Amaha, and Kokeb as well as their other two sisters, Jote and Yeshi. We were, as you may know, Jote and Yeshi's guardians for several years. Some of the money from several pieces of the jewelry was used for their education. However, we have sold only a few pieces of the jewelry. Given a little time, I'm certain we can raise ten thousand dollars to help with the escape. I feel there is no better use for the money than to rescue the children."

I told the Bromleys about the message I had received from the Princesses before I left Addis.

"The mothers said they were willing to pay any price for their children's freedom. I am certain they were referring to their lives, but given an opportunity, I know they would confirm the decision that you have made, Sir Thomas. I cannot thank you enough."

"That will deplete the funds," Sir Thomas commented, almost to himself. Then, sitting up straighter and looking resolved in his decision, he said to me, "I have no doubt the Princesses would desire the money to be used in this manner. I had always assumed it would be used for their education, but certainly it goes without saying that this is a matter of life and death. I will be in touch with you, Michael, as soon as I have something to tell you."

The matter concluded, Michael reminded me that we planned to meet his brother, Seyoum, in Oxford. Lady Bromley asked if she could take some photographs before we left. When we finished, Sir Thomas took us into Oxford. As we departed, he assured us again that he would be in touch with Michael as soon as he had some information for us.

I was so elated by our afternoon's accomplishments that I could hardly keep my mind on the conversation later that afternoon as we met Seyoum. Like other family members, Seyoum was overtly happy to meet us. It was obvious he had heard a great deal about us, and he knew that his young sister was in our care. I wasn't certain how much he knew about an escape plan; in fact, it didn't appear he knew anything about it. Michael directed the conversation away from any specifics about my present visit to England, other than to mention that I was on my way to the States because my mother was having surgery.

As darkness enveloped the English countryside we were back aboard the train, heading for London. Seated beside me, Mimi dozed, her head against Michael's shoulder. The train pounded its way along the track. I did not realize until after I boarded the train for our return trip, how tired I was and how stressful the day had been.

My mind absorbed with the thoughts about the escape, Denton, and the children, I looked off into the darkness and smiled to myself. We had only been in London twelve days. A lot had been accomplished in those days. Wouldn't Denton be amazed if he knew plans were this far along? It appeared likely that we had just raised ten thousand dollars. I was thrilled. Last night we had discussed the escape route at length and tentatively decided where Denton should go to meet the plane. Michael had said today that they knew a man who would be willing to go to Addis as the doctor. Ras Mengesha was leaving in a few days and would make arrangements for a relative of his in northern Yemen to help us. Denton and the children would drive to northern Ethiopia, to a mission station with a small landing strip. The plane would land there and fly them to northern Yemen, where this unnamed relative would assist Denton and the children with the legalities of seeking political asylum. As the plan stood, I would fly to northern Yemen and meet Denton and the children, more for moral support than anything else, because Ras Mengesha felt they could be in no better hands than his relative, a former ambassador to northern Yemen from Ethiopia. Discouraged by the present Ethiopian government's brutality, this man had defected and sought political asylum himself. Ras Mengesha felt certain he knew the ropes and would be of great help to Denton.

Yes, several things were actually coming together. We hoped we would soon hear from Sir Thomas that he had sold the jewelry and we would be able to proceed with the plans for the airplane.

Michael and Mimi went with us on the Underground from the train station to our hotel. Shellie and Brent were barely awake as we guided them into the hotel lobby, where Michael and Mimi said good night and went on their way.

Michael had encouraged me to rest the next day, but he had promised to call the minute he had word from Sir Thomas. I made up my mind to do just that! I was exhausted. I will do something special with Shellie and Brent tomorrow, I thought, as I tucked the covers around them and kissed them good night.

My plans were altered when Michael telephoned Sunday morning and invited us to lunch at Rebecca's at one o'clock.

After lunch Ras Mengesha took his two grandchildren, Abraham and Asede, and Shellie and Brent swimming. I spent the afternoon with Rebecca. It was late when we returned to our hotel, and there was a telephone message from Carol marked "Urgent." I tore open the envelope. The message was brief but explicit: "Conditions worsening." Fear raged through my entire being. I was upset that I had missed the phone call.

I had given Carol my telephone number when I had written to her eleven days ago. I considered telephoning her, but called Michael instead.

"I hope this doesn't mean the children have been arrested," I said after reading the short message to him.

"I certainly hope not! We trust that Sir Thomas will arrange something in the next couple of days, and we will hear from him. Be strong, Mrs. Collins! We've come this far," he said, trying to encourage me. "I will call you tomorrow."

I didn't sleep well that night. Sometime during the early

hours of the morning I made the decision to send Shellie and Brent to the States to stay with my mother and Ben.

Before seven o'clock I telephoned my mother in California.

"Of course, you can send Shellie and Brent home. I only wish you were coming with them, Jodie! When do you think you will be coming home?"

"I hope it will be in the next couple of weeks, Mom. I really want to wait for Denton. We hope we can come home together."

I purposefully avoided any mention of what I was really doing in England. There was no reason to upset everyone at home and cause them to worry. I would explain things once we were safely back in the States.

"I will explain everything when I get there, Mom. Right now I think it is best if Shellie and Brent get settled into school. They have already missed two weeks by staying here with me. We have had a wonderful time and seen many sights. They will tell you all about the things we have done when they get there. I am going to arrange their flight as soon as a travel agent opens here this morning. I will call you back in a few hours and give you the time of their arrival. I am going to call Jean and Moe Hernandez and ask Jean to find a school near her for Shellie and Brent. I'm sure Jean won't mind keeping the children during the week, and you and Ben can keep them on the weekends. Does that sound OK?"

"It's fine, honey. Just let me know what you arrange. We'll do whatever we can to help."

After talking with my mother, I called Jean and Moe.

At ten o'clock that morning I found a travel agent near our hotel and booked Shellie and Brent on a 1:10 flight leaving London.

When I returned to the hotel less than an hour later, Shellie and Brent squealed with delight when I told them to pack their suitcases because they were leaving for the States within two hours. We were just leaving our room when the telephone rang.

I didn't recognize the woman's voice but she introduced herself: "I am the wife of Asfa Wossen, the Crown Prince of Ethiopia. Mrs. Collins," she continued, "I was wondering if you would be kind enough to meet me today at the St. George's Hotel? There is a restaurant on the fourteenth floor."

"I'm just taking my children to Heathrow. They are flying to the States today. Perhaps I could meet you there at three o'clock this afternoon."

"That would be fine," she said. "I will see you then."

I didn't have time to wonder why she wanted to see me until after I had put Shellie and Brent on the airplane and caught a taxi.

"The St. George's Hotel, please," I said, directing the cab driver.

Leaning back in the seat to catch my breath, I considered the reasons why the Crown Princess of Ethiopia might want to see me.

As I stepped off the elevator on the second floor of the restaurant, the matriarch of the Ethiopian royal family was seated on a small settee. I'm not certain if she recognized me, but as I approached her, she extended her hand and said, "Mrs. Collins, thank you for coming." She motioned for me to take a seat beside her.

She was dressed in black, and I assumed she was still in mourning for the Emperor, as well as other members of the royal family who had died in the revolution—most recently, her daughter, Princess Ejigeyehu. We spoke to each other only in Amharic.

She signaled to the maitre d' and, turning to me, she asked, "Would you like coffee?"

"Yes, please," I said, accepting her invitation.

"May we have two cups of coffee served here, please," she requested.

"Certainly," the maitre d' responded, repeating the order to a nearby waiter.

I was surprised that she did not want to go into the restaurant rather than sit there in the foyer where we were much more conspicuous than we would have been inside. I wondered why she spoke to me in Amharic when she could obviously speak English.

Until the waiter came with our coffee, she asked me about Loly, Kokeb, Menen, and Amaha. After our coffee was served, she got to the point of why she had invited me to meet with her.

Her voice was gentle and soft. I had to listen carefully to hear her. I was impressed with her self-assurance and poise.

"I am concerned for my daughter's two youngest boys, Bekere and Issac," she explained.

When I only nodded my understanding, she continued. "There is a missionary who has an airplane. His name is Dr. McClure. Do you know him?"

"Yes, I do."

"I am wondering about asking him to help us get the children out of Ethiopia. Do you think your husband could contact him?"

"Your Highness, I am not certain that my husband is in a position to contact Dr. McClure. I received a message from Addis just yesterday, warning me that conditions are worsening. I am not certain what that means at this point. Perhaps it means it is too late for an escape."

She looked alarmed. "We are greatly concerned about all the children. We want nothing more than their safe deliverance out of Ethiopia. I do hope that we are able to find some way to bring this about." There was a sense of urgency in her voice as she continued. "If you and Mr. Collins are in a position to help us, we would be grateful."

"Yes," I replied, trying to sound reassuring, "if it is possible to help you, we will do our best." I was sincere. There was nothing I would have wanted more than to find a way to rescue all ten of those children. In reality, however, it looked impossible.

"Thank you very much, Mrs. Collins," she concluded, extending her hand. I understood our conversation was completed, and after shaking her hand, I stood up to leave. She remained seated, and I assured her that if I found a feasible way to arrange an escape for all of the children, I would get in touch with her immediately.

CHAPTER FOURTEEN
All Signals Go

On Tuesday morning, just two weeks after I had arrived in London, Michael telephoned me with the best news I had heard so far!

"Sir Thomas just phoned to say the jewelry has been liquidated. We have an appointment with him in Oxford on Thursday to pick up the check." I could tell from his voice how pleased and excited he was.

I joined in his excitement. "Oh, Michael! It's wonderful. It is another answer to prayer. I'm thrilled!"

"My father and I will meet you at your hotel tonight about seven o'clock. We will go to dinner and discuss final details."

"Fine! I'll see you then, Michael. Goodbye."

After I hung up, I was so excited I couldn't sit still. I paced up and down the room, talking to myself, "We've done it! We've actually done it! This thing is coming together. O God, you are so good. You have actually answered my greatest prayer. I can't stand it, I'm so excited."

After breakfast I decided to spend the day visiting the National Gallery. I needed something to keep my mind occupied until seven o'clock.

Just before seven I returned to the Queensbury. At seven-thirty Michael and Ras Mengesha still had not arrived. I was getting restless and hungry. I realized today how much I missed Shellie and Brent's company.

Suddenly someone pounded on my door. More than a little alarmed, I jumped from my chair and moved closer to the door. "Who is it?" I asked, trying to sound firm.

"It's me, Mrs. Collins—Michael!"

I unlocked the door and Michael and Ras Mengesha fell into the room, both breathless.

"What's wrong?" The shock registering in my voice matched the fear on their faces. Michael was obviously shaken. Ras Mengesha was surprisingly calm.

"Two men in the bar . . ." Michael said, pointing in the direction of the bar, just around the corner from my room. "The gunmen from Addis, remember?"

Of course, I remembered. "Oh, no!" I whispered. "Did they see you?"

"No, I don't think so," Ras Mengesha answered calmly. "But we cannot go out that way. We must go through the fire escape. I saw one at the end of the hallway. Get your things, Mrs. Collins."

Ras Mengesha opened the door and glanced cautiously down the hall. "It is clear," he said taking my arm and leading the way. Michael followed. Ras Mengesha opened the door carefully, listening for an alarm. Silence. He carefully peered outside to see if the way was clear. "Follow me closely," he whispered. They kept me between them as we ran to an alley a half-block from my hotel. Once hidden in the shadowy darkness, we slowed our pace and walked a few yards, emerging onto a well-lighted street near the Underground. We continued without speaking until we came to a small Italian restaurant where we had eaten together several times.

"Let's go in here," Ras Mengesha instructed, breaking our self-imposed silence.

It felt good to be in the crowded, noisy little restaurant, at a secluded table in the back of the room. I was impressed by Ras Mengesha's outer calm. I realized then that he had probably survived many attacks on his life, and it was undoubtedly his ability to remain composed and unperturbed, and to think clearly in these situations, that had enabled him to stay alive. I thought of Emama Ruth telling me about Ras Mengesha's escape from the palace at Mekele with his youngest son, Seyoum. Yes, he was no doubt a man of great inner strength, resolve, and equanimity.

We mentioned nothing more about the incident, and during dinner we talked over the final plans for the escape.

"You wrote Mr. Collins about taking the children on a holiday up north to your missionary friends' home?"

"Yes, I suggested that he spend a couple of days there and then Bob could take them on a picnic to the mission compound near the landing strip. That way Denton would not have to leave a car at the mission compound. Bob would just drive back home. This would also give Denton an alibi if he and the children were caught. He could just say that they are taking a mission plane back to Addis. You said you would have the plane painted like the mission plane. I just hope Denton will get the photographs to us in time."

"The pilot I have in mind will be a foreigner, an Italian. If the plane is stopped for any reason, or the pilot questioned, I'm sure enough outside pressure could be applied to get him released," Ras Mengesha said reassuringly.

"Mrs. Collins, I am going to leave London Friday."

"Yes," Michael interrupted, "he plans to take the money from Sir Thomas so that he can arrange for the airplane, pilot, and doctor."

"I think the most important thing is sending the doctor in to see Denton and having everything explained to him clearly so there is no mixup," I said. "We want to leave nothing to chance."

They both nodded their agreement.

"I will stay in touch with Michael. If Mr. Collins writes you, or you hear from Carol, get the information we need to Michael immediately. If we know the landmarks, coordinates, potential obstacles, and security near the landing strip, it will make our job a lot easier," Ras Mengesha added.

After dinner we decided that it was best if Michael and Ras Mengesha did not come back to Queensbury with me. Ras Mengesha took my hand in his, bowed deeply, and kissed my hand.

I smiled to myself, recalling the first night he had kissed my hand. I had not even recognized who he was.

"Goodbye," he said in his gentle way. "I cannot tell you

what a pleasure it has been to meet you. I hope that we meet again very soon. May God bless and keep you."

"Thank you, Ras Mengesha. Thank you for everything. You have been very kind." I could say no more. The tears were welling up.

Michael asked, "Will you have any problem finding your hotel?"

"Heavens, no, Michael," I said, smiling. "This is my neighborhood now. I feel right at home."

We all shook hands one final time and went our different ways. Will I see Ras Mengesha again? I wondered as I made my way back along the quiet streets.

As I neared the hotel, I hoped that those men, whoever they were, hadn't seen me with Michael and Ras Mengesha. I walked past the door of the bar quickly, not bothering to look inside. I was relieved as I turned the lock in my hotel room door.

On Thursday Michael and I took the train to Oxford for the second time and met with the Bromleys. There was something about receiving the check from Sir Thomas that made me feel our plans had finally commenced.

On Friday morning Ras Mengesha left according to schedule. I had not thought to ask where he was going. From the way he had talked, I assumed it was Italy or northern Yemen.

Friday afternoon I met Michael for lunch at the Italian restaurant. As we ate our dessert and sipped our last cup of coffee, I asked, "Michael, what do you think about my going on to the States to wait out the airlift?"

Reflecting on what I had asked, he peered into his cup and stirred the coffee gently with his spoon. "Actually, I see no reason why you can't return to the States," he answered.

"If your father is sending in the doctor to meet with Denton, there is no reason why this man can't get the information that Denton has gathered. I could just call Carol and tell her to get a message to Denton that the doctor will be in touch with him, and to be sure to have all the necessary information regarding Catherine's surgery. What do you think?"

"It sounds reasonable to me. You are planning to fly to

northern Yemen to meet Mr. Collins and the children, aren't you?"

"Yes. I want to."

"When do you intend to leave here?"

"I thought I would check on reservations for tomorrow if that seems all right to you."

"It is fine with me. I think the most important thing is that we stay in touch with each other. I should have the telephone number of the place you plan to stay."

"Yes, I thought of that. I will give you two numbers. I will be either with my friends the Hernandezes or my mother. Both are in California."

I made my plans and telephoned Michael to let him know that I would be leaving London at noon the following day, Saturday, March 19.

I then telephoned my mother with the good news. I would be home by Thursday, March 24. My plans included a layover in Oklahoma City, where I wanted to visit my friends Guenet and Assamentch. Both girls were Ethiopian students attending Central State University. Guenet had been like a member of our family in Ethiopia. I had known her for twelve years. I had met Assamentch only two years ago. It would be great to see them again, and better yet to be on my way home. I could hardly wait to see Shellie and Brent. Mom had mentioned during our last telephone conversation that Shellie was having difficulty settling into school.

Guenet and Assamentch were there to greet me when I arrived in Oklahoma City. It seemed we had so much to catch up on, although it had been only eight months since I had seen Guenet.

On Sunday, the three of us went to a small church in Seminole, Oklahoma, where we had gone to visit other friends. Monday, Tuesday, and Wednesday mornings while the girls were at school, I rested and wrote letters. During the afternoons we would shop in the large shopping mall and have dinner together. The four days passed quickly.

On Wednesday when the girls and I arrived back at the Holiday Inn after dinner, I telephoned the United Airlines desk at the airport to confirm my flight to San Francisco the next morning.

"Well, I'm all set," I said as I hung up the phone. "My

flight's confirmed, nine-thirty tomorrow morning."

We said our final goodbyes, since I had planned to take the hotel bus to the airport in the morning. The girls had school, and I had insisted on getting to the airport on my own. "I've done it a few times before," I assured them. "Please, don't worry!"

After Guenet and Assamentch had left, I watched television for awhile. My mind wandered, and I couldn't concentrate on the program, so I turned it off.

Denton and the children had been in the back of my mind all evening like a small, dark cloud shifting from time to time over the bright sun. Were they all right? It's Thursday morning in Addis right now, I thought, glancing at my travel clock and calculating the time difference. I'll call! I thought, excited, as I scurried across the room toward the telephone. First I'll write out my message. Three minutes isn't very long to talk, and once I hear his voice and verify Catherine's surgery, I chuckled, I know I'll feel a lot better.

I still sensed the exhilaration of knowing the escape plan was all set. As Michael had said during our last telephone conversation together before I left London Saturday morning, "All signals go!"

I dialed for the operator and placed my call to Addis. The operator would call me back as soon as she could get through to Denton.

I tried to read. I was restless. I put my book down and paced the floor, waiting for the call and reviewing the code in my mind once more. The telephone rang. I grabbed my paper and pencil from the bedside table and sat down by the telephone trying to calm myself. After letting it ring once more, I lifted the receiver slowly. I finally heard Denton's voice coming through the static-filled receiver. His voice faded in and out. He sounded tired and strained as he assured me that he and the children were well.

I read the code carefully and distinctly so he would catch each word. "Denton, listen. Catherine's surgery is scheduled. It is scheduled for April 22, eight o'clock in the morning. The doctor will contact you with all the details about Catherine's surgery."

Then had come his devastating message, "Cancel Catherine's surgery!"

Even now, on the plane to San Francisco, fourteen hours after our conversation, I still sensed the numbness of my mind and the disbelief of last night's conversation with Denton. He had insisted, "If you don't cancel Catherine's surgery, she will die!"

I had sunk to the floor beside my bed and cried for hours. My eyes were still smarting and stinging from crying most of the night.

Fortunately I had been able to reach Michael, and he had assured me he would contact his father and Zetaos Gebre-Michael in northern Yemen, as well as the Bromleys.

I had sat there on my bed for hours after talking to Michael, too heartsick to move. Only the Bible verses I had read had brought me any solace and comfort. I would have to cling to those verses on trust during the weeks and months ahead, I reminded myself.

Just meeting my family at the San Francisco airport was going to be difficult.

I closed my eyes, reclined my seat, and tried to put all thoughts of last night out of my mind for a few minutes. I took a deep breath and quietly let out a deep sigh. I knew I couldn't sleep, but if I could just relax my cluttered, troubled mind momentarily, I was sure I would feel better. My heart still throbbed from my final hours in Oklahoma City.

PART TWO

CHAPTER FIFTEEN
Denton Is Threatened

I had cancelled the escape. I wouldn't know why until Denton could get a message to me explaining what had gone wrong. I would be landing in San Francisco within the next hour, and I still had no idea what I would say to my family and friends about what I had been doing in England for the past three weeks, why I had left Denton in Ethiopia with four children, or when Denton was coming home. I had a lot of questions myself, and very few answers.

The flight attendant announced that we were beginning our descent into the San Francisco International Airport, and she asked us to fasten our seat belts.

I was so uncertain about the future. I didn't even know whether I should rent an apartment, stay with Mom and Ben, or stay with Jean and Moe. I felt extremely tired, almost depressed. I hoped it wouldn't be too obvious. I wasn't even certain how much I should tell my family and friends. Maybe I would be able to sort things out in my mind after a few days' rest.

My depression lifted as I saw Shellie's and Brent's blond heads bobbing through the crowded waiting room at the end of the concourse.

"Mommy! Mommy!" they shouted working their way through the crowd. I was enveloped in their hugs and kisses before I saw Mom, Ben, Jean, and Moe moving more slowly through the crush of people. Suddenly Ethiopia, England, escapes, all seemed remote as I was encompassed by those I loved so much. "When's Daddy coming?" Brent asked, hanging onto my arm as if he was afraid I might leave again. Ben hugged and kissed me and offered to carry my hand luggage. Mom held my other arm as we moved with the throngs of people down the escalator toward the luggage carrousel. After we collected my suitcases, I decided that I would stay with Mom and Ben for the night. Since Shellie and Brent had school the next day, I would pick them up after school and go to Jean's for dinner, and I'd spend a few nights there. Perhaps by then I would have my bearings and could make the appropriate decisions. Shellie and Brent seemed to sense that I was extremely weary, and after kissing me goodbye once again, they went along with Jean and Moe without a word.

Driving home with Mom and Ben, I realized that Michelle, Jean and Moe's daughter, had not been at the airport. In all the confusion I hadn't noticed.

"Mom, where was Michelle?" I inquired.

"Jean said that she was at play practice. She will be there tomorrow night when you go for dinner, Jean said."

I slept until nearly one o'clock the following afternoon. Mom peeked into the room just as I sat up.

"I was just coming in to wake you up," she said, as she carried a beautifully arranged breakfast tray. "Breakfast in bed, anyone?" she said smiling.

"What a treat! You will spoil me to death," I exclaimed.

I could tell that Mom was greatly relieved that I was home safely. It is difficult to understand how worried mothers can get until you have daughters of your own, I thought, as she sat on the white wicker chair beside my bed.

Yes, it was marvelous to be home again. The past few weeks seemed dream-like and unreal as I settled into the routine of picking up Shellie and Brent from school each day, helping Jean with dinner, and sitting around the table, chatting easily with close friends.

I explained to everyone who asked that Denton had business to settle for the Mission before he could leave Ethiopia. When asked about the royal children, I said we were uncertain about their future.

If they had only known how my heart ached to have some word from Denton and the children. One evening as Moe and I sat in the living room, talking, I spoke about the children and the good times we had camping and doing things as such a large family.

"You really love those children, don't you, Jodie?" he commented.

"Yes, I do, Moe. More than anyone realizes, I think. We really want to get them out of the country," I began, opening up for the first time since I'd been home. Jean joined us, and wrapped in our *gabes* (Ethiopian blankets), we sat together as I told Jean and Moe about the last three weeks in England. Moe brought an atlas and I showed them how we had planned to send a plane from northern Yemen across the Red Sea into northern Ethiopia to pick up Denton and the children. "It wouldn't be a long flight, but it would be risky. But now all of that's been cancelled, and I'm just waiting for some word from Denton about what happened that made him cancel it."

Jean and Moe marveled at the ingenuity of our code. "That's great, Jodie! It sounds just like something you would do," Jean teased. "But weren't you scared?"

"Jean, I'm still scared! We aren't through this ordeal yet. I'm so anxious to hear from Denton. The longer I don't hear from him, the more worried I am that something has happened to him or the kids."

Denton's letter arrived ten days after I arrived in California. It was dated March 24, the day after he had told me to cancel the surgery.

Dear Jodie,

I wish that I could have talked more on the telephone last night, but I know now it is tapped. Things really have gone bad. I'll try to reconstruct it in the order that things have happened.

Things went well for a few days after you left. Everything in general was very quiet. Then on Saturday, March 12, the kebele officials came with a summons from Security saying I had to come on Monday, March 14, for questioning. Then all of a sudden they said, "Come now. Don't you have some children here? They must come, too."

Honestly, Jodie, my heart went through the floor. They
were armed and there was nothing I could do. They were
standing right at the back door of our house. It wasn't like
I could get the children and run away. I told them to wait
while I got the children. I called Carol's husband, Bill,
and told him that I was being taken to Security and to
notify the authorities at the embassy. I was hoping to get
Carol so that she could call Brad, but Carol wasn't home.
The armed guards took us into Security. They questioned
the children first. They asked them their names and how
long they had been with us. They asked me several
questions, then told me to come back on Monday and to
bring someone who could translate for me. I was so
relieved when we left that place.

On Monday I took Joseph with me. That is when the
real interrogation took place. It lasted for hours. They
finally told Joseph and me we could leave, but they made
Joseph sign as my guarantor so that if I leave the country,
they will arrest Joseph. Before we left Security on Monday,
they said I had to bring Tsige in for questioning on
Tuesday. That was worse than the two previous days.
After they had questioned me in one room and Tsige in
another, they brought us back together and said that our
stories of how and why we got the children did not match,
and they ordered me back for a fourth day and told me to
bring an interpreter other than Joseph. Tomorrow I must
go again, and I am taking one of the deacons from the
church, Tegne. When I asked why they were questioning
me like this, one man spoke up and said that the kebele
officer had reported that I was planning to leave with the
children. I'll bet dear Feyesa knows something about this!

Before I ever went to Security on Monday, I met with
Carol and Brad. Brad was in favor of hiding the children
immediately, and so plans were made that on Monday
morning I would drop them off on my way to take them to
school, and Brad would see to it that they were hidden in
homes with diplomatic immunity. I was to return to the
English School and, unable to find them, I would report to
the authorities that they had been kidnapped. Brad said
two families had volunteered to hide the kids. Later,

*however, when Carol mentioned the plan to her husband,
he hit the ceiling and said we were endangering their
whole family, and that there would be no way to keep the*
kebele *from knowing. So Carol called me back and said
that the plan was off. She also said that she and Brad had
taken a man called Lou into their confidence. He is the
second in command at the embassy after Mr. Tinken, the
Chargé d'Affairs.*

*Lou said he doubted if the children were in any more
danger than they had been prior to the interrogation, and
that if they suddenly disappeared, it might cause more
problems than it would solve. So we decided to go ahead
with the plans and wait for the doctor to contact me.*

*Lou also said that there was an American lady from
Namru whose Ethiopian husband escaped from here some
time ago. She has been asking around for someone who
wanted to get four kids out of here. This information got
right to the top man, Tinken. He called her in and told
her to keep quiet and to stay out of politics or she would
be sent out of the country.*

*Then Tinken called me in and asked if I was planning
to escape with the children. He was furious, and said that
he was contacting our Mission board, and if I pursued
this he would see that I was sent out of the country. He
threatened to send anyone who was helping me out of the
country with a "black letter in his file." In other words, it
could mean the end of a diplomatic career for Brad and
anyone else involved, if we go ahead with this.*

*Jodie, it was right after all this had happened that you
phoned me with Catherine's surgery scheduled. It was just
too risky. The Ethiopian government was having me
watched, and so was the American government.*

*The landing strip you were planning to use is too near
the Mission hospital and several houses where foreigners
and Ethiopians live. There are several Ethiopian guards
on duty at all times. It would be much better if you could
arrange for the pilot to land on the road about ten
kilometers outside of Robi. That way I could drive it in
one day. If I have to wait two days, the workers would
have time to report us. If we do it on a school day, the*

workers will just think I've gone to school, and there would be no reason for them to suspect anything.

As if all of that wasn't enough, the government has put on a city-wide search for illegal weapons and hoarded grain and gasoline. Curfew is seven o'clock in the evening. Only cars with special passes can be on the roads after seven. Going in and out of each neighborhood kebele *you must stop and be searched. I was searched six times in one morning. Today they searched our house and took away my shotgun, even though I had permission to have it. Everything in this country seems to be upside down right now.*

Yesterday kebele *officers took eleven workers out of the government printing press and shot all of them, men and women. One had been a student in our night school for several years. Their bodies were left in the field next to the church and were there when I came to work this morning. Today government officials came and arrested the* kebele *leaders. One of them is Olani, Joseph's cousin. I am sure the government intends to execute them and no doubt Olani is finished. On my way to work this morning, I saw two bodies on our road, and four other bodies had been dumped over the bridge where our lane joins the main road. Berhanu saw ten bodies on the street as he came to work this morning. The windows of his house were all shot out last night and one man was killed on his compound. Another missionary was arrested for storing gasoline.*

Everything has fallen apart at once. Things are as tight as they can possibly be. It's horrible! All our missionaries have their exit visas and will be leaving in the next week or two. That will leave just me. I will miss everyone, but it is better they are getting out now.

Before I had seen it with my own eyes, I would have said life could never be like this. Life is sure cheap. A British man was killed this week and so was a Belgian diplomat. The government's excuse for killing them is always the same. They accuse them of espionage.

The American embassy called all the mission directors

in last Tuesday and issued a warning. The embassy officials said they no longer have any influence; therefore, everyone must be very careful. They warned against tourists coming to Ethiopia and asked us to pass the word along.

Jodie, I just don't know what to do. What was a fairly simple plan has become tremendously difficult. If we do anything at this point, even Joseph's life is in danger, because he had to sign as my guarantor. The circle of those involved broadens and broadens.

Right now my steps are trailed too closely for me to do much that is not circumspect. I don't know what to do except pray that some new opening might come. Brad says that if there is a mass evacuation there will be a chance to get the kids out in all the confusion. It seemed so much was opening up, only to slam shut so fast. Let's pray together that we will have another opportunity to do something at a later date.

I really want to leave this place the second I can sell our house. If nothing develops regarding Catherine's surgery before August, I would like to leave anyway, even if I can't sell the house.

Pray for a miracle, Jodie, and for a guardian angel's protection on all of us. I feel I've learned so much through all of this, but the lessons seem so cheap when lives are involved. I did see how God does give us help as He promised when His children are taken for questioning. I hope you can make something out of all of this. Pray, pray, pray!

My love, Denton

I telephoned Michael in London and read him the letter. Neither one of us knew what to say to comfort the other, so we just agreed to keep in touch and hung up. Just as I set the receiver down, I dissolved into tears. Why, Lord, why this? Why did everything have to fall apart? It had been such a good plan.

I heard no still, small voice reminding me of my earlier desire to trust God. The only evidence of God's help in my life was that I had the courage to go on with the routine of my everyday life. That, I assumed, in the light of my heavy heart, was God's grace and provision to me.

My happiest days were those when I got letters from Denton. His letters gave me a glimmer of hope, although they were filled with horrifying snatches of the deteriorating political situation in Addis. Each time he mentioned the children, my heart revived, and I knew there was still time to do something—but what could we do?

March 26, 1977

Dear Jodie,

Today and tomorrow the Derg has ordered everyone to remain at home. There is to be a house-to-house search. Not even government cars are allowed on the road without special permits.

The American embassy called me today, emphasizing the importance of staying inside. We were supposed to play our last baseball game of the season, the all-star game, and have the award ceremony. Needless to say, it was all cancelled because of the search going on in each kebele. *I guess they are looking for guns or anything that looks the least bit suspicious. Recently a missionary doctor was arrested, Dr. Canada. The* kebele *searched his home and found his hunting rifles. He had his permission papers, but it made no difference to the authorities. One rifle had a telescope. They found cameras, film development paper, and a reloader for rifle shells. They spread all this out and photographed him with it and then made him stand beside everything they had found while the townspeople passed by, sneering at him and telling him he was an antirevolutionary. They brought him and his wife and family by armed guard to Addis, and he is in jail. It is obvious our American passports won't exempt us from imprisonment!*

Yesterday while I was in the Ministry of Security for my third interrogation, I heard officials questioning a Finnish missionary, Mr. Lehardiho and his wife. They gave them twenty-four hours to leave the country. Mr. Lehardiho said they didn't have the money to leave, so the

Ethiopian man interrogating him called the Finnish embassy. He said they must either leave or go to jail within twenty-four hours. Not much of a choice, is it?

Continue to pray. God opens doors in many ways and at strange times. A total, earthshaking collapse one week does not have to mean defeat. God's Word and work go on.

Love, Denton

CHAPTER SIXTEEN
The Clouds Grow Darker

On April 6 I found a small, comfortable townhouse and began the arduous task of sorting through the maze of barrels and crates stored at the Home of Peace. I was thankful that we had postponed shipping our household goods and furniture to Ethiopia after our third furlough. Each furlough we bought furniture for one or two rooms of our home in Ethiopia. We had bought a bedroom set for the master bedroom and one for Shellie's room during our last furlough, and many other new household items for the home we had just built over there. In spite of all the unsettling news of strikes, rioting, and political upheaval in Ethiopia, we had decided to return to our work and home, but not to ship our crates and barrels. The workers at the Home of Peace were wonderful. They broke all the locks off of the barrels, since I had forgotten to bring the keys with me from Addis. They opened the ends of all the crates, and I spent days deciding what would fit into the small townhouse, packing the remainder away until Denton arrived home and we could make a decision on what we were going to do with the rest of our lives.

I didn't want to hire a truck to transport my things from the Home of Peace until I had gone through everything. I stayed with Jean and Moe in order to take Shellie and Brent to school each morning. They were happy in their schools, and I didn't want to transfer them.

I was delighted when Jean said, "Jodie, please, don't transfer these kids. They've been through enough! Let them stay here while you get your place settled. School is almost out. We only have a few more weeks!"

After taking Shellie and Brent to school each morning, I drove from Fremont to Oakland, where our goods were stored. In the afternoon I would pick the children up from school, and we would go to Jean's for dinner. After dishes, I would help Brent with his multiplication tables until bedtime. At nine-thirty I tucked Shellie and Brent into bed and drove back to the townhouse. The work was therapeutic, but each evening when I crawled into bed, exhausted, I could think of nothing but Denton and the children.

April 10, 1977

Dear Denton,

Today was Easter Sunday. We were all at Mom and Ben's for the day. Ben hid the colored Easter eggs at least ten times for Shellie and Brent. It was a lovely day, but how I wished you all could have been there.

I have found a two-bedroom townhouse. Can you believe it has more bathrooms than bedrooms? It has three baths! Moe and Jean are going to help me move our things from the Home of Peace next weekend. I'm going to rent a U-Haul. It should be a busy weekend. Our things in storage were in excellent condition. I can hardly wait for you to see everything. I had forgotten so many of the things we bought for our new home. I guess they will still be for a new home, just not in Ethiopia. Sad, isn't it? Do take care of yourself. We love you all.

Love and prayers, Jodie

April 18, 1977

Dear Jodie,

Sounds like you've been busy apartment hunting. I can hardly believe that apartments are five hundred dollars a month. Remember when we first got married? Our first apartment was only fifty dollars a month. Of course, that was Springfield, Missouri, not the San Francisco Bay area in California.

The kids are still in school and doing fine. They all had

*their school pictures taken the other day. Amaha has had
a bit of a cold, but other than that, they are great!*

*I haven't been called into Security for nearly two weeks.
I hope that is all behind me.*

*Sorry to hear Catherine's leg and hip are giving her so
much pain. It will be good when the operation is over. Do
you think she will ever get in shape enough to have the
surgery? If it is rescheduled, how long do you think it
would take?*

*Last Friday a man was shot right beside our house.
Three young men came to kill our kebele leader, and,
according to what I heard, the plan was foiled. One was
killed right beside our fence and the other down by the
river. I didn't hear what happened to the third.*

*Later this week I may go up north to the Mission station
at Kombolcha. The scenery is so nice on that road. It is quiet
there, too.*

*I doubt that I can finish all the Mission business and
close the remaining Mission schools and stations before
June or July.*

*Please take care of yourself, and keep the letters
coming. I love hearing from you about all you and the kids
are doing.*

Love, Denton

I understood from Denton's letter that he wanted us to
consider an airlift near the Kombolcha mission compound,
possibly on the main road. What I hadn't told him was how
remote it seemed that we would ever be able to reactivate
the plan, with all of us so scattered around the world. It
didn't seem likely to me at the moment that the conditions
would ever come together again as they had been when I
arrived in London in March.

April 19, 1977

Dear Denton,

*Your letters seem to be arriving regularly now. It is so
good to hear from you, and to know that the children are
still with you.*

*I am settled into the new townhouse in Walnut Creek.
Jean helped me hang all the pictures and many of our
Ethiopian things. They look great! She is so clever, and it*

took her no time at all. Moe and our new landlord, Vic, moved all the heavy pieces of furniture. I'll bet there aren't too many landlords that would help you move into their place. His wife's name is Diane, and she is really nice, too. Vic has offered to fix the garage up as a third bedroom for Brent. Brent is so excited. He said, "Now I can ride my bike right into my bedroom!" He's crazy. Must take after his dad!

Moe has offered to help Vic with the garage. I will buy the wallboard, and they will hang, seal, and paint it. We had that nice piece of brown carpet stored at the Home of Peace, and it will just fit in the garage, so the room will be completely carpeted. Can't wait until you are home to see it. It's starting to feel a little bit like home.

My days are becoming more routine. Ethiopia and all I've been through these past few months seem like a dream.

Please take care of yourself. Give the children my love.

Love and prayers, Jodie

April 20, 1977

Dear Jodie,

We are all well. I just wanted to write and tell you not to worry. We are fine. The newspapers here are filled with accusations against Somalia for invading Ethiopia. An all-out war with Somalia looks inevitable.

The Morrows and Singletons are leaving within the next six weeks. Morrows are here in Addis now. They were held by armed guards on their mission station at Haik for four days. As soon as they were released, they came into Addis. Dr. Canada is still in jail. Take care.

Love, Denton.

April 22, 1977

Dear Jodie,

I just got your letter telling me all about Easter at your mom and Ben's. I also received the cards from Shellie and Brent.

The townhouse sounds really nice. I'm glad you were able to go through the things at Home of Peace and get the things you needed to set up housekeeping.

It's great to have friends like Jean and Moe. We'll never be able to repay them for all they have done for us. They have really been good to you and the kids. I guess sometimes in friendship you just can't pay things back. It's just part of being friends.

Yesterday the radio announced that two holding tanks at the oil refinery in Assab were bombed by antirevolutionaries. The fires are still burning, according to the last reports. Lines were already forming at the gas stations today, because everyone is worried about more gas shortages. The local newspapers have asked all churches and mosques to turn in the tents that they use for weddings, wakes, and funerals. They need them desperately for the war. I guess no one is supposed to die or get married until after the war!

I heard today that two hundred Cuban advisors arrived. Remember that big apartment building next door to the Hilton Hotel? It has been newly renovated for the Cubans.

The radio and newspaper are trying to arouse the people so they will enlist for the war now rapidly escalating between Ethiopia and Somalia.

There is a great deal of propaganda against the United States right now.

Since there were no missionaries living in the apartments at the Headquarters, I was worried that the local kebele might take them over. I filled them with church families and gave Joseph the small one, number eight. I figured if anyone deserved it, he did. He has been so faithful through the years.

Richard Konnerup is coming back to Ethiopia. He wants to visit his mission at Kombolcha to pack his belongings and ship them home. He is supposed to come around the first of May.

We sure do miss you. Please keep writing! Your letters are great!

With love, Denton

April 26, 1977

Dear Jodie,

What a nice surprise! I just walked into my office after taking the kids to school and Joseph had slipped a letter *from you under the door. So I'll just sit now and answer it. Two of your letters and a card from Shellie came yesterday. They are not coming in order, but I'm thankful they are coming. Last night I put them all in order to read them again. I really do enjoy hearing from you.*

I wonder if you have heard yet that all U. S. organizations with the exception of U. S. Aid have been given seventy-two hours to get out of the country. That included the American military, United States Information Service, our big military base in Asmara where Brent was born, and the consulate in Asmara. They are only going to be allowed to have a skeleton crew at the American embassy. I was shocked when I heard the announcement. Can you imagine trying to get all the Americans out of here in seventy-two hours? It will be hectic. As soon as I heard I tried to call Carol. When I couldn't reach her, I went over to their house, but no one was home. I want to tell them goodbye and thank her for all she has done for us.

They have also closed the Italian, British, Belgian, and French consulates in Asmara. Yesterday they gave the Washington Post, *Reuters, and a French agency twenty-four hours to leave.*

The Derg is sending soldiers up north as fast as possible. I guess the Eritrean Liberation group that has been trying to secede from Ethiopia for the last ten years or more have decided to launch an all-out offensive since Ethiopia is distracted in the south by Somalia's invasion. It looks as though Ethiopia is expelling the Americans and her allies and calling in the Russians and Cubans.

I was at the Hilton Hotel swimming yesterday and there was a large East German delegation there with all their bodyguards. It looked like the Hilton was under siege!

Here in Addis all the bridges, train station, and airport are being guarded by old pensioned soldiers, because they are sending the younger ones to Eritrea up north and the Ogaden in the south. Bob Morrow came into town from Kombolcha yesterday and passed forty busloads of soldiers going north. There are new restrictions about leaving the city. The Derg is requiring a special permit for traveling. That could complicate life even further!

The girls have been quite upset lately, and I felt it was best if I explained a little about what has happened in light of Catherine's surgery and the cancellation. It had become obvious that they were expecting something and the uncertainty seemed to be getting to them. I think Loly was particularly disappointed. Maybe she just showed it more than Kokeb and Menen. They are fine, aside from that. They were supposed to visit Tsige yesterday, but for some reason it was called off.

The Mission Headquarters in Springfield wrote a letter instructing all of the remaining missionaries to leave together. I guess they don't realize that that is impossible. Jim and Barbara are planning to leave May 11. Morrows will go just as soon as Richard comes and takes over the responsibility for Kombolcha again.

Well, I must close and go buy some groceries. We are really getting low. This Sunday is May Day. There is a huge parade scheduled at Revolutionary Square. I won't be able to get out because of all the crowds, I'm sure!

With love, Denton

April 28, 1977

Dear Jodie,

I received a letter from you today. It always makes my day! I was really happy to hear that the boxes Carol sent to you arrived safely and in good condition. That's great! At least our Ethiopian souvenirs and slides are safe.

The last of the American military, USIS, left yesterday. The killings continue. One of the teachers in our night school was killed yesterday. He was vice-chairman of his kebele. There is a group called Ethiopian People Revolutionary Party (EPRP), and they are killing off all the kebele officials. The newspapers list the names of those who have been killed each day. The government is out to find and eliminate the EPRP, believe me. Jim saw two corpses on his way to school yesterday, a student and a policeman. The newspaper told of eleven more people who were executed for opposing the revolution.

Morrows still plan to leave May 6 and Singletons on the

*11th. I thought Richard would probably be coming May 2
or 3, but we haven't heard from him.*

*The weather here is as crazy as everything else. One
day it is beautiful, the next day rain. Amaha is nearly
over his cold. The girls are fine. Amaha is over playing
with our neighbor's boy Michael. They have become good
friends.*

*I am writing this letter while waiting in an office to get
Bob Morrow's tax clearance. I can't figure out why it is
taking so long.*

*Well, I hope things continue to go well with you, and
that the kids are still enjoying school.*

With love, Denton

May 4, 1977

Dear Jodie,

*Happy Mother's Day! I realize this will be late, but
nevertheless. . . . I looked for cards yesterday, but none
were available!*

*Morrows are staying with me; they leave in two days.
The kids have enjoyed having them, too. I got word that
Richard is coming Sunday.*

*I feel better today, but I tell you—yesterday all I
wanted was out! out! out! not caring about anything or
anybody. When I get out of here, I think I'll get off the
plane at the first stop, get a hotel, and unwind for a week
before I go on! I don't know why, but some days seem far
too much. I feel as if I'll explode, but then I get a good
night's sleep and it's better the next day. I don't know how
to explain it in a letter.*

*How are we ever going to make arrangements for
Catherine? I don't trust anyone anymore. If I have to
leave by myself it will be the hardest day of my life, but it
is going to be very difficult to come with others.*

*I have packed a big package of Ethiopian seasonings for
you, and I will mail it airmail tomorrow.*

*Please keep praying for us. I don't know all the reasons,
but my nerves are shot!*

Love, Denton

May 6, 1977
Dear Jodie,
    Richard Konnerup called this morning at four o'clock. I
was sound asleep. He asked if he should come, in light of
all the recent changes. I wasn't sure which changes he was
referring to. There are so many every day, it seems. He
might have been referring to all the U. S. organizations
being expelled, but maybe he heard about last Friday's
massacre. More than one thousand students were killed. A
friend of ours saw the bodies of two hundred students
near his home. In the city it looks like everyone is
wearing black. The whole city is in mourning.
    You mentioned that you thought Frank's station at Robi
was not a good place for me to get away and rest. You
suggested the lake where we usually go camping. I wonder
why you say that. It seems Robi is more quiet.
    Richard has asked me to go with him to Kombolcha
when he comes. Of course, there will be no time to rest
then, but I can see I'll have time for some relaxation after
Richard leaves.
    Last night the Singletons, Morrows, the kids and I all
ate at the Chinese restaurant. It was a nice evening.
    Thousands, thousands, thousands are being sent north
for a big offensive. The government has confiscated all
vehicles with four-wheel drive from the mission station in
Ambo. They also ordered the hospital cooks to the battle
front.
    It's been a long time since I have said it, but because I
always want you to know, I will say it now, I love you very
much. I've thought that if something out of the way would
happen to me, I'd want you and the kids to know my real
feelings. Remember it always.
                                                  Denton

May 10, 1977
Dear Jodie,
    Well, Richard came in Sunday morning. Saturday
morning at seven-thirty the Derg announced that there
would be another house-to-house check and everyone was
ordered to stay at home. There were no buses, taxis, or
private cars permitted on the roads. Only diplomatic cars

were allowed to move about, and they could be stopped and inspected whenever the soldiers felt so inclined. Richard was to arrive on British Airways, but because of the situation, British Airways cancelled their flights into Addis, and Richard flew in on Ethiopian Airlines. Fortunately, he saw a lady diplomat at the airport. Her children and Richard and Jeannine's kids had gone to Good Shepherd School together. She offered to bring him to our house. I had no idea how he would get here since I couldn't leave the house to get him.

Singletons were to leave tomorrow, but because of the situation they couldn't finish their paperwork and they are going on Friday. Jim is very sick. I think it is a relapse of hepatitis. I have been trying to help him with some of his business transactions. I'm writing this at the customs office, waiting for them to sign a paper for him.

As I told you, I am going to Kombolcha with Richard to close the mission station. I will have to make arrangements for the kids to stay with someone. Tsige has been enlisted to cook for the army. It is supposed to be for three days, so maybe they can stay with her. If not, I hope I can find someone to come here and stay with them. Maybe the Dutch lady.

Feyesa has been arrested. You won't believe it when I tell you the charges. Selling tin cans! Yes, that's right! He is supposed to give all our empty tin cans to the commune. You know how he always used to sell them for a few cents each. Well, he got caught doing it after an order went out from the kebele to turn all tin cans in to them. I don't know when he will be released. Assefa, the night guard, was arrested over some radio that the officials say was stolen. They will not release him until the original owner of the radio is found and identifies it. Strange world!

Today the government announced that anyone in any kebele that is not working must go to the war and fight. Addis is going to be a quiet place.

Sunday night at five o'clock, however, shooting started and continued all night. It was especially heavy down near the river. The next morning until eleven, the whole

*area was completely covered with army. Jim and
Barbara are staying at the Mennonite Guest House, and
they said all night bullets were flying over the house.*

*Our house wasn't searched this weekend, but they
searched a lot of other houses in our kebele.*

*I will write again later to answer the questions you
asked in your last letter. I don't have it with me here at
the Customs Office.*

Love, Denton

May 11, 1977

Dear Jodie,

*Tomorrow Richard and I are planning to leave for
Kombolcha. I won't be writing again until I get back. The
children will be staying with Tsige.*

*I will stay there and help Richard pack what he wants
to ship. I will bring that load back to Addis, and Richard
will stay at Kombolcha to work on selling what he doesn't
want. Then I will probably go back for four or five more
days when I go to get Richard. He is on a forty-five-day
excursion ticket, so we don't have much time to settle
things there at Kombolcha. I have really enjoyed having
Richard stay with me.*

*Jim is really very sick. I don't know if they will be able
to leave when planned or not.*

*Monday morning Richard and I set a record. We got his
work permit, alien registration, and driver's license all
renewed in one morning, plus we bought a battery to take
to Kombolcha for Richard's car. I couldn't believe it. It
usually takes a whole day to get one signature.*

*The Chairman of the Derg came back from Russia
yesterday. Richard and I were just coming home, and we
were forced to stop until he passed. Security was
unbelievable. Tanks and all!*

*I told you that the Derg told everyone to turn in their
tents to be used for the war. Well, now there is a new
order. They are collecting pots, pans, and Ethiopian
baskets for the war. Can you believe it?*

Must close for now. Keep the letters coming!

Love, Denton

May 12, 1977

Dear Denton,

I have settled into the routine of American life: getting kids to school, picking them up, helping Jean fix dinner, doing dishes, helping kids with homework, Saturday shopping in the mall for the latest style jeans, tennis shoes, and shirts, trips to Toys-R-Us to buy the latest toy advertised on television.

Before I had arrived in the States Jean had bought Shellie a hamster and Brent a pet rat. When I raised my eyebrows and said, "You didn't, Jean?" she made such a case about these two lonely children sent home by their mother from England, that I dissolved into laughter and couldn't say anything else about our newly acquired menagerie.

I felt vindicated when Jean invited guests over last Saturday afternoon. I heard her in the bedroom talking to Brent.

"Now listen to me, Brent. My friend would not even come into this house if she knew there was a rat here. Cage or no cage, it wouldn't make any difference. She hates rats! Don't take your rat out of his cage once while she is here. This has to be our secret today, all right?"

Brent gave her a serious nod. He loves Aunt Jean, and he had no intention of upsetting her or her guests.

When the company arrived, Jean and Moe greeted them at the front door and Jean took their coats. As she was walking down the hallway past Brent's bedroom, she saw Brent's rat run across the back of the sofa. She nearly dropped the coats she was carrying as she dashed into the room and closed the door. Minutes later she appeared in search of Brent. I had just been introduced to the guests, when Jean appeared looking like she'd seen a ghost, not a rat!

"Jodie," she asked calmly, "have you seen Brent?" That was my first clue something had gone wrong.

"He and Michelle just went out in the back yard with the skateboard."

"Would you call him and tell him I need to see him in his bedroom for a minute?" she asked, as if it were absolutely nothing.

I remained suspicious.

"Brent," I called, through the screen of the sliding glass door, "Jean needs to see you for a minute."

As soon as I heard Brent go into the bedroom, I excused myself from the guests and joined Jean and Brent. They were both on their hands and knees crawling around the bedroom floor.

"What are you guys doing in here?" I asked, nearly ready to collapse into laughter.

"Jodie, help us. Brent's rat is loose. If Judy finds out there is a rat in this house, she will leave and probably never come back."

I joined the search party, trying to look sufficiently upset with Brent for forgetting to lock the rat's cage. It wasn't the first time his pet had gotten out, but I was afraid it might be the last.

"I've got to get back out there, or everyone is going to get suspicious. Brent, don't you leave this room until that rat is found," Jean ordered in her firmest whisper.

Tinker the rat was rescued, returned to his cage, and no one was the wiser. I later had a good laugh, and told Jean it served her right for getting that rodent in the first place.

Wouldn't you think that was enough for one Saturday! Not so! Jean suggested I spend the night there rather than drive back to Walnut Creek since Judy and her husband left late. Shellie volunteered to sleep on the couch in the family room so I could sleep in her bedroom. Normally I would have thought that was a very nice gesture. However, as it turned out, she slept peacefully all night while I spent the night on my hands and knees looking for Teaky, her hamster. I just couldn't bear the thought of Jean finding out that the hamster got out, too.

I had no sooner gotten into bed and was reading a few minutes when I heard this funny scratching sound. I looked over at Teaky's cage, and guess what? No Teaky! I just couldn't believe it. Out of bed I went. Every time I moved, the noise stopped. Finally, I just sat on the floor and read, listening for the sound again. At last I heard it. I opened the bottom drawer of the dresser and guess who I found? Teaky! He had made the nicest little nest from all the angora off Shellie's newest sweater. I felt like skinning him, but who would wear a hamster coat! When I picked him up and he looked at me with those tiny brown eyes, I knew I had to tuck him back into his cage, although that wasn't my first thought! I'm still debating whether or not to tell Jean "the rest of the story" tomorrow.

Well, I must sign off for now. I hope you and the children are well. You are all in our prayers.

Love and prayers, Jodie

CHAPTER SEVENTEEN
A New Plan

On Friday, May 20, I picked Shellie and Brent up from their schools for the weekend. I had planned to spend the weekend at our townhouse to give Jean, Moe, and Michelle a weekend alone as a family. Shellie hadn't been feeling well all week, and I had made an appointment with the pediatrician in Concord for late Friday afternoon.

"I'm sorry, Mrs. Collins. It is mononucleosis," the doctor confirmed. "Shellie will need complete bed rest for at least a week, and then I should check her again."

Shellie was so disappointed. Her eighth grade graduation was just four weeks away. I assured her that if she listened to the doctor and stayed in bed, she would be fine by June 13.

I called Jean and told her the news. "I'll just keep Shellie here with me. I will bring Brent back Sunday evening."

I was disappointed Saturday morning when the mailman brought no letter from Denton. It had been nearly a week since I had received his last letter. I am getting spoiled, I chided myself. He writes so faithfully. He is probably in Kombolcha with Richard, I reasoned. It would be difficult to mail a letter from there. He probably decided it would take longer for mail to come from Kombolcha than if he just waited to mail it when he returned to Addis. I had sent him our new telephone number in my last letter. Maybe he will call me when he gets back from Kombolcha to let me know he is all right.

As I sat reading and having my second cup of coffee early Sunday morning, before the kids got up, the telephone rang. "Ah, ha," I said out loud. "Maybe that's Denton." I hurried to the kitchen to answer before it woke up Shellie and Brent.

"Hello."

"Hello, Mrs. Collins. This is Seyfou in London."

"Seyfou?" I repeated, shocked that the Crown Prince's son-in-law was calling me. I hadn't talked to Seyfou or Mary since our one visit together in London when he asked me to consider helping the other six royal children still in Addis. How had he found my new telephone number? I wondered.

"How are you, Mrs. Collins? I have just been talking with Michael. In fact, he gave me your telephone number," he said, as if reading my thoughts. "Have you heard from Mr. Collins and the children?"

"Yes, I have had several letters, Seyfou. They are doing fine. Have you heard any news from Addis lately?"

"No, not recently. But I do have some good news. We have found another airplane. I think it is larger than the one you planned to use in the first escape plan."

It seemed peculiar to me that he knew we had even concluded our first plans for escape. Michael! I thought to myself. He and Michael must have discussed it together.

"We can plan another escape, Mrs. Collins. Are you interested?"

Trying not to appear overanxious, I said, "Yes, of course. What do you have in mind, Seyfou?"

"Mrs. Collins, there are two conditions we must meet in order to get this airplane. First, Mr. Collins must agree to bring out the children of Princess Ejigeyehu."

I was so startled by this first condition, I nearly forgot there was a second.

"Seyfou, listen to me. We are now talking about an escape with ten children. Do I understand you correctly?"

"Yes, Mrs. Collins, that is the first condition for the plane. There is no problem, the plane is large enough."

"The plane may be large enough, Seyfou, but how will I ever get Mr. Collins to agree? He is leery about escaping with *four* children."

"The second condition is that you look after all ten children until other arrangements can be made for them. We want them all to go to the United States. It isn't safe for them to come to England."

Raise ten children? *Twelve* children? Oh, my goodness! It was too much.

"Are you still there, Mrs. Collins?"

"Yes, Seyfou, I'm still here. Listen, there is no way I can make this kind of a decision without talking to Denton first," I insisted. "I am going to have to phone him in Addis and try to find a way to ask him about this. We are going to have to send a contact man into Addis to sit down with Denton and go over the details for this plan carefully. There will be no way I can relay all the details over the telephone."

"That is not a problem. We have someone who can go to Addis and meet with him. You arrange it, and we will send him. There is just one other thing. The war between Somalia and Ethiopia is escalating fast. This could complicate our plans. We must move quickly. Call me as soon as you have talked to Mr. Collins." He gave me his telephone number.

"All right, Seyfou. I will try to contact him, but he was going up north to Kombolcha with another missionary. He should be back in Addis by now. I will try my best."

"Fine. I'll talk to you tomorrow, May 23."

As soon as I hung up the receiver I said to myself, "Tomorrow? How do I even know I can reach Denton by tomorrow?"

I tried to calculate the time there. I could never remember exactly the time difference between Addis and San Francisco. I guessed they were approximately twelve hours ahead of us. That meant it was Sunday night, May 22.

It might be a good time to reach him, I thought, reaching for the receiver again. I had to stop a minute to recall our home telephone number in Addis. I dialed for the operator to place the call. There was no direct dialing to Africa as there was to London. I would have to place the call and wait for the operator to call me back.

Once the call was placed, I waited. I tried to occupy myself by picking up the book I had been reading when Seyfou first called.

"Our faith must continually go through the death-resurrection cycle. Our old faith must die, eaten away by doubts and fears, but only so that a new and deeper faith may be born." The words were written by Paul Tillich. I felt they were written especially for me.

Ten children, I thought. Is it really possible?

The telephone rang.

"Hello," I answered.

"Is this Mrs. Collins? Did you place a call to Addis Ababa, Ethiopia, to Mr. Collins?"

"Yes, I did, Operator."

"I'm sorry, there is no answer."

"Operator, would you please continue to try the number throughout the day? It is extremely important that I talk to Mr. Collins."

"Yes, I can do that. I will call you when I reach him."

That's good, I thought. *Surely I will get through sometime today.*

By two o'clock in the afternoon, the operator still had not called me back. I phoned Jean and told her something urgent had developed, and that I was waiting for a call from Denton. I asked if she and Moe could come over for dinner and pick up Brent while I waited for the operator's call. She agreed immediately.

When Jean, Moe, and Michelle arrived for dinner, I told them about the call from Seyfou. They were overwhelmed with the thought of escaping with ten children.

"What are you going to do?" Moe asked incredulously.

"I don't know yet. I must wait and talk to Denton. Can you imagine his enthusiasm when he hears this plan?" I said.

When Jean, Moe, Michelle, and Brent left for Fremont at eight o'clock that evening, I still had not heard from Denton.

I tried placing the call with another operator, only to be told that there was still no answer at our home in Addis.

Most of the evening I sat on the edge of Shellie's bed. I cautioned her against talking to anyone about a possible escape, and for the first time, I told her of our aborted plan in April. "Daddy's life could be in serious danger," I warned her. "We must not tell anyone, Shellie. It is a family secret," I said, patting her on the shoulder.

By ten o'clock Shellie was asleep. I decided to try to call Joseph at the Headquarters. I calculated it would be ten in the morning there.

It was so good to hear Joseph's familiar voice.

"Joseph, this is Mrs. Collins. I must get in touch with Mr. Collins. Where is he, Joseph? I have tried calling him at home all night and there is no answer."

"Yes, Mrs. Collins. Mr. Collins went up north with Mr. Konnerup. We were expecting him back before now, but he hasn't returned."

"Joseph, listen to me carefully. I must talk to Mr. Collins. It is urgent. I want you to take the bus to Kombolcha, find Mr. Collins, and tell him to telephone me. I must talk to him!"

Always so gracious and obliging, Joseph agreed to go immediately. I knew the bus ride to Kombolcha was a rugged twelve-hour trip, and Joseph wouldn't be able to get a bus until early Tuesday morning, May 24. I estimated that Denton should call me within twenty-four hours. If Joseph was able to leave Tuesday morning, that meant Denton should call me by Tuesday night or early Wednesday morning.

The hours of waiting nearly undid me. Shellie was a doll. She read and watched television, and, sensing my anxiety, she stayed in bed according to the doctor's orders. I took our meals to her bedroom, and we talked together as we ate. Most of our conversations were about our fun times in Ethiopia together with Menen, Loly, and Kokeb. Her voice was filled with love and concern as she talked about Amaha, and how happy she was when he was able to join the family. Shellie and I laughed together and sometimes we cried. I was happy for Shellie's company during this long vigil.

I tried to stay busy reading, straightening my closet and drawers, watching television, and caring for Shellie, but my mind was restless. Was all of this a mistake? Was I asking too much of God? Escaping with four children had seemed impossible enough at times. Now an escape with four children sounded remarkably uncomplicated. But *ten?*

By Wednesday evening, May 25, I still had not heard from Denton. I telephoned Seyfou to tell him what I had done. At ten o'clock the same evening, I placed another call to Addis. This time Berhanu, another of Denton's assistants, answered the phone.

"Berhanu, have you heard from Mr. Collins or Joseph?"

"No, Mrs. Collins. Joseph left Tuesday morning on the six o'clock bus for Kombolcha to try and find Mr. Collins."

"Yes, yes, I know, Berhanu, I sent him!" I felt the impatience in my voice. "Berhanu, listen to me! I want you to take the bus up north and try to find out what has happened to Joseph and Mr. Collins. Try to get a bus this morning. I must talk to Mr. Collins. It is extremely important. Tell him to telephone me immediately. Do you understand, Berhanu?"

"Yes, Mrs. Collins," he assured me.

I waited. Two more days passed—May 27 . . . May 28. No word came from Denton, Joseph, Berhanu, or Richard. On Sunday morning, May 29, a week after Seyfou had first called me, I decided it was time to inform Seyfou of the complication I had run into, looking for Denton.

"I can't locate Denton. I've sent two young men to Kombolcha to tell Denton to phone me. I haven't heard from Denton or either of the young men."

"We are running out of time, Mrs. Collins. Thousands of soldiers are being sent south to fight with Somalia. Thousands more are going north to the war in Eritrea. We won't be able to fly a plane in there for much longer. You must find Mr. Collins!" Seyfou concluded emphatically.

"I'm trying my best. I will call you when I know something new." I hung up, exasperated with Seyfou, myself, Denton, everyone!

Sitting in the living room alone, I tried to think whom I could call next. I remembered Guenet's sister, Asselefetch. She lived in Dessie, a city very near Kombolcha. Maybe her husband, Tariku, would drive to Kombolcha and give Denton a message. I called Guenet in Oklahoma City to ask her for Asselefetch's number. I explained that I needed to get a message to Denton and was hoping that Tariku could drive to Kombolcha and ask Denton to phone me.

I knew it would be Sunday evening in Dessie. I hoped they hadn't gone to Addis, and I was relieved to hear Tariku's deep voice.

"It's wonderful to hear from you," he exclaimed.

I was brief and specific. Without hesitation he agreed to go. He would leave as soon as the morning curfew was lifted, six o'clock Monday morning, May 30.

After talking to Tariku, my vigil continued. Paging

through my Bible, I knew I had read a verse about waiting. Where was it? I checked the concordance of my Bible. There it is, I said to myself. There's another one! I leafed through my Bible until I came to the familiar Psalm 37. Verse 7 said, "Be still before the Lord and wait patiently for him . . . do not fret. . . ." It seemed the Lord kept taking me back to that chapter again and again. It had become like a dependable friend, constantly reminding me of what I needed to do to survive these difficult hours of waiting and hoping for the best. . . . It was a vigil.

Slowly I turned to the other reference I had found in my Bible concordance—Isaiah 40:27-31: "Why do you say . . . and complain, 'My way is hidden from the Lord; my cause is disregarded by my God?' The Lord is the everlasting God, the Creator of the ends of the earth. He will not grow tired or weary, and his understanding no one can fathom. He gives strength to the weary and increases the power of the weak. Even youths grow tired and weary, and young men stumble and fall; but those who hope [wait] in the Lord will renew their strength. They will soar on wings like eagles, they will run and not grow weary, they will walk and not be faint."

I hung onto the words during the hours that followed. I slept restlessly on Sunday night. Early Monday morning, May 30, Tariku called. "I'm terribly sorry," he explained, his voice heavy with disappointment. "Mr. Collins and Mr. Konnerup arc both under house arrest. The compound is surrounded by soldiers, and the guards have refused to let them leave. They are being held as antirevolutionaries. They allowed me to talk to them briefly, and Mr. Collins explained that the local group calling themselves the Committee for the Defense of the Revolution came to the compound and searched the house for nearly three hours. They found a small map on the stationery of a former missionary. I think Mr. Collins said the missionary had been gone for nearly five years. The map was very small, printed on the letterhead. It appeared not to have the province of Eritrea on it, and the Committee accused Denton and Richard of conspiring with the Eritrean Liberation Front for the secession of Eritrea from Ethiopia. It is terribly unfortunate for Mr. Collins and

Mr. Konnerup, but they both assured me, and asked me to assure you, that the matter is nearly resolved. Mr. Collins said he will phone you as soon as he gets back to Addis."

So there it was! My greatest fear. Denton had been arrested. And what was worse, it was in the countryside where each committee, group, and association was a government unto itself.

Tariku assured me that he would check on Denton and Richard each day until they were released. He said that the members of Richard's church had been bringing food to them each day. The soldiers inspected the food, but allowed Denton and Richard to have it after inspection.

I called Seyfou again Monday after Tariku's call. It was like hearing a taped recording, "Mrs. Collins, the contact man is waiting to leave for Ethiopia to meet with Mr. Collins. Time is running out!"

My patience was waning. "Seyfou, we can't send anyone in there to talk to Denton until he is released from Kombolcha and back in Addis. Don't you realize he is twelve hours from the capital city on a remote mission station at the mercy of some overzealous, irrational committee for the defense of Ethiopia? If we send someone to Kombolcha to talk to Denton, the committee might be suspicious, and just angry enough to kill both Richard and Denton." I heard my voice rising, and my irritation was only thinly disguised. "We must wait to hear from Denton," I insisted.

Denton's call came the next morning. It was four o'clock and I was sound asleep when I heard the ringing. I thought at first it was the alarm clock. When I realized it was the telephone, I nearly bolted out of bed. Only bad news comes in the middle of the night, I thought, pessimistically.

My voice was groggy with sleep. "Hello."

"Jodie, is that you? This is Denton."

Thank God, the connection is clear, I thought instantly.

"Denton!" I screamed. "Are you all right? Where are you? Where are Joseph and Berhanu? Are you all OK?"

"Yes, we are fine. I am still in Kombolcha. They are taking Richard and me back to Addis under armed guard tomorrow morning early. I have written you. I'll call you from Addis. I just wanted to let you know that we are on our way to Addis."

"Denton, Catherine's surgery has been rescheduled. The doctor is going to contact you once you are back in Addis. How are you feeling?"

"Jodie, my nerves are shot!"

"Please listen to me, Denton. You need to get some physical exercise. When you get back to Addis, play tennis. It will help you a lot. Play with anyone who asks you. Do you understand? Play tennis," I emphasized it again.

"Tennis?" he asked haltingly, not certain what I was trying to say.

"Yes, Denton, please. For your health's sake, play tennis!"

"All right, Jodie, I'll play. I'll talk to you again when we get to Addis."

I decided against waiting until later in the morning. I called Seyfou as soon as I hung up from talking to Denton.

"I don't know if they will release them once they get to Addis, Seyfou," I said, in answer to his question. "He is going to call me once he is in Addis. Just have the contact man ready to go."

"Did you tell Mr. Collins the 'doctor' was coming?"

"Well, not exactly. I told him he needed to play tennis. He was telling me about how his nerves were shot, and I stressed that he should play tennis with anyone who invited him. We have a tennis membership at the Hilton Hotel. When the contact man flies to Addis, tell him to stay at the Hilton Hotel. Our home telephone number is 73501. Tell the man to call Denton early in the morning, around eight o'clock, before he leaves to take the kids to school. He should ask Denton to play tennis. I hope Denton will remember he is supposed to play tennis. They can meet at the Hilton, and the man can explain the details of the new plan."

"That's fine, Mrs. Collins, fine. We will get things ready on this end. Let me know the minute you hear from Denton again."

At last things were moving again. I could hardly wait for Shellie to wake up the next morning. I was so happy she was there. I was eager to share the news with someone. How would Denton take the news of the new plans? I would know soon enough.

Shellie squealed with delight when I told her the news of Denton's release. "Why didn't you wake me up so I could talk to Daddy?" she asked.

"There was no time, honey. He seemed to be in a hurry. You can talk to him if you are here when he calls again. You have a doctor's appointment this morning. You might be back in school by Monday. Wouldn't that be great!"

"Do you think Daddy will call before then?" she pursued.

"I hope he will call Saturday. Then you and Brent could both talk to him. Wouldn't that be great?"

She bustled with excitement as she dressed for her doctor's appointment. Her tests showed her greatly improved, and she was cleared to return to school Monday morning. "Now I'll get to graduate, Mom," she announced excitedly. "Can we go shopping for my graduation dress this weekend?"

"We will if Daddy calls by then. I don't want to be away from the telephone until after I talk to him. We will go and get Brent on Friday afternoon. If Dad has called by then, we will shop Friday evening. If not, we will wait."

She seemed satisfied with my explanation.

Shellie occupied herself during the remainder of the morning. After lunch, while she was taking a nap, the telephone rang.

"Yes, Mrs. Collins, my name is George Hawk. I am with the State Department in Washington, D.C. I am calling regarding your husband, Denton Collins."

Oh no, I thought. No! Surely nothing has happened to Denton. I talked to him just a few hours ago.

"Yes, Mr. Hawk."

"It seems your husband is missing in Ethiopia. It has been reported to the American embassy in Addis Ababa that Mr. Collins went to northern Ethiopia on mission business. It seems he has not been heard of since. We just wanted to inform you, and let you know that we are involved in locating him."

It was the first chance I had to say anything. "Mr. Hawk, I

talked to my husband just this morning. He phoned me from Kombolcha, where he and another missionary, Mr. Richard Konnerup, went to close Mr. Konnerup's mission station. He was detained and placed under house arrest, but he said the government was transporting him and Mr. Konnerup back to Addis in the morning under armed guard."

"That is good news, Mrs. Collins. We just wanted you to know that we are on top of the situation, and I will be getting back in touch with you if there are any new developments."

I thanked Mr. Hawk for calling. When he had hung up, I wondered if the State Department was really on top of the situation or if he had learned more from me than I had from him.

It was Thursday, June 2, when Denton called again. He was back in Addis. I told him about Mr. Hawk's telephone call, hoping that if our telephone was tapped, the listeners would understand that the State Department was in touch with me and looking into Denton's situation.

"I've written you about everything, honey," Denton said, wearily. "Nothing is settled. The Ethiopian government has confiscated Richard's and my passports and Richard's airline ticket. He was to have left June 10, but now things are very uncertain. We are not under house arrest now, but we have been told not to leave the city. They even made the American embassy sign as our guarantor in case we try to escape. Now I have two guarantors: Joseph and the American embassy."

This was depressing news in light of what I was about to tell Denton.

"Catherine's surgery is being rescheduled. The doctor should be contacting you soon to explain the new procedure that he feels certain will save her life. I hope you will listen with an open mind. She must have this surgery or I'm afraid it is all over for her. It could be within the next week or two if you just agree to it."

"All right, Jodie. I will listen to what the doctor has to say and then decide if it's best. Did I tell you that I haven't played any tennis lately? I just haven't found anyone to play with me. Most everyone who plays is gone, and Richard doesn't play tennis. I am still looking forward to a good game."

I was pleased he had understood that I was trying to relay a message to him on Tuesday when he had called me so unexpectedly from Kombolcha.

"Good, Denton. I hope you get a chance to play tennis real soon. It will help your nerves if you'll just follow through with it. And, Denton, please keep an open mind and listen to the doctor!"

Minutes later I was talking to Seyfou.

"Yes," he assured me, "we will have someone go to Addis and talk to Denton. Because of the delay, the man we had hoped would go in cannot go at this time. We will find someone else. We are planning to send a plane in from Kenya. We will pick Denton and the children up from Lake Langano. It's a whole new plan. Once they are safely in Kenya, we hope you will meet them and help process all their papers. Even Denton will be there illegally."

"That's not a problem; I'll go!" I said, without hesitation.

Seyfou promised to call as soon as they found someone to go to Addis. I thought the days would never pass. My days were filled with the routine once again: dentist appointments, haircuts, doctor's appointments, vaccinations, grocery shopping, banking, post office.

On Wednesday, June 9, I went to a travel agent and bought an airline ticket to Kenya. I checked my passport to make sure it had not expired and applied for a visa to Kenya. My vaccinations were in order. For the first time in months it felt as though things might work out again.

Shellie's graduation from junior high was June 13. It was a special evening, commencing with dinner at Jean and Moe's. We all piled into the car and headed for her school after dinner. My mom, Jean, Moe, Michelle, Brent, and I were all there to cheer as Shellie received her diploma. She beamed with delight as I snapped a picture of her. Following a lovely reception, we said goodbye to Moe, Jean, and Michelle. Shellie and Brent came home with me, ending my daily commute from Walnut Creek to Fremont. We all missed the Hernandezes, and once in awhile, Brent still called me Aunt Jean.

We had a wonderful surprise the weekend after Shellie's graduation. My father and step-mom, Ivy, called me from Singapore. Dad said he had called Addis thinking I was still there, and Denton had given him my phone number. Dad had lived in southeast Asia for nearly thirty years. He had decided to send Ivy and her two boys, Lukie and Monde, to the States. He was planning to retire from the oil company, but they had decided it was best if Ivy and the boys left immediately. They had bought a mobile home in Santa Rosa last year when they were home for vacation. He said he would explain things when he got home. It sounded so familiar that I was reluctant to ask any questions.

"Dad, Ivy and the boys are welcome to stay with Shellie, Brent, and me. I would be happy to pick her up from the airport and help her get settled. I have a car, and Santa Rosa is only an hour north of Walnut Creek."

"That would be wonderful, sweetheart. I know Ivy would appreciate the help. She's only visited the States, you know; she's never lived there. You would be a big help to her. She and the boys are flying into San Francisco Sunday evening on Philippine Airlines flight PR106."

"I'll be there to pick them up, Dad. Don't worry about a thing. There's nothing I'd rather do than shop with Ivy and spend all your money before you get here!"

His laugh was contagious, and we both chuckled.

It would be nice to see Ivy and the boys again. I had met them only once, in 1975, when we all happened to be in the States at the same time.

Dad had lived in Sumatra, Borneo, as well as Singapore. He could keep me spellbound spinning stories of his adventures in jungles, flying helicopters, and forging snake-infested rivers.

I loved his jolly Irish manner and great sense of humor.

I do hope Ivy arrives before I have to leave for Kenya, I thought hopefully. I was still waiting to hear if Seyfou had found someone willing to go to Addis to talk to Denton.

I began receiving Denton's letters again by mid-June.

Some had been written from Kombolcha and were nearly a month old. I didn't mind. They described in detail Denton's frustration and experiences at Kombolcha during the final weeks of May.

May 19, 1977

Dear Jodie,

I haven't written for a week, so I had better get on the stick. We're at Kombolcha. Things have not gone as well as we had hoped. We were wanting to sell and pay severance and salaries through this school year. I didn't think it best for Richard to come alone, and it has proven true. First the Farmer's Association insisted we get permission before we sell any of Richard's things. They are insisting that they get first choice. They said they are not allowed to buy in the city at the kebele shops, and therefore, the city people should not buy in their area until they have a chance to buy what they want to. This is what started it all. Then the local administrators wouldn't give us the permission that the Farmers' Association insisted we acquire. We went to Dessie, since it is the main center for this area. The local officials there gave us permission to sell Richard's things, but when we came back here, the Farmers' Association refused to accept it. Complicated, isn't it?

Night before last about six-thirty Richard and I were working to pack the barrels that he wants to ship home, when we were suddenly surrounded by people with guns pointed at us. They were fanned out all around us. They said they were the Committee for the Defense of the Revolution. For three hours they searched the house, reading all the letters and papers, looking through everything. Then they sealed up all the buildings except his house, where we were sleeping. They came back again yesterday and searched again. They took all Richard's duplicators, stencil makers, and other office machines, seven in all. They kept questioning us about the Bakers. We told them we knew Bakers, and that they had been in Ethiopia three or four years ago. Last night they arrested

*all of the mission teachers. It will certainly be best when
we can get out of here. Poor Richard—of all people who
worked to have good relations with the community, and
now look what has happened. Now people will be afraid
to come to church here and be associated with the
mission.*

*Jim and Barb were to leave yesterday. I tried to call
them from here, but the line was down. I was finally able
to get a message through to Tsige that I would not be back
in Addis as quickly as I had expected to be.*

*I guess to expect peace and quiet for more than two or
three days is just expecting too much. I hope there are a
lot of letters from you and the kids waiting for me when I
get back to Addis.*

May 22, 1977

Dear Jodie,

*Well, you'll never guess what's happened now. The
closing of every mission station has gone differently, and
so I should have expected something new, I guess.*

*I last wrote you on Wednesday, May 18. Thursday
morning when Richard and I went outside, there were
police guarding the house. They informed us we were
under house arrest, so for the last three days we have
been sitting in the house. The local officials have come to
question us several times. Neither Richard nor I can
believe the accusation. It seems they found a piece of
Baker's stationery with a small map of Ethiopia on the
letterhead. They insist the map does not have Eritrea on
it. They have concluded we are associated with the
Eritrean Liberation Front. Can you believe it?*

*The people from Richard's Ethiopian church have been
just wonderful. They are bringing us much more food than
we can eat.*

*I feel terrible about the teachers' being in the local jail.
I'm glad they let us stay here instead of putting us in jail
too. The teachers have really done nothing. Their only
crime is being friends with us.*

I hope we will find out in the next couple of days what

they plan to do with us. Don't call the headquarters in Springfield unless you don't hear from me again within a week or so.

May 25, 1977

Dear Jodie,

We are still under house arrest at Kombolcha. Word has come to us that the officials in town are waiting for word from Addis about what to do. There is an airplane flight today, so hopefully it will bring them instructions about what they should do with us. The teachers are still in jail too. I suspect they will forbid us to sell any of Richard's things and give us twenty-four hours to get out of the country. I hope that is the worst that can happen! The problem we will have if they do that is that Richard will not have the money to pay his teachers their severance pay and wages if he is not allowed to sell his things. It is amazing to both of us how this whole incident has been blown completely out of proportion. People are still bringing food: tea, eggs, bread, injera *and* watt. *Last night the owners of the Agip Restaurant brought us soup and roast beef. It was a welcome change.*

I have sure caught up on my reading while being confined to the house. I think I've read more books during this past week than I've read during the whole last term in Ethiopia. Don't worry about us. We are fine, just bored! I keep wondering what you are doing. Does Brent enjoy his school as much as Shellie has enjoyed hers? One nice thing is there will be lots of mail in Addis when we get back there. Be sure and let me know how everyone is doing.

May 27, 1977

Dear Jodie,

The teachers have been released. Isn't that great! Richard and I are still confined to the house, and the teachers cannot come to visit us, but at least they are out and with their families.

Joseph came to visit us. He brought a letter from you and one from Brent that had arrived the day before he left. He had put all the other mail under the door of my office, so he couldn't get it out to bring it to me. He was planning to catch a bus and return to Addis. I assume he did. I gave him the keys to my office and our house so he can get in and water all the plants. I told Joseph to go to the English School and tell Loly what had happened to us so she can tell Tsige. I didn't want them to worry that something serious had happened to us.

We heard there was trouble in Dessie this week. Some school teachers were executed and students jailed. The way the military was checking people coming and going in Kombolcha, I was afraid for Joseph. I hope he got out of here all right. They have let us go out of the house, but not off the compound. Richard and I have been using his golf clubs and hitting balls back and forth across the mission station. Today I have stayed inside. I have a headache and I ache all over from head to toe. Probably something I ate. It will be a great relief when this station is closed, and we can get out of here. The only station left to close will be Addis. One thing for sure—I'm glad I came with Richard. It would be worse to be kept in a place like this alone.

We have a radio, and the news said that an American was found to be a CIA agent in southern Ethiopia.

Well, I'll close and write later.

June 4, 1977

Can you believe it? We are finally back in Addis. Berhanu and Joseph are fine. Today the group of American embassy workers, Marines, and the military attaché left. There was also a very large group of missionaries leaving, too. Many more are scheduled to leave tomorrow. All diplomats and military personnel must leave by commercial planes. No military or private planes can fly into Ethiopia now. Missionary Aviation took their five planes out, too.

We were brought back to Addis by armed guard. We are not confined to the house, but we cannot leave the city. We have gotten no reply from Security regarding the case

*against us. They said it had been referred to the Derg. I
just can't believe it!*

*Jeannine called Richard last night. She said our
Mission director was trying to get the State Department to
force us out of here. It is impossible without our
passports.*

I will close for now and get this ready to post.

June 14, 1977

Dear Jodie,

*I'm writing this from beside the pool at the Hilton Hotel
in Addis. Amaha and I came here to swim while Richard
tries to get some gasoline. There are long, long lines for
gas. Yesterday I waited in line for one hour and just as I
got to the pump, they ran out of gas.*

*Ami sure does enjoy swimming. Yesterday he fell down
and scratched his face. He is all right, though.*

*We still have no news regarding our case, but we've
heard that the Chairman of the Derg and all those top
guys are so busy with the two wars that they don't have
time to consider cases like ours. It is rather lonely coming
to the Hilton. No one ever calls to play tennis. I wonder
why? So many people have left that I guess there aren't
that many around who play tennis. How are the kids? Are
their schools out for the summer yet? Did you get the
package of spices I sent to you? How is your mom?*

*I still don't have my passport back yet. We have been
told not to leave Addis, but I would sure like to take a
short rest at Sodere or Lake Langano. I don't know how
the road is, since it has been so long since I traveled that
way.*

*I haven't had any letters from you in a few days. I hope
I get one tomorrow.*

June 22, 1977

Dear Jodie,

*I really don't think our mail is going out, but
nevertheless, I'll write, hoping that eventually it will*

*reach you. I have not gotten one letter from anyone in the
States since coming from Kombolcha. I can't help but
wonder if they have stopped mail coming from the States.
It seems peculiar. I feel like the government here is
playing games with us. We've still heard nothing about the
accusations made against us. If they think we are
subversive counterrevolutionaries, we are in trouble. How
can such a small matter turn into something like this? It
seems unbelievable when I stop and think about it all! The
kids are just fine. Feyesa is out of jail. Today Loly and
Menen are out of school, because it is study day for exams
next week. They are studying right now, but if we get any
sunshine today, I plan to take them to the Hilton
swimming.*

*I heard today that the Sudan Interior Mission has
scaled down to five mission stations with fifty
missionaries. They will have only thirty missionaries
soon, and most of them will be in Addis. Seems incredible
after their having over 400 a couple of years ago.*

I'll write again later. Hope you are writing, too.

I waited every day to hear from Seyfou. The waiting went
on and on. A self-imposed house arrest, I thought, cynically.
I read and waited, waited and read, afraid to leave the
house because the telephone might ring.

One day while reading a book by Oswald Chambers I
came across a paragraph which seemed to describe my situation perfectly:

*There are times when there is no illumination and no
thrill, but just the daily round, the common task. Routine
is God's way of saving us between our times of
inspiration. Do not expect God always to give you his
thrilling minutes, but learn to live in the domain of
drudgery by the power of God. We say we do not expect
God to carry us along on flowery beds of ease, and yet we
act as if we did. If I do my duty, not for duty's sake, but
because I believe God is engineering my circumstances,
then at the very point of my perplexity, I can look to the*

Lord and know He is mine through faith . . . His promises are mine, through faith.

"At the very point of my perplexity. . . ." That best described my moment! The domain of drudgery! My back ached from cleaning closets, cupboards, moving furniture. My heart ached at the thought of starting our lives all over again. Is it really possible to live through moments, days, months, like these by the power of God?

I resolved once more that I would try to trust God, but I knew it would always be difficult, because I was one of those people who liked to work things out for myself, find my own answers, and push forward as quickly as possible. This business of waiting for the Lord, trusting Him, well, I just wasn't sure I was cut out for it!

Ivy and the boys will be here in four more days. That will be great, I thought, trying to cheer myself up.

I had nearly given up when the call finally came. It was June 23.

"It's Seyfou, Mrs. Collins. The doctor has gone to see Denton. You should hear something soon. Let me know."

He was brief. I could hardly contain my excitement. The contact man was on his way to Addis. God, hear me, please let Denton go for this, please!

I ran to the swimming pool to call Shellie and Brent. I felt as if I had been let out of prison. "Come on, kids, let's go get pizza. We are going to celebrate."

They jumped out of the swimming pool and came running. "Come on, I'll race you to the house," I called, full of energy and ready to take on the world again. Unfortunately Shellie and Brent were in much better shape and I huffed and puffed into the house yards behind them. Collapsing into a chair in the living room, I said, "The contact man has gone to Addis to talk to Dad about the escape plan. We should be hearing something from Dad in a few days. Let's go celebrate."

They were in my arms, hugging and kissing me. We were all excited beyond words.

Ivy, Monde, and Lukie arrived on Sunday, June 26.

The house was full of activity. I felt alive again, and hope filled my heart.

Brent, Monde, Luke, and Shellie piled into sleeping bags in Brent's room in the garage. They loved it. Ivy stayed in Shellie's room. The first night they arrived, long after the kids were tucked into their sleeping bags, Ivy and I sat and talked.

"My brother was killed by the communists," Ivy explained. "He was ambushed. I was afraid for Luke and Monde. Monde is so young, but they were going to draft him into the military. Your dad and I thought it would be better for us to wait for him here. It is better for the boys to finish school here."

I told Ivy our whole story. I don't think we slept until dawn.

I hadn't been asleep more than a couple of hours when the telephone startled me awake. It was daylight, but I could barely get my eyes open.

"Jodie, this is Denton. I have just talked to the doctor." I bolted out of bed and began pacing, holding the telephone in my hand.

"Jodie, listen to me. Catherine's surgery is too complicated. The operation is too complex. There is no way she can have this surgery!" My heart nearly stopped beating for fear he meant it. His voice was rigid and firm.

"Denton, please," I begged. "You know she will die if she doesn't have this surgery. Be reasonable, Denton, please. Listen to the doctor."

"I have listened. I can't believe it. This new procedure is outrageous. She doesn't stand a chance."

"Denton, please!"

Neither of us spoke for nearly a minute. Denton broke the silence. Suddenly his voice sounded resigned and softer. I heard him sigh deeply, as if he were exhausted. His voice was barely a whisper, but I heard him clearly, "All right, Jodie. Catherine will have her surgery."

I collapsed onto the bed, holding the telephone in my lap.

"OK, Denton. Thank you," was all that I could utter.

"I'll write you, Jodie. The surgery is scheduled for three

weeks from now." That was all he said, and he hung up.

I was too shocked to move. I must have sat on the side of the bed for an hour, thinking about all this meant.

Twelve children. We were going to have twelve kids! It went without saying, we wouldn't be staying in this townhouse. Three weeks. I tried to calculate the date. It would be the 17th or 18th of July. I would know more when I talked to Michael or Seyfou.

As the immediate impact of Denton's call wore off, I decided to call Seyfou.

"He's heard, Seyfou. The doctor arrived, and he has agreed to go through with the operation. Can you believe it? Catherine is going to have surgery."

We were both ecstatic.

"All we can do is wait," I heard him say.

That brought me back to earth in a hurry. Wait? Again? That seemed like all we had been doing for months. There seemed to be one minute of exhilaration and weeks of waiting. The cycle was repeated again and again.

I told Shellie as soon as she woke up. We danced all over the living room. Brent rarely showed much excitement, but he forgot himself and joined in a moment of hilarity. I think our noise must have awakened Ivy, because it wasn't long until she joined us downstairs, and we all excitedly repeated the good news for her. Later, Shellie and Brent told Lukie and Monde the whole story from the beginning.

Over coffee, Ivy and I organized our day. We would leave a refrigerator full of food for the kids, and we would set off for Santa Rosa to see if their mobile home had been delivered and set on the lot. The utilities company, water, and telephone company needed to be notified that Ivy was moving into the home. Our list of things to do kept growing. We knew we would never get everything done in one day, but we had to start somewhere. For me that always meant a list.

During the next few weeks Ivy and I worked to get her and the boys settled into their home. We bought beds, mattresses, bedroom furniture, washer, dryer, sheets, towels. We left the kids with instructions for the day and plenty of food to keep them happy. Monde was sixteen and Luke was twelve. They were good boys, and Shellie and Brent enjoyed their company.

On July 6 I received Denton's letter confirming Catherine's surgery.

June 27, 1977

Dear Jodie,

Last Wednesday, June 22, I got two letters from you and two from Brent and Shellie. I was sure getting worried, and was ready to call you. I even went to the post office and complained Wednesday morning, and then Wednesday afternoon all your letters arrived. It had been nearly a month since I had heard from you.

I finally got to play a game of tennis last Friday. I enjoyed it. Hope to play again in a few weeks. It's very hard to get the time. Rest and relaxation are very important, though. I'm hoping to take off for Lake Langano by myself later this week or next if I can get gas. It is a real problem now. Then about July 15 I'd like to go again for a longer time (maybe eight days or so). This should be just what the doctor ordered.

Feyesa went to the countryside for a wedding a week ago and was to be back on the 24th, but he hasn't returned yet. Richard's and my case is still unresolved. Your registered letter arrived, and I sure enjoyed the snapshots you sent. It was so good to see our Ethiopian souvenirs arranged so nicely on the walls of the townhouse. You're right. Jean did a nice job arranging them. I could tell from the picture Brent had gained weight. He always does put on weight when he's in the States. What is it? All the ice cream? I was surprised to hear you started taking golf lessons. You've always played tennis, but I didn't know you were interested in learning to play golf. I think it is a great sport and more relaxing in a way than tennis.

I'm really quite homesick. I really miss you guys, and I'm getting quite tired of all the tension here. It seems it's a never-ending problem.

The kids are all fine. They have really grown since you left. They get out of school tomorrow for the summer holiday. Amaha is really speaking English well now. You'd be surprised. It seems to have blossomed since we got back from Kombolcha. It's amazing to listen to him chatter away.

Well, must close for now and get this ready for Joseph to mail. I have really been giving him a bad time about not bringing me any letters from you!

Really pray for us, as we remember you all too. God's timing, I'm sure, is always perfect if we have sense enough to wait on Him.

Unexpectedly on the evening of July 6, my dad called and said he was coming home. He missed Ivy and the boys too much to wait six months or a year to retire. He would take an early retirement rather than be away from them that long. We picked him up at the airport on July 10. I teased him, saying, "You couldn't stand thinking of Ivy and me doing all that shopping! I didn't know the Irish were so tight-fisted!" He'd chuckle and usually have a quip or two in order to have the last word.

The furniture Ivy and I had bought for the home was all delivered, and their mobile home began to take shape. Two days after Dad arrived home, he had to go to Los Angeles on business and wanted Ivy to go with him. I offered to keep Monde and Luke. They were going to be gone only a couple of days. They planned to return Saturday or Sunday. I hoped they would be back before I got a call from Seyfou telling me to head for Kenya. It would be close, but Dad assured me that the boys could stay with friends of theirs in Santa Rosa if I had to leave before they got back.

CHAPTER EIGHTEEN
The Reunion

As the weekend of July 15 drew near I could feel my anxiety intensify. I was glad that Shellie and Brent had Monde and Luke to play with. I spent time each day alone in my bedroom praying for Denton and the children's safety. I read my Bible and marked the most meaningful verses. I wrote the verses out in my prayer journal so I wouldn't forget them.

On Saturday evening July 16 Jeannine Konnerup called and said Richard and Denton had gotten their passports back and Richard was leaving Addis within four hours. I nearly shouted with glee! What timing! What timing! Denton had no doubt been concerned that Richard would be left behind with no passport. I'm sure Denton is rejoicing in this answered prayer. It looked as if Richard would be safely on his way to the States before Denton and the children were airlifted out of Ethiopia.

Sunday morning, July 17, I took Shellie, Brent, Monde, and Lukie to church. When Pastor Carlson saw me in the congregation, he motioned me to the platform. I joined him, and he whispered, "Why don't you give the folks an update on Denton. How is he doing, and when do you expect him home?"

There was no way I could explain all that was taking place. Pastor Carlson had no idea Denton and the children were escaping this very day, possibly at this very moment! I had gone to Pastor Carlson when I returned home after the first escape plan had been foiled. He had always been such a source of encouragement to me, and I knew he sincerely cared about Denton and our family.

I began, choosing my words carefully. I just couldn't let slip a word that would disclose the escape plan.

"As many of you know, Denton has been released from house arrest in the countryside, and he is back in Addis Ababa. I just received word last night that he and the other missionary with him have had their passports returned to them. The Ethiopian government had appropriated their passports when they took them to Addis Ababa under armed guard from Kombolcha. I am still not certain when Denton will return to the States, but I hope it is very soon. Please continue to pray for his safety and for the safety of the four children in his care."

Only Pastor Carlson knew that the four children were the great-grandchildren of the late Emperor.

As I walked down from the platform, I felt the tears streaming down my cheeks.

The strain of the next few hours was unbelievable. After church I fixed the children's lunch. I went up to my bedroom and took my suitcase out of the closet. It had been packed for weeks. I took my ticket out and looked at it. I felt like an expectant mother. I did a handwashing, and was out on the patio hanging it on the clothesline when the telephone rang. It was three o'clock in the afternoon.

I sensed it was the call I had been waiting for for months. Were they safe? Were they alive? I let the phone ring once more. My hands were cold with fear. I lifted the receiver.

"Hello."

"Hello, Mrs. Collins. Seyfou here." It seemed an eternity before he continued. I hung on his every word, waiting.

"Mrs. Collins, Mr. Collins has just played the most beautiful set of tennis!" The tone of his voice told the whole story.

"God!" I whispered softly, collapsing against the kitchen wall. "Thank God. Are they all safe? How many sets of tennis did he play?"

"They are safe in Nairobi, Kenya. He played ten sets!"

"Oh, my goodness! Ten! That means I have twelve children!"

"I have more good news. There is a gentleman here with us from Sweden. He was a missionary in Ethiopia as well. He has told us that a Swedish man in Stockholm wishes to give you twelve airline tickets—for you, Mr. Collins, and the children—from Kenya to San Francisco. Can you leave for Kenya today?"

"Yes, of course, I will try to get a flight this evening. That's wonderful news, Seyfou." I was crying again. The tension of the last few hours burst like an avalanche of freshly fallen snow. Just one more instance of God's looking after His own, I thought to myself. "I'm so grateful," I whispered through my tears.

"We want you to come through London to get the tickets on the way to Kenya, but there is also someone else who might be very helpful to you—a Dr. Simonson in St. Paul, Minnesota. We have talked to him, and he has offered to help you. If you call him and arrange to meet him in St. Paul before you fly to London and on to Kenya, it would be useful, I'm sure. He was an ambassador to Ethiopia, and he has many connections. He may give you some invaluable advice." Seyfou gave me Dr. Simonson's telephone number.

"Yes, I'll telephone him immediately. I hope to see you in a few hours, Seyfou. This is a day we will never forget!"

When I hung up the telephone, my mind was reeling. Could any list contain all I had to do in the next few hours?

I grabbed a handful of tissues and ran outside to find the children. They were at the swimming pool.

"Shellie, Brent, Mon, Luke, come quickly," I called from just outside the wrought-iron fence.

Once back inside the house, my joy and tears burst. "Daddy's safe! He's out of Ethiopia with all ten children! I'll leave tonight to fly to Kenya to meet him." Shellie, Brent, and I fell into each other's arms, laughing, crying. Poor Mon and Luke were speechless.

Turning to Monde, I said, "You boys get your things together. I will call Jean and Jim Allison. Dad said you could stay with them if I had to leave unexpectedly. We will leave for Santa Rosa as soon as I make a few more phone calls."

Since it was Sunday, the travel agency was closed. I telephoned the airport to make reservations to fly to Minnesota, London, and Kenya. I then called Dr. Simonson. Seyfou had talked to him earlier, and he was expecting my call. He would meet me at the airport tomorrow morning. My plane was to arrive at six o'clock. That would give us a full day to discuss the best procedures to follow once I arrived in Kenya. He suggested we go to the offices of Senator Humphrey and Senator Frenzel and make a visit to the Office of Immigration.

Next I called my mother. "Denton's out of Ethiopia, Mom! He has escaped with all ten of the Emperor's great-grandchildren. I'm flying to Kenya tonight to meet him. Can you take care of Shellie and Brent?"

Nearly overwhelmed with my excitement, she said calmly, "Of course, honey. Will you be all right? I mean, is it safe in Kenya?"

"Kenya is safe, Mom. We won't have any problems there," I said confidently. If I had known what lay ahead, my voice might not have been filled with such certainty.

"Can you take me to the airport, Mom? My flight leaves at one o'clock this morning, but, if possible, I would like to be there around ten o'clock. I think my ticket will have to be rewritten, and this is one flight I don't want to miss!" I concluded enthusiastically.

I called Denton's parents in Kansas. My same enthusiasm spilled over into every conversation. "They're out! They're safe!" Mom Collins suggested that I send Shellie and Brent to them for a few weeks. "We would love to have them," Mom encouraged me. I called my mother back, and she said she would make their flight arrangements and get them to the airport on Monday or Tuesday. "The important thing right now is to get you safely on your way, honey. We'll take care of Shellie and Brent tomorrow."

I called Jim and Jean Allison to tell them I was bringing Mon and Luke. I was happy it was Sunday afternoon. Everyone I needed seemed to be home.

One more call, I thought, as I dialed Jean and Moe's number. Michelle answered.

"Are your folks there, Michelle? Can I speak to your mom? Jean! They've done it! Denton's out and they are safe in Kenya! I leave tonight, well, actually at one o'clock in the morning. Mom's taking me to the airport. The kids are going to Kansas to stay with Mom and Dad Collins until I get back."

When I told Shellie and Brent they were going to visit Grandma and Grandpa Collins in Kansas, Brent was overjoyed. "That's great. We can ride horseback, feed Grandpa's pigs, play in Turkey Creek!" They loved to visit the folks' forty-five-acre rancho, and I felt sure they would be kept busy enough that they wouldn't have time to miss me while I went to collect the rest of the family!

My mother drove me to the airport. My mind and heart raced as I thought over what lay ahead of me that day. I tried to anticipate my meetings with Dr. Simonson, the American embassy officials in Kenya, Seyfou in England.

It was one o'clock in the morning when my plane lifted off from San Francisco International Airport and headed for Minneapolis.

I watched the sunrise from the window of the airplane. It was six o'clock in the morning as we circled to land at the Twin Cities' airport. Dr. Simonson spotted me first. We had never met, but he was such a warm, kind gentleman that we had instant rapport. After a quick breakfast at the airport, several cups of coffee to keep me going, and a strategy session, Dr. Simonson drove me from one office to another in search of information that would be helpful to me once I arrived in Kenya. Our greatest help came from Senator Bill Frenzel. His assistants took an immediate interest in my situation and telephoned him in Washington. I talked with the Senator on his conference phone from his private office. He instructed his secretary to type letters of introduction to the American ambassador in Kenya for me to carry with me. He instructed his aides to offer me any assistance possible, and asked me to stay in touch with his office even from Kenya. I felt fortified and encouraged when we left Senator Frenzel's office.

Dr. and Mrs. Simonson took me to a lovely luncheon hosted by one of the many organizations that Dr. Simonson belongs to, and following the luncheon we went to their home, where Mrs. Simonson encouraged me to get some rest. I was weary. I hadn't slept on the plane, and we had been busy every moment since I arrived. It felt good to shower and stretch out on the bed for two hours before Mrs. Simonson called me for supper. My flight for Chicago left at five o'clock that evening. My layover in Chicago was only long enough to make a connecting flight to London. I had just time enough to call Guenet in Oklahoma City and tell her the good news. I had planned to fly to Oklahoma in two weeks for her college graduation. She planned to come and stay with us after her graduation.

"Gunny, if I am not back for your graduation, you are still welcome to come out to California. We are going to have a houseful of people, but we will just add one more sleeping bag. You can stay in the townhouse until I get back. In fact, it will be a help if you do. I will keep in touch with you from Kenya and let you know when we plan to come home. Maybe you and Jean can get sleeping bags together from people at church. I've got to catch my plane now, but I'll be in touch." There were no two more dependable people than Jean and Guenet. I knew they would have the logistics for accommodating twelve kids all worked out when I got home. Just getting us all home from the airport would be no small feat.

I arrived in London at nine o'clock on Tuesday morning. Michael met me at the airport. It was like a reunion of old friends. "Oh, Michael," I said, throwing my arms around him, "we've done it! They're safe! Can you believe it has finally happened?" His enthusiasm matched mine. He was all smiles. After collecting my single suitcase, we caught a taxi. On the way to the Sheraton Hotel near Heathrow Airport, Michael explained that Seyfou was going to the Pan Am office as soon as it opened, to pick up the twelve airline tickets that Mr. Lindquist had so generously provided. "Seyfou will bring the tickets to the Sheraton. I have reserved a room for you for the day. I thought you might want to get some sleep. Doesn't your flight for Nairobi leave at six o'clock this evening?"

"Yes, it does, but I don't feel as if I could sleep. I'm much too excited! It's a long flight to Nairobi. Maybe I will sleep then."

My room at the Sheraton wasn't ready when we arrived,

so we went to the coffee shop. It was good to be with Michael again. We had known each other only a year, and yet we had lived through what seemed a lifetime during these past six months. We talked about the apparent failure of our first plan and the miraculous success of our recent accomplishment. We had been through one of our lives' greatest moments together, and we were radiant.

The desk paged me when my room was ready, and Michael left to meet Seyfou at the Pan Am office. They would come back to the hotel with the tickets.

I went to my room, showered, and lay down on the comfortable bed. I was sure I wouldn't sleep, but as a precaution I set the alarm on my travel clock. At four o'clock the alarm jarred me into consciousness. I sat up in the bed, forgetting momentarily where I was.

Where are Michael and Seyfou? I wondered nervously. *My plane leaves in two hours.*

By five o'clock I was pacing the floor of my hotel room. Where were they? Why hadn't they phoned? I *had* to get to the airport. I didn't want to miss my flight.

I decided to take the airport bus back to Heathrow. Fortunately, it was not far.

It was five-thirty when I heard the boarding call for my flight over the intercom. I walked toward the Immigration desk, sick with disappointment. I had just handed my passport to the man behind the desk when I saw Seyfou running down the corridor toward me. As the immigration officer handed back my passport, I stepped out of line.

It was obvious from the way Seyfou acted when he saw me that he didn't want to talk to me directly. Maybe he has recognized someone in the airport and he is afraid for us to meet. I watched him. When he was certain that I had seen him, he walked into a gift shop. I remained outside. I noticed a packet in his hand—the tickets, I thought!

He looked through some clothes hanging on a circular clothes rack. I watched intently as he set the packet on top of the rack and left the shop. He walked right past me but didn't even look at me. I hurried into the shop. The cashier was busy at the desk, but I hoped she wouldn't think I was shoplifting when I lifted the packet from the rack and quickly left the shop. My heart was beating so fast by the time I got to the concourse and began to board the plane, that I thought I was going to faint. I stopped to catch my breath, letting other passengers go ahead of me. Nervously I opened the packet. There were the twelve airline tickets! Without taking them out of the envelope, I counted them. Tucked between the tickets I saw five one-hundred-dollar bills. *Money, too,* I thought exuberantly. I had brought only a hundred dollars cash with me. I was thankful for this additional blessing.

Once aboard the huge 747 jumbo jet, I settled into my seat, leaned my head back, and sighed deeply. As I felt the enormous aircraft lift off, I thought, *Maybe this trusting business isn't so bad after all!* Little did I know that within forty-eight hours I would be put to the test of trusting once again. Fortunately, for the moment, I thought the worst was behind me.

The two seats next to mine were empty. I removed the chair arms and asked the hostess for a pillow and blankets. She told me they would be serving dinner shortly, but I assured her I was much too tired to eat. I had never slept on an airplane before, but I curled up on my short, three-seated bed and fell sound asleep. When I awoke, the hostess handed me a steamy hot towel for my face. Raising the window blind, I could see the sun rising over Africa. The moment was exhilarating as I thought of my imminent arrival in Kenya and reunion with Denton and the children. The hot coffee and warm breakfast did even more to bolster my spirits. I was ready to take on the world. I felt surprisingly rested, as I sipped my second cup of coffee and began outlining my strategy for the day. Nothing would do but a list!

I jotted down: exchange money, check into hotel, go to American embassy, and in capital letters, FIND DENTON AND KIDS. My agenda for the day, I thought proudly! I was still uncertain about where Denton and the children were staying. In the envelope that Seyfou had given me there had been a small paper that said, "Call Franco at 50798." I assumed this Franco would know where I could locate Denton. I reasoned that I would rather go to the American embassy before I contacted Denton and the children, because I wanted to be able to give them some good news about when we would be heading home.

I watched from the window of the plane as we circled over the city of Nairobi, making our final descent into the capital city of Kenya.

I passed through immigration and customs quickly and lined up to exchange my U. S. currency for Kenyan money. Within one hour I was standing in front of the airport, waiting for a taxi. As the cab driver put my suitcase into the trunk, I slipped my attaché case into the small back seat beside me. As he slipped back under the steering wheel on the right-hand side of the front seat, it was just one more reminder that I was back in Nairobi.

"American Embassy," I said to the driver.

In spite of the intense African sun, my hands were cold and clammy as I stepped into the quiet, cool entry hall of the American embassy.

The stoic-looking woman sitting behind the reception desk could have been carved from Amboseli meerschaum. I felt my head pounding as I stepped up to the window of the reception desk.

"May I help you?" the receptionist inquired sternly.

"Yes, please. I have a letter addressed to the ambassador from Senator Frenzel of Minnesota and from the Crown Prince Asfa Wossen of Ethiopia. May I talk with the ambassador, please?"

"I'm sorry, we do not have an ambassador here in Kenya at this time."

A flutter of panic shot through me. "Then may I see whoever is in charge here?"

"In regard to what matter?" she asked coldly.

I could see that I was not getting anywhere with this woman, so I decided to play my highest card right then. If she didn't respond to that, I wasn't sure what my next move would be!

"My husband has just escaped from Ethiopia with ten of the deposed king, Emperor Haile Selassie's, great-grandchildren. They are all hiding here in Nairobi. We have good reason to believe their lives are in danger. I must talk to someone here about this matter. Please!"

Her calm crumbled. "He what?" she screamed.

I was relieved that she did not wait for me to repeat myself. Without another word, she began pushing and pulling cords and buttons on her switchboard. Within minutes two men appeared.

"Good morning. Mrs. Collins, is it?"

"Yes," I answered.

"My name is Mr. Bennett. This is my assistant, Mr. Henning. Please come with us."

I followed them into the inner sanctum of the American embassy.

I was oblivious to everything around me. We moved quickly into an elevator. My head was still throbbing from jet lag, and I felt like my forty-eight-hour trip might be catching up with me. I pulled my purse snugly under my arm, a habit I had acquired while living thirteen years in Africa. *I hope I have all the papers I need to convince these men I need their help,* I thought anxiously. We stopped in front of an impressive-looking double door. Before my eyes could focus on the brass sign on the door, I was ushered into a large and elaborately furnished office.

It looks like an ambassador's office, I mused. *I wonder if it is?* Across the room was a large brown overstuffed leather couch, two matching leather chairs, and a coffee table. At the far end of the room was an impressive desk and executive desk chair, all neatly in place. No one spoke until the door closed softly behind us.

Neither man impressed me as being an ambassador. They were obviously embassy officials, neatly groomed and in business suits and ties.

I was relieved when Mr. Bennett ended our silence.

"Please, Mrs. Collins, have a seat," he said, motioning toward the couch. Obviously used to giving orders, he motioned for Mr. Henning to sit in the chair opposite me, and he joined me on the couch.

"How can we help you, Mrs. Collins? The receptionist mentioned your husband and an escape?"

"Yes, that's right. My husband has just escaped from Ethiopia with ten of the former Ethiopian Emperor's great-grandchildren. We have reason to believe they are still in danger."

I knew these men were trained to appear calm, but I wasn't disappointed when they seemed alarmed and more than a little interested in my story.

"The receptionist, Mrs. West, mentioned letters. Do you have them?"

"Yes," I said, opening my purse. "There are two."

"Maybe you should fill us in on some of the details, Mrs. Collins," Mr. Henning suggested, speaking for the first time since we had met.

"Yes, I would be happy to do that," I said, sitting forward on the couch. They listened intently for nearly an hour as I told them the entire story.

Concluding, I leaned back against the couch. I felt weary; I had just relived the entire past year.

Mr. Henning sat forward in his chair. "Mrs. Collins, this is an overwhelming story. Have you made any contact with your husband or the children yet?"

"No, I haven't. I wanted to talk to you first. I want to take them news of what is going to happen next. They have lived with uncertainty for months. I want something concrete to tell them."

"You mentioned that you thought they might still be in some danger. Can you explain that?"

"Yes, of course. The children had another relative who escaped into Kenya. He was hiding here in Nairobi when terrorists broke into his room, firing an automatic rifle. He and his friends barely escaped by leaping through a window. The leg of his trousers was riddled with bullets, but he escaped injury. He was lucky! I would hate to see anything like that happen in our situation. It isn't likely we could all get away. I'm sure you'd agree."

"Mrs. Collins, why don't you get in touch with your husband? We will contact President Carter, Brzezinski, his assistant in foreign affairs, and Secretary of State Vance. I will have some word for you first thing in the morning. Come back here alone tomorrow morning at nine o'clock, and I will have some information for you."

"Thank you very much!" I said with a new burst of energy.

Sensing my optimism, Mr. Bennett continued. "Mrs. Collins, I would imagine that you, your husband, and the children will be on your way to the States within twenty-four hours." For the first time since I had met these two men, they both smiled.

I immediately felt some of the tension easing from my body as I sat up straighter. "I want to thank you both. I feel much better than I did when I first came into the embassy."

Both men stood, and I understood our meeting was over.

"Then we will see you first thing in the morning," Mr. Bennett concluded. Both men shook my hand. "Mr. Henning will see you out."

Mr. Henning and I retraced our steps to the entrance of the embassy. "This is one of the most remarkable things I have ever heard, Mrs. Collins," he said as we stood together near the receptionist's desk. Even Mrs. West smiled now.

"Yes, Mr. Henning, it is remarkable. I can still hardly believe it myself. I am so eager to see my family, I don't think I can stand it!"

"Good luck to you, and have a wonderful reunion. You all surely deserve it. I hope we have good news for you tomorrow."

I hailed another taxi. "Norfolk Hotel," I said, climbing into the back seat.

I had not really known what to expect at the American embassy, but I was not disappointed. I had been deeply interested in President Carter's human rights policies and efforts. In fact, just as a matter of personal interest, I had been clipping out all the articles about President Carter and human rights. *Perhaps Mr. Bennett's and Mr. Henning's reactions today represent the Carter administration*, I thought, as my cab weaved through the crowded streets.

Once back in my hotel room, I fumbled through my briefcase, looking for the envelope that Seyfou had given me. I took out the small piece of paper with Franco's phone number on it.

I didn't know who this Franco was, but I was about to find out. A woman with a thick accent of some kind, possibly Italian, answered the telephone. I asked to speak to Franco.

"Who's calling?" she asked gruffly.

"This is Mrs. Collins. I am looking for my husband, and I understood I might find him here."

"Franco isn't here right now," she replied, as if she hadn't even heard me ask about Denton.

"Please have Franco call me when he comes back. I am staying at the Norfolk Hotel."

I felt terribly disappointed when I hung up. My body ached from sleeping on the uncomfortable airplane seats all night, and I was restless. I stretched, and tried to decide what to do next. Maybe a hot shower would help relax me.

After my shower, I slipped into my robe and lay down on the twin bed. I listened to the familiar African sounds. I heard the gardeners calling to one another in Swahili; the birds' songs seemed louder and more urgent than in America. Outside it was warm, but in my room I pulled my Ethiopian *gabe* around my shoulders. I never went anywhere without it. Denton always laughed and teased me about my security blanket. During our first years in Ethiopia I had learned to wrap the soft white blanket around me Ethiopian style. I owned several of them, but I always carried at least one with me everywhere I traveled. Curled in its softness, I fell asleep.

The phone jarred me awake. Disoriented, I sat up and listened. The phone rang again. Jumping up, I ran across the room to answer it. I heard a man's voice, and I almost held my breath until he identified himself.

"Mrs. Collins?"

"Yes?"

"My name is Franco. I will pick you up at eight o'clock this evening. I will take you to Mr. Collins. He and the children are safe."

He, too, had an accent. I was certain that with the name Franco, he must be Italian.

"Shall I meet you in the lobby at eight o'clock?"

"No, I will come to your room. What is your room number?"

"Four-thirty-three," I said, reading the number from my room key.

Precisely at eight o'clock, there was a knock on my door.

When I answered, a short, dark-haired man was standing there. "Are you Mrs. Collins?"

"Yes, I am." I felt quite nervous.

"I am Franco. Come with me. I will take you to your husband."

Strangely enough, I trusted him. I didn't have much

choice, if I wanted to see Denton. We drove for approximately fifteen minutes. It appeared to me that we were going into the countryside.

I was relieved when he pulled into the parking lot of the Jacaranda Hotel. The parking lot was dark, and for some reason I felt we were in another world. As we walked up the front sidewalk toward the lobby, a window on the second floor of the hotel opened and I heard a woman's voice call, "Jodie Collins, what are you doing here?"

I squinted toward the upstairs window and saw someone waving frantically in my direction. As I walked closer to the building, she called again, "Jodie, how are you?"

I couldn't believe my ears or my eyes. It was Audrey. We had played softball together in Addis Ababa. She was an American woman married to an official at the Kenyan embassy in Addis. I just couldn't believe it. How could I run into someone I knew in such a remote place in the world?

I waved her away from the window, hoping she wouldn't call my name again. Actually, I was hopeful she would get the hint that she shouldn't be seen with me. She must have caught on, because she quickly closed the window and disappeared. I didn't see her again. I could only assume that she had understood by my signal that it was best that we didn't meet. I knew that, married to a Kenyan diplomat, she would be returning to Ethiopia. If she were seen with me or with Denton and the kids, it might be assumed that she had helped in the escape. That might be very costly in terms of their lives or her husband's career. I would learn more later.

As I followed Franco into the foyer I glanced across the brightly lit lobby and coming down the staircase was my youngest daughter, Kokeb. She saw me just as I saw her.

My first instinct was to run toward her. When she saw me, she screamed, "Mommy!" then threw her hand over her mouth and disappeared back up the stairs. Stunned by her reaction, I stood looking at the place where she had been standing just seconds ago.

In less than a minute I saw her running down the stairs again, followed by Denton and nine more children. Before I knew it, I was surrounded. We were hugging, kissing, crying, laughing, and talking all at once. "Mommy, Mommy,"

Loly squealed with delight. Her arms were around me. Denton lifted Amaha and he stretched his little arms out to me. I held him to me. The six other children stood awkwardly until I turned toward them. Loly ran to them and said, "This is my mom, you guys. Mom, these are our cousins, Sammy, Meheret, Aster, Rahel, Bckere, and Issac."

"I'm happy to meet all of you," I said, shaking their hands warmly. "Why don't we all go up to your room, and I will tell you the latest news and developments," I said to everyone as they gathered around me.

People in the lobby were beginning to watch us, and I didn't want to draw any more attention to our presence. They were, after all, in Kenya illegally. I was eager to hear how their trip to Lake Langano had gone. I followed as they led the way upstairs.

"Mrs. Collins," said a voice behind me. Turning, I saw Franco. I had forgotten all about him in the last few minutes. "I will be back in about three hours to get you. For safety's sake, it is best if you and Mr. Collins stay in separate hotels. We never know what to expect."

I thought of Seyfou's experience and his bullet-riddled pantleg. I didn't argue. I just nodded my head and thanked him for bringing me to Denton and the children.

"I'll see you later," I said turning to join Denton.

Once in the room, Amaha climbed onto my lap. "We went on an airplane today," he said in fluent English. All I could do was stare at him as he chattered away in perfect English. "He doesn't even have an accent," I said in utter amazement. I had never heard him speak in English except for a few words the girls taught him from his ABC book and the daily object lessons on the way to the English School. Loly and Kokeb sat beside me on the bed. After her initial welcome, Menen settled into the background beside Meheret.

Denton looked weary and drained. His face was pale. I could hardly imagine the pressure he had been under during the past months. No one could know, I was certain, who hadn't lived through it.

"We have five rooms in the hotel," Denton explained. "Franco arranged it. He said it is safer this way. Amaha and I are staying in this room; the boys, Sammy, Bekere, and

Issac, are staying in one room. Kokeb and Aster are together, Loly and Rahel, and Meheret and Menen."

The evening passed quickly as we talked and shared the experiences of the last few days. I told them how Seyfou had called me and said, "Mr. Collins has played a beautiful set of tennis!" They all laughed and enjoyed the inside joke. They were excited, too, as I related the story of Mr. Lindquist and our twelve airline tickets home. They listened intently as I shared how I almost missed Seyfou at Heathrow airport.

"Mom, wait until you meet Georgio. He is Franco's friend. He flew on the airplane with Dad, Ami, Aster and me. Last night he took us to a movie."

"A movie?" I asked. "Denton, is it safe for them to be going to a movie?"

"It was a drive-in movie, Mom. No one saw us. We were in Franco's car."

"Franco thought it would be all right for them to go," Denton added.

I had reservations about it, but I decided not to say more.

"I've been to the American embassy. It looks as though we will be on our way to the States within twenty-four hours!" I said enthusiastically. Everyone cheered at the good news. "Do you think they'll send the presidential jet?" I joked. "Maybe President Carter will come, too!" We all laughed, and it felt good to hear them all giggling.

Before I realized it, Denton reminded me that it was eleven o'clock, and Franco had said he would pick me up. I kissed the children good night, and as I walked past the desk, I noticed a small notebook lying open. "Denton, what is this?" I asked, pointing to the notebook.

"I have been writing down some notes about the last few weeks," he answered.

"Have you finished?"

"Yes, I have written about everything up until today. That's what I was doing when Kokeb called me that you had arrived."

"May I take it and read it tonight? I'll bring it back tomorrow."

"Sure, I don't mind. But I haven't written the most exciting part."

"What's that?"

"Your arrival!" he said, giving me another big hug and kiss. The kids all giggled.

"I'm going to walk Mom down to the lobby to meet Franco. You guys can all wait here or go to your rooms if you want."

"Can we go back to the television room?" Sammy asked.

"Yes, that's fine, too. Just try to stay together. I think it's best if you don't walk around alone," Denton cautioned.

As we walked down the stairs to the lobby, I said, "Denton, why don't you come to the Norfolk and meet me for an early breakfast tomorrow morning, say about seven o'clock? I'm supposed to be at the American embassy at nine o'clock, and they stressed that I should come alone. You could be back here by nine. Do you think the kids will be OK here for a couple of hours?"

"That would be nice. Maybe Franco would come over and keep an eye on them. I'll ask him," Denton quickly volunteered.

CHAPTER NINETEEN
Denton's Diary

Arriving back at the Norfolk at eleven-thirty, Franco opened my car door and walked me into the lobby of the old hotel that had once been Ernest Hemingway's residence.

"Good night, Franco," I said, extending my hand to meet his. "Thank you very much."

"No, Mrs. Collins, it is better if I walk you to your room. It is very dark in the courtyard, and we don't want to take any chances."

Although I felt in no particular danger, I didn't argue. When we arrived at my room, we shook hands again, and I thanked him for all he had done for Denton and the children.

"It's all in a day's work," he said, smiling from ear to ear. "I will bring Mr. Collins here in the morning at seven o'clock and then go back and stay at the Jacaranda with the children. Maybe he can catch a taxi back to the Jacaranda when you go to the American embassy?" he suggested.

"That's fine, Franco. Good night."

Alone in my room, I undressed, showered, and wrapping my *gabe* around my pajama-clad body, I climbed between the chilly sheets to read Denton's journal. Surprisingly, I wasn't the least bit sleepy. *Of course not,* I reminded myself, *your days and nights are reversed. Normally you would just be starting your day.*

As I opened the notebook, I saw Denton's neat handwriting and smiled to myself, recalling how I had begged him to address our wedding announcements sixteen years ago, because his script was so much neater than mine.

He began on the day the "doctor" or contact man first telephoned him:

June 22: *The kids and I had just finished eating breakfast, and I was getting ready to take them to school, when the telephone rang. I didn't recognize the man's voice, but he said, "Denton how would you like to play some tennis today?" My first thought was,* This must be the doctor. *I told him I'd like to play, but I would have to drop the kids at school first. He suggested I meet him at nine-thirty at the Hilton Hotel. As I hung up, I wondered if anyone listening to our conversation would have been able to figure out what we were doing.*

I immediately went to the storage room to get my tennis gear. As I put it into the car, Loly looked surprised and asked, "Are you playing tennis today, Dad?"

"Yes, Loly, I thought it would be a good way to relax and get some exercise. I haven't played since Mom left, and I want to stay in shape."

I tried to sound as natural as possible. I had no idea whom I was going to meet, what he looked like, or anything else. I was just going on the fact that Jodie had said to play tennis. I knew it had to have something to do with the escape.

I was nervous, but I remember my determination not to show it. It had become a way of life since the revolution, repressing fear, anger, and anxiety. I knew that any emotional display could cost me my life and possibly the lives of the children. I had learned to present a very controlled, calm-looking exterior, even though I felt extremely nervous and uncertain within.

I dropped the children at the English School and headed down the hill toward the Hilton Hotel. Once inside the lobby, I sat with my tennis racket and my Adidas bag placed very conspicuously at my side. I hadn't waited more than fifteen minutes when a short, plump Italian man approached me with his hand extended.

"Denton, are you ready to play?" he asked
enthusiastically, as if we met to play tennis every day.

"Yes, I am, but how about a cup of coffee before we start
our game?" I replied in the same matter-of-fact tone.

We went into the coffee shop and I asked the hostess for
a table near the back. I saw there were fewer people
there, and I wanted to be as far away from people as
possible so we could talk without being overheard. I sat
where I could see all the activity in the room and watch
the people coming in and out as well as the waiters and
waitresses as they came near our table.

Whenever our waitress came to the table, we talked as
though my companion were a tourist visiting Addis. He
asked me questions about what to buy for his wife or as
souvenirs. "I'd like to take my wife some amber prayer
beads," he commented as the waitress poured us each
another cup of coffee.

Outside, near the swimming pool, I recognized three
officials from the East German embassy, which was
located next door to our house. They looked out of place
in their three-piece business suits, walking around and
around the swimming pool, deep in discussion. The
thought crossed my mind that they probably suspected
that their rooms were wiretapped and preferred holding
their secret discussions outside. I had to give them credit
for being cautious. It was something I could identify with
at this particular point in my life. Filled with my own
suspicions, I hoped that our table wasn't bugged. I had
misgivings about our home. It would be so easy for a
servant to place a small microphone nearly anywhere in
the house without its being detected.

As I sipped my coffee, the contact man told me about
the new plan. "We have a larger plane, but there are ten
children. With you and me, that makes twelve
passengers."

I couldn't hide my shock. "Ten children! Where did we
get ten?"

He explained that the additional six children were the
Princess Ejigeyehu's children, and that their lives would

*be in even more jeopardy if they were left behind, and we
escaped with just the four children in my care. He
continued before I had time to register all of my
objections.*

*"We will fly the plane into Lake Langano. Your wife
thought you would be familiar with the place. She said
you camp there frequently. It is near the bridge, exactly
twenty miles beyond the entrance to the hotel. Do you
know it?"*

I only nodded, and he continued.

*"If there are any complications—for example, if the
weight is too much for the airplane—you will have to
remain behind with two or three of the children, and we
will have to pick you up the next day."*

*I couldn't keep quiet any longer. "There is no way that I
am going to spend a second night at that hotel after some
of the children have left. It would be suicidal. We must all
go out at once!" I kept my voice low, but my determination was evident.*

*He registered no surprise. I continued. "I don't see any
way we can get out of here with ten children. Where are
these other six, anyway? Where do they live? Who are they
staying with?"*

"Don't you know?" he asked, surprised.

"No, I can't recall ever hearing that much about them."

*We sat there for a moment, each expecting the other to
say something.*

*"Wait a minute," I said softly, recalling a dinner party
Jodie and I had attended at the Canadian embassy
months ago. "I did meet the oldest girl once. Her name is
Rahel. If I remember right, she mentioned that she worked
at the Iranian embassy. Listen," I interrupted my own
train of thought, "before we pursue this plan any further,
I want to get in touch with Jodie, my wife. It is nearly
ten-thirty. Why don't I meet you back here after lunch,
about three o'clock? Everything is closed between one and
three o'clock anyway. I will probably have been able to
contact Jodie by then, and we can continue our discussion
at that time."*

He seemed to understand my reluctance and surprise

*about the new plan and agreed to meet me at three
o'clock. I went to my office to place a call to California. I
was eager to clarify all of this with Jodie!*

*It was four hours after I first placed the phone call that
the operator called me back again.*

"Mr. Collins, I have your party on the line."

*"Hello, Jodie? Can you hear me?" I had hoped for a
clear connection. I didn't want to have to yell so loudly
that the workers could hear me. The connection wasn't too
bad, and I heard Jodie's voice.*

"Yes, Denton, I can hear you fine. How are you?"

*"We are all fine here. I've just come from playing tennis.
I am calling regarding Catherine's surgery, Jodie. I have
talked to the doctor, and I think it is too complicated. I
don't like the sound of the new procedure he described. It
is far too risky. The surgery is too complex, Jodie!"*

*"Denton, please be reasonable! You know if she doesn't
have this surgery she will die. There is no more time. She
just must have the operation. We've cancelled one, hoping
for a new technique. We must trust the doctor. Please,
Denton, please!"*

*I didn't like the plan at all. It seemed overwhelming to
me. I was angry, thinking that Jodie was not considering
my feelings or welfare at all, but I knew she was right
about the children. Their lives were in danger. They
wouldn't be safe if they remained in Ethiopia. I had to
risk it!*

*I heard myself take a deep sigh. I could hardly bring
myself to say it, but I knew I must.*

"All right, Jodie. Catherine will have the surgery."

*Her voice was barely audible. "Thank you, Denton."
I think I detected tears.*

*"Jodie, pray for this surgery. As the doctor described it,
it will be complicated and involved. The surgeons will
need wisdom and endurance."*

*"I'm praying, Denton. I haven't stopped, believe me,"
she assured me.*

"I'll be in touch, Jodie," I said as we concluded our call.

*As I set the receiver down, I felt as though I had an
enormous weight placed on my back. I could barely stand*

up, it felt so heavy. I stared at my watch for several seconds, so deep in thought my eyes refused to focus on the hands.

I blinked. "Good grief, I'm late," I said out loud. "It's 3:10, and I was supposed to meet the doctor again at three o'clock. I ran downstairs, calling for the guard to open the gate for me. Quickly I drove back to the Hilton.

On the way I realized for the first time I didn't even know the name of the contact man. Maybe he preferred it that way. I wondered how Jodie had put all this together. Who was helping her? I knew if anyone could do it, she could. I don't think I would have trusted another person on this earth to put a plan like this together. I just wouldn't take a chance like this for anyone else. Of course, I knew the Lord was the master planner, but humanly speaking, I would only go through this for Jodie.

As I hurried into the lobby I saw the contact man sitting near the door to the coffee shop. We shook hands and went back into the shop to talk. I asked for the same table. The hostess seemed to remember us. After she brought our coffee, I said, "I talked to Jodie. I have decided to go ahead with the surgery."

He nodded his head knowingly, and I detected a slight smile. I continued. "I think we should go to the Iranian embassy and try and find Rahel. Rather than leave here together, why don't you walk down the hill toward the Palace? I will pick you up near the hospital just one block beyond the Palace. Let's hope neither of us will be followed." I left the hotel first.

As we drove to the embassy, the man took a letter out of his sock. I tried not to look too surprised as he explained that Rahel's grandfather, the Crown Prince, was living in London, and the Crown Prince had written a short note to Rahel, assuring her that he favored the escape and that this man could be trusted.

As he held the small piece of paper up to show me, I noticed it was written in English and on the Crown Prince's personal stationery so that Rahel would know it was really from the Crown Prince personally.

He folded it up again and tucked it safely into his sock.

"If I am caught with this letter, I'm dead," he said as calmly as if we were discussing the latest football scores.

Our first problem came when we arrived at the Iranian embassy. The guard there refused to let us go inside. He insisted on knowing our business. I said I had business there, and that I must see someone. I didn't want to give him Rahel's name. After fifteen minutes of arguing with him in Amharic, I stated emphatically that I had to get in there to get a visa. Seemingly more satisfied with that answer than others I had given, he reluctantly allowed me to go inside, but still steadfastly refused to let the contact man go with me.

Inside the entry hall of the embassy it was ghostly quiet. I hadn't walked more than five feet into the waiting room when I heard someone's footsteps on the tile floor. When the person came around the corner into the foyer, I was shocked to see it was Rahel. She looked as surprised to see me.

I moved very close to her, afraid once again that we might be overheard or the room might be bugged. "Rahel, I'm Mr. Collins. My wife and I have been caring for your four cousins."

In a hushed voice she said, "Yes, Mr. Collins, of course, I remember you. We met at a dinner party some months ago."

I was relieved that she recalled who I was. As quietly as I could, I whispered, "Rahel, there is a chance for an escape; are you interested?"

"Definitely!" she responded, as if she had been expecting me.

"Meet me at the Wabe Shebelle Tearoom on the roof of the Wabe Shebelle Hotel at six-thirty this evening," I instructed.

She nodded her head and shook hands with me. I returned to the car. The contact man was sitting in the car waiting for me as I climbed in. "I saw her," I said as I started the engine and drove quickly down the bumpy road. I was relieved to get away from there, and to have made the initial contact.

I dropped the contact man off near the Palace and

agreed to pick him up at the same place at six o'clock. That would give us adequate time to drive to the Wabe Shebelle Hotel where I had agreed to meet Rahel at six-thirty.

That evening I picked up the contact man, and we drove to the hotel. We were early and decided to wait in the car until time to go inside. We saw Rahel arrive in a taxi and go into the main lobby. We followed and took the elevator to the top floor. I spotted Rahel standing near the entrance to the tearoom and we joined her. Again I asked for a table away from everyone else.

As we were seated, I sensed Rahel was uncomfortable with the contact man's presence. "Do you have the letter for Rahel?" I asked him.

He looked around the room before he nonchalantly crossed his legs and removed the small piece of paper from his sock. He unfolded it and slid it across the table toward Rahel. She read it quickly, nodded her head, and he quickly returned the note to its hiding place. Rahel looked relieved, and I felt we could continue our conversation.

The contact man began, "We have set the date for Sunday, July 17. I will return to Europe tomorrow morning to finalize the plans. Rahel, you and your sisters and brothers will go with Mr. Collins to Lake Langano on Saturday. Tell no one that you are going."

Rahel interrupted, "What about my grandmother? We are living with her. I must tell her something so she doesn't worry."

"Why don't you tell her and your sisters and brothers that I am taking you all to Lake Langano for the weekend along with your cousins?" I suggested. "That way no one will be suspicious until late Sunday night or Monday morning. We expect to be out of the country by that time."

The contact man looked pleased with my suggestion and nodded in agreement. "Rahel, please don't bring any keepsakes or photographs along. We will have to go through the army checkpoint as we leave the city. Pack only your nightclothes and swimming suits and one set of extra clothes. When we are searched leaving town, I don't want to arouse any suspicions. Watch carefully what your sisters and brothers pack, although it is best if you don't even tell them we are escaping. Just let them think we are going to spend the weekend at Langano."

"That's a good idea," the contact man agreed.

"Rahel," I went on, "you meet me at the English School Saturday morning at nine o'clock. It should be fairly quiet there, and we won't be conspicuous. We will leave from there."

The contact man looked at me and said, "If anything goes wrong and you feel we must cancel the escape, you will call me in Rome. I will give you the number to call, and you just leave a message to cancel the surgery. I know how to contact you. I will try to arrange a second airplane so that you won't have to wait until Monday to be picked up, as I mentioned to you earlier."

Rahel looked puzzled, but he didn't stop to clarify what he had said. He just continued, "You will all be flown to Kenya. There will be vans there to pick you up and drive you to Nairobi from the game park where we will land. If there are any questions asked at the hotel, Mr. Collins, you will just tell them that you are an American school teacher, and you have brought a group of children to visit the game parks. There is a man there who will help you. His name is Franco. He runs a safari company; he will make arrangements to get you all to Nairobi, and he will see that you are taken care of while you are in Kenya. Rahel, do you have any questions?"

"No, I don't," she answered softly.

"Mr. Collins?"

"No." Turning to Rahel I said, "If you need to contact me, my telephone number is 73501. Don't discuss any of this on the phone, but I will meet you somewhere. Otherwise, we will meet on Saturday morning, July 16, at nine o'clock," I repeated.

Ten minutes later the contact man and I were driving toward the Palace. He wrote on a small slip of paper the phone number where I could call him if I should have to cancel the escape. He suggested that I drive to Langano in the next few days to scout out the area and to drive up *and down the beach to see if I thought the plane would be able to land in the sandy soil without getting stuck. He also directed me to park the car in the direction of the wind the day of the actual airlift. I was to have it parked in the opposite direction of the wind if we were to abort the landing. When he finished giving me all the details for the day of the escape, he took the note from the Crown Prince out of his sock, tore it in tiny pieces, and ate it.*

"I can't afford to take any chances," he said, still trying to get the last small piece down his throat. I was too shocked to say anything.

As I pulled up to the curb he looked toward the dark palace grounds and asked, "Is this where their grandfather used to live?"

"Yes, it is," I answered sadly. "It was called Jubilee Palace, but the new government changed the name and now it's called The People's Palace."

As we shook hands, he said, "If all goes well we will play tennis again in three weeks, July 17, nine o'clock in the morning at Lake Langano. I hope they have good tennis courts there!" He turned and was gone.

C H A P T E R   T W E N T Y

The Trip to Lake Langano

The next entry in Denton's journal was Wednesday, July 6.

It has been twelve days since I played tennis. After I took the kids to school today, I went to the Ethiopian Tourist Organization to see about renting a car. I rented a small Volkswagen for today, but I know I will need a much larger car when I take all the children to Lake Langano for our weekend outing. Today I wanted to drive to Langano to find a nice camping spot. It was a long, tiring day. I left town at eight-thirty this morning and didn't get back until nearly ten o'clock tonight. I was glad I had arranged for Richard to pick the kids up at school and get them home. I found a nice picnic area. I was glad that the sand seemed to dry out quickly after the morning rains.

The only thing that concerns me is that Richard is still here. I hate to leave him alone in Addis when I take the kids to Lake Langano. I received permission to leave the city, but Security has refused to give Richard permission. I wish the Derg would settle our case so we would know what they are going to do with us. This uncertainty is draining both of us. Richard is so restless and bored he can hardly stand it. We still do not have our passports back, and Richard's airline ticket was confiscated by

Security as well. I cannot believe this matter has gone all the way to the Derg. It's ridiculous! I'll be relieved when it is settled!

July 10: *Today is Sunday. I am so proud of Bekele, our pastor. He is such a man of God and provides the church with such leadership. Last Sunday afternoon we all met together to discuss the future of the church. They understand, although nothing has been said specifically, that my time here is limited. They have labored very hard to organize and prepare for when I am gone. They had election of officers, and although I did not participate, I was very pleased with their choices for the six deacons. Of course, Bekele will remain as their pastor. During the meeting last Sunday afternoon, the deacons asked that I preach this Sunday for the Amharic service, and Bekele volunteered to translate in Amharic for me. He usually does the preaching for the nine o'clock Amharic service and Ethiopian Sunday school, and I preach for the English service at eleven o'clock and teach the English-speaking Sunday school class. Of course, both services consist mostly of Ethiopians. I don't think we have ever had more than a handful of foreigners in our English services.*

Today we had the installation of the new deacons, and then I preached for both services. It was great speaking to a full house. I was so happy that we had arranged it for this weekend, because next Sunday I will be gone. That is when I plan to take all the children to Lake Langano for the weekend. It will be good to get out of Addis and get some rest. I'm even hoping I can play some tennis.

Thursday, July 14: *I am so exasperated! I have gone to Security every day this week hoping to hear some news about Richard's and my case, but the officials there just keep saying the Derg has other things to do besides decide what to do with us. I did get permission to leave for three days this weekend, but they still refuse to let Richard leave town. I hope I can get enough gas to get to the lake. The lines at the gas station are longer than ever. It seems I spend most of my days at Security or in line for*

gasoline. All this waiting is harrowing to say the least!
Today was the kids' last day of school. They asked if
they could go to the Headquarters tomorrow to visit
Joseph and the workers there, but there has been so much
trouble and shooting lately that I didn't think it was best.
Then they asked if they could go shopping downtown, and
I just didn't feel comfortable about it. They seemed very
disappointed, but I just felt it was best for them to stay at
home where nothing could go wrong.

Friday, July 15: *Today was a busy day. I rented the car for*
our trip to Lake Langano tomorrow. It was a relief when
the secretary at the Organization of Tourism recognized
me from when I rented the smaller car two weeks ago. She
said she wouldn't even bother to fill out new papers. She
would just pull out the information and forms I filled out
last time. I was shocked when I went outside to get the
car. I had told them I needed a larger car than last time,
so she suggested a Volkswagen Kombi bus. What she didn't
tell me was that the Kombi was painted black and white
zebra stripes, obviously a tourist van. I stood aghast,
wondering if I really needed such an ornate car for this
particular trip. Not wanting to shock Assefa and Feyesa, I
took the zebra Kombi to the Hilton Hotel and left it there
for the night. I hardly needed to draw attention to myself
by driving it around Addis all day.
After renting the car, I went by Security. I was
overwhelmed when the man there recognized me and
said, "One moment, Mr. Collins." He went into the other
room and came back with Richard's and my passports
and Richard's airline ticket. I was speechless! "The Derg
has decided to drop the case against you and Mr.
Konnerup. Mr. Konnerup is free to leave Ethiopia
whenever he likes. You will be staying to finish the
Mission's business."
I wasn't certain if it was an order or a statement, but I
nodded in agreement, accepted our papers, and left as
quickly as possible. The timing couldn't be better. Now
Richard can leave, and he won't have to stay in Addis
when I go to the lake with the children.

Greatly relieved, and eager to let Richard know, I went directly home from Security. Richard was elated when he heard the news. He had not been too pleased about my proposed trip to Langano since he would have had to stay behind.

After lunch I had several more errands to run. Feyesa needed some groceries to prepare our picnic. One of my greatest concerns was how to tell Feyesa that he really didn't have to go on this picnic with me. I really wanted to get away from everyone, workers included. Feyesa has gone on every picnic and camping trip that our family has gone on for as long as he has worked for us. I wasn't certain how he would react when I asked him not to go.

At dinner tonight the strangest thing happened. Amaha started saying, "Daddy, my teacher says we are going to America tomorrow." The first couple of times I just laughed, but he wouldn't stop saying it. I was afraid Feyesa would take him seriously, so I took him into the other room and tried to tell him that we could all get in trouble if he talked like that. He seemed to understand, and he didn't repeat it again. I don't know where he would hear a thing like that! It hardly sounds like something his teacher would have said, but you never know.

Late this evening something else came up. I am still not certain how we will resolve this situation. It could throw a monkeywrench into my plans for the weekend. I hope not!

Tsige called me and sounded happier than I had heard her in months. "Mr. Collins, I have finally gotten permission for the children to visit their mothers at the prison tomorrow morning at nine o'clock." I hardly knew what to say. She knew we had been planning to go to Lake Langano, but I couldn't bring myself to remind her about our trip. I was afraid she would never understand why our trip should take precedence over visiting their mothers. They have not seen their mothers for nearly three years. All I could say to Tsige was, "Yes, of course, I understand." I hope the children will come back early enough for us to leave and drive to the lake before curfew.

I surely would like to be there before Sunday morning; after all, we weren't planning to stay there that long. I guess I will know more tomorrow when Tsige picks up the children. Maybe I will remind her that we are planning to leave and suggest that she bring them back as early as possible.

I still have not talked to Feyesa about not going tomorrow. I hope he won't be too offended when I tell him in the morning.

Tonight after he went to bed, the children and I really cleaned house. There were a lot of papers I wanted to burn, and I thought we could take care of that while we were packing for Langano. I am tired, and tomorrow is going to be another busy day!

Saturday, July 16: *I got up very early this morning, several hours before I woke the children to get ready. I just wanted to sit in the living room and enjoy my coffee. I love our home so much. We had dreamed of building our own home for years. We finally got it built and furnished, and it is so comfortable. I will miss it terribly when we leave Ethiopia. I can't help but wonder who will live here when we're gone. Feyesa came in about seven-thirty, and I could hardly believe my ears!*

"Mr. Collins," he began, rather embarrassed. "I have not been well all night. I need to go to the doctor today. I don't think I should go to Lake Langano with you." I'm sure he thought I would be upset, but I could have hugged him.

"That's perfectly all right, Feyesa. Go ahead and go to the doctor. There is no problem about your staying here." I had difficulty keeping the enthusiasm I was feeling out of my voice. Now I can get away from workers, too! This was my dream!

I was still sitting there enjoying myself and the good news when the telephone rang. Feyesa answered it and then called for me.

"Hello."

"Hello, Mr. Collins. This is Tsige." Her voice sounded terribly depressed.

"Good morning, Tsige. How are you this morning?"

"Mr. Collins, I have some terrible news. The officials from the prison just telephoned me, and they have cancelled the children's permission to visit their mothers today."

I knew I had to be extremely careful. I was still reveling in the good news about Feyesa, and now this! I could have shouted for joy, but instead I stated very calmly how sorry I was. "Perhaps they will be able to see them another time in the near future, Tsige. I know you have tried very hard to get the permission, and I'm sorry. Nevertheless, I'm certain it will work out." I was truly sorry that the children wouldn't see their mothers before we left, but I did hate to postpone our plans for today. Now we would be able to leave according to schedule.

Feyesa had prepared our picnic basket and left it sitting on the kitchen sink. He left for the doctor's office almost immediately after he talked to me.

I woke the children and told Loly to dress Amaha and to take their suitcase out to the car. I finished getting all the last-minute things together, packed the car, and told Assefa that we would be gone until Monday morning.

He waved us all out the gate, and we were on our way. I had arranged the swimming gear, towels, snorkles, swim fins and masks on top of the suitcases so that the kebele guards who usually congregated outside the gate to keep a watchful eye out for people coming and going in the community, would see our things and know we were going swimming. I was surprised when I drove by the kebele office to see that no one was standing outside.

I drove our car to the parking lot behind the Chinese restaurant. The kids stayed in the car while I caught a taxi to the Hilton Hotel, where I had left the rented zebra Kombi overnight. I didn't want anyone at the Hilton to see me transferring the kids into the zebra van. We were all fairly well known at the Hilton. We had been going there to swim and play tennis for over a year. I thought if I transferred everything from our car into the van behind the Chinese restaurant, no one would see us.

As I was leaving the parking lot to go and get the other

car, I noticed a group of soldiers milling about the parking lot. They appeared to be watching us. I warned the children to stay in the car. I told them I would be right back. "I am just going to the Hilton to pick up another car. I am afraid this old clunker won't make it to Langano," I said, trying to keep concern from my voice. I was certain the girls had noticed the soldiers, too.

I caught a taxi to the Hilton and was headed back to the China Bar Restaurant within twenty minutes. I hope the kids are all right, I thought, as I sped down the hill. I was relieved, when I got back, to see that the soldiers were gone. As quickly as we could, we carried our suitcases and gear to the van. "I like this car, Daddy," Amaha quipped. "It looks like a big zebra!" I lifted him into the zebra, and ran back to check our car once more to make sure we hadn't left anything behind. I didn't realize at the time that we had left our picnic on the kitchen sink at home. I don't think I would have returned to get it even if I had remembered. Once again I told the kids to stay in the car. I was going to drive our car to the English School to get the other six children, and I didn't want to take them with me. "Ami, you be a good boy and mind Loly, OK?" I admonished. "Daddy will be back in just a few minutes and we'll be on our way!"

I approached the English School about fifteen minutes early. I didn't want to arrive early, so I decided to stop by the Rajahs' house and tell them that I couldn't keep the dinner date we had for Sunday evening. The Rajahs were an Indian family living in Addis. Mrs. Rajah had been a math teacher in our night school at the Mission for years. Several weeks ago she had invited the children and me to dinner, and I had forgotten to tell her that we had planned this trip. I was disappointed when no one was home. I left her a note, and headed back for the school. I had driven only a short distance from the Rajahs' house when the car stopped right in the middle of the road. I was baffled when nothing I tried would make it start. A young boy helped me push it off the road. I didn't know what to do! It was time to pick up the kids from the English School. I caught a taxi and went back to the *rented car and the children. Just as my taxi turned the corner near the China Bar Restaurant, I saw a police car and people standing all around as if something had happened. I was petrified! Remembering the soldiers I had seen watching us earlier that morning, I was certain they had come to arrest the children. I observed them for several minutes before I hurried over to the van. I was so relieved to see that the children were not involved in whatever was going on. My knees were weak with fright as I started the van and drove slowly out of the parking lot. I went to the Mobil station, and fortunately there were not too many people in line for gasoline. I bought gas and headed up the hill toward the English School, praying that the other children had not left. We were nearly half an hour late.*

Next door to the English School was another kebele office. Rather than risk being seen with the ten royal children and a zebra van, I drove back to where my car had stalled.

"Loly, you walk down to the English School and see if the other kids are still waiting. If they are, bring them here."

While she was gone, I poured gas over the carburetor of our car and it finally started. I got back into the van and waited for Loly to return. I was glad now that I had told the girls the significance of this trip. After Feyesa had gone to bed last night, I went to their room and explained about the trip and how important it was. They seemed to understand and took it real well. After I left the room, I heard them talking and giggling. It finally got so loud I was worried that Feyesa and Assefa might hear them, so I went back in to tell them to be careful not to disturb Feyesa and Assefa.

When Loly had been gone for about twenty minutes, I began to get worried. Maybe the other kids had decided we weren't coming and had left, I thought anxiously. I hope I don't have to drive around trying to find where they live. I had almost decided to walk up to the English School myself and try to find Loly when I saw her coming. She was in the front seat of a Land Rover. I was terribly alarmed, because the military use Land Rovers, and I thought she might have been picked up by the army. I didn't recognize the driver. I saw six other children in the back seat as they drove closer. I was speechless when they stopped beside me and the driver stepped down and came toward me. He was smiling as if he recognized me.

A few feet from me he said, "Hello, Mr. Collins. I am Gebre Wolde-Mariam. I was a student in your school for four years."

Of course, I recognized him. We shook hands and greeted each other. "What are you doing now, Gebre?" I asked calmly, hoping he wouldn't ask me too many questions.

"I am a chauffeur for the children's grandmother," he said, nodding toward the six children just getting out of the Land Rover. "She asked me to bring them to the English School to meet you. It is nice that you are taking the children to Sodere for the weekend."

I glanced at Rahel. She had a slight grin on her face.

"Yes, I thought it would be nice to get away for a few days. Since the children are all out of school, it will be a nice change. It should be warmer there and not as rainy as here."

He looked in the direction of the van and our car.

"I've been having some trouble with the small car starting. It stalled on my way to meet the children. That's why we were a bit late. I rented the other car, thinking ours might not make it."

"Is there anything I can do to help you, Mr. Collins?" he offered graciously.

"It might be better if I left our car down near the Ghion Hotel. I can pick it up when we get back on Monday and have it serviced. It would be helpful if you drove the van down to the Mobil station on the Debre Zeit Road."

I looked at Rahel's oldest brother. "Does your brother drive, Rahel?" I asked, turning toward Rahel.

"Yes, Sammy can drive."

"Then, Sammy, why don't you drive your grandmother's car and follow me to the Ghion Hotel? Do you know the Rivera Apartments behind the Ghion? I'll park this car

there and ride with you to meet Gebre. Gebre, just wait
for us at the Mobil Station, all right?"

"Fine, Mr. Collins. We'll be there."

It was a strange procession. The zebra van led the way.
We had to drive right past the police headquarters, the
Security office, where I had spent so many long, tedious
hours, the Palace, and Army Headquarters.

It was a relief when Sammy and I pulled into the Mobil
station and I saw Gebre and the children. I had no reason
to distrust him, but I hardly trusted anyone these days!

What happened next was very strange. Gebre and the
children all got out of the car, and one by one he kissed
them all goodbye. That wasn't so strange, but he cried like
a baby. I couldn't understand why he would cry when we
were only going on a picnic to Sodere. And I was glad
that he thought it was Sodere!

It felt like a major accomplishment just being on the
road. I would have felt a lot better if I had not had to
worry about the army checkpoint ahead of me just a few
miles.

I think the most discomforting thought of the whole
morning was the checkpoint. We had had to suffer through
the delays and aggravations of that checkpoint since the
first weeks of the revolution. It was annoying to have
soldiers search your body, your car, and all of your
belongings.

I told the kids to get their identification ready, but not
to show it until the soldiers asked them for it.

"I will try to flash my American passport. If we are
lucky, they will just look at that and let us through
without a thorough inspection. Otherwise, if they ask you,
show them."

I heard someone whisper, "Daddy," and I assumed it
was Menen.

"Yes, Menen," I answered.

"I forgot my identification card."

My heart sank. The soldiers always wanted to see
everyone's ID card. They checked it against the list they
had of people who were wanted by the government.

"Menen, it's all right. We aren't going back to get it. We
will just try to get through without it. Everyone else be

*ready to show his, and maybe they will get tired before
they get to you, Mini," I said, trying to cheer her up. I
knew she felt bad, but there was nothing we could do
about it at that point. I certainly wasn't going back!*

*As we left Addis Ababa, we passed many buses filled
with soldiers en route to the war with Somalia. When we
arrived at the roadblock, I saw fifty or sixty buses
waiting to go through the inspection point. I didn't want
to wait behind all the buses, so I drove cautiously along
the side of the bus caravan until I was nearly to the
checkpoint. The guards seemed preoccupied, inspecting a
taxi. I slowed almost to a standstill, when one of the
armed guards turned from searching the taxi and walked
toward our zebra van. My heart was beating so fast, I
could hear it pounding in my ears. Suddenly the guard
stopped. He waved his arm, signaling that I was to move
on through the checkpoint. No stopping, no search, no
delay! It was more than I could comprehend! It was as if
God had opened the Red Sea for us as he did for Moses
and the children of Israel thousands of years ago. I
shifted the van into low gear and moved through the maze
of cars, buses, and soldiers. We weren't more than fifty
yards from the checkpoint when I let out a loud
"Whoopeee!" and really startled the ten children.*

*"Daddy!" Loly called from the back seat, "you scared us
to death!" They were all laughing by this time.*

*I felt an enormous weight roll off my back. It seemed the
most significant thing that had happened all morning. As
we drove along the narrow asphalt road, the children
talked quietly in the back seat. Sammy rode in front with
me. I guessed his age to be about eighteen. He was very
tall and slim, a nice-looking young man. "What are your
brothers' names?" I asked Sammy.*

*"The older one is Bekere. He is fifteen. Issac is thirteen.
I am a year older than Rahel; I'm twenty-one."*

*I was embarrassed to tell him I had thought he was
only eighteen. Instead I asked, "What about your sisters?"*

*"Well, I told you about Rahel; she's twenty. Meheret, the
taller one, is eighteen, and Aster is the youngest girl, she's
seventeen."*

When I had first seen them at the English School, I had

been surprised. For some reason I had expected them all
to be younger. They were very nice-looking young people,
but I could hardly call them children.

"It is really nice of you to take us out of town like this,
Mr. Collins," Sammy continued. "We never get a chance to
get out of Addis much, and the place really gets on my
nerves. It hasn't been easy since the revolution. I can't
believe Rahel, Meheret, Aster, and I were all out of the
country, and when we heard that trouble was beginning,
we called our parents and told them we wanted to come
home. They warned us not to come, but we came anyway.
And now look at the mess!"

His anger and frustration were apparent. He didn't
mention the recent death of his mother. I was sure it was
much too painful to talk about. The girls had their hair
cut in very short afros, and when I met Rahel, the first
thing I noticed was that she was dressed completely in
black, according to Ethiopian tradition. I had told Rahel
when we met at the Wabe Shebelle not to wear black when
we were leaving town. I didn't want them to call attention
to themselves, and Ethiopians would normally not go on
an outing or picnic while they were in mourning. Today I
noticed when I first saw them at the English School that
they were wearing sports clothes over their black
mourning clothes. I hoped no one else noticed.

We made excellent time getting to Lake Langano. We
drove into the hotel just before three o'clock. I parked
some distance from the registration desk and told the kids
all to stay in the car. I registered for five rooms. The clerk
did not seem surprised.

When we unpacked the car, I realized that I had
forgotten our picnic lunch. I was annoyed with myself,
because that meant we had to eat in the hotel restaurant.
I decided that we should not all eat at once, so that we
would not call attention to ourselves. I told the girls to go
first. The boys and I would wait and eat later. Amaha
was so hungry I sent him with Loly. I thought it was best
if I ate alone, so that I wouldn't be seen with the kids.

The boys and I had just gone back to carry some of our
gear into the room when Rahel came hurrying toward us.

I could tell by the look on her face something was wrong.

"What's wrong?" Sammy asked, the minute he saw her coming.

When she got close to us, she said, "You won't believe this. Sammy, remember I told you that I had to tell my boss something because I couldn't work today and you suggested I tell him that I had to go to the dentist?"

"I remember," Sammy answered.

"Well, I walked into the restaurant, and I saw my boss. I didn't want him to see me, because I had told him I was going to the dentist. I turned to leave, and who do you think was sitting across the restaurant? My dentist!"

"Oh, my goodness!" we all exclaimed in unison.

"You're right, Rahel! I can hardly believe it. Did they see you?"

"I don't think so. I told Loly to bring me something to eat. I will eat in my room later."

Other than Rahel's close call with her boss, the afternoon passed uneventfully. The only problem was, I thought it would never pass.

I saw Loly, Bekere, Kokeb, and Issac walking down the beach. I called to Loly, "Don't go too far away." She nodded her head to acknowledge that she had heard me. Amaha took a nice long nap, and then I took him to the beach away from the hotel and restaurant. Rahel, Sammy, Meheret, and Aster stayed close to their rooms, talking and playing cards.

We went to dinner, using the same plan as we had for lunch. Meheret ate with Rahel so she didn't have to eat alone in her room. We weren't certain if her boss and dentist were spending the night or had just stopped to have lunch and were traveling on, but we didn't want to take any chances.

We all decided to go to bed early. I don't know about the others, but I cannot sleep. I was thankful that in spite of his long nap, Amaha went right to sleep. His long afternoon swim must have tired him out.

Maybe tomorrow morning I will get to play some tennis.

CHAPTER TWENTY-ONE
Our Dream Comes True

Sunday, July 17, 1977: *Catherine's surgery was scheduled for this morning at nine o'clock and in spite of the new and dangerous procedure I hoped the operation would be successful!*

What a day! It is one that I will never forget. I wasn't certain I would live through the tension of the final hours.

Last night I lay awake most of the night. I heard every little sound. The generator always goes off at midnight, and there are no electric lights after that; we had only candles. I couldn't read by candlelight, so I just lay there, listening. It was eerie. I heard every car that drove in and out of the parking lot, and each time I felt sure it would be someone looking for us.

I was just in the twilight zone, half asleep and half awake, when I heard a knock on the door. I knew it was all over and they had come for us. I jumped out of bed. "Who is it?" I asked, my legs weak with fear and my voice quivering. In spite of the warm evening, I shivered.

"Daddy, it's just me, Loly. We thought we heard something and we were scared. We were knocking on Sammy's door, not yours."

I relaxed. "All right, Loly, try to get to bed and get some sleep. Tomorrow will be a full day."

It wasn't long after that that I fell asleep.

My alarm clock woke me up at seven o'clock. My appointment to play tennis was at nine o'clock. It would take me at least a half hour to drive to the courts. I woke the kids up and told them to get ready. They all grumbled about getting up so early. I didn't want them to go to the hotel restaurant for breakfast. Luckily I hadn't forgotten the sack of fruit and cookies that Feyesa had packed. We ate from that as we drove around the lake toward the rendezvous point. I clocked the mileage, although I felt certain I knew the place. I had driven here two weeks ago to check the layout. I saw the familiar roadmarker and turned down an unpaved road toward the lake. During our ride to the prearranged meeting place, I listened while Rahel explained to Sammy that we were going to meet a plane.

"You're kidding," Sammy exclaimed, taken completely by surprise.

"See, I told you," I heard Loly say. "Daddy, I told Issac and Bekere that we were going to escape today, and Bekere bet me five dollars we'd never make it."

I laughed nervously and said, "Well, Bekere, this is one bet I hope you lose!" Everyone laughed, and Bekere said uncomfortably, "I hope I lose, too."

"Rahel, try to open the suitcases and put everything you can into one suitcase. I don't know how much we can take with us. Weight could be a problem. In fact, I may have to stay behind with one or two of you until tomorrow morning if we have too much weight for the plane to lift off. We won't know until after the plane arrives.

"Loly, in my carry-on bag there is a sack of coins and dollar bills. Take it out and hold onto it. I thought that if there are a lot of shepherd boys standing around when the plane lands, I would toss the money as far away from the airplane as I can so that the shepherd children would run after it and we can get away. I've never been to Langano and tried to have a picnic when we weren't surrounded and watched the whole time we ate. Today will probably be no exception."

I was surprised by how quiet it was. I saw no one from the time I turned off the main road until we stopped the

car. *Usually there were women looking for wood, or going
to the lake for water or to bathe. Young children were
usually watching their herds of goats. Today no one was
around. It was just another small miracle!*

*I parked the car on the beach. Sammy, Amaha, and I
got out of the car. I checked the wind direction and got
back into the car. Ami and Sammy waited on the beach
while I drove up and down the beach to see if the sand
was firm enough for the plane to land. I was pleased that
the car had barely left an impression on the sand, it was
so solid, but troubled that the longest angle I measured for
the plane to land was three-tenths of a mile. The contact
man had said we needed four-tenths. I maneuvered the
car into the direction of the wind as the contact man had
instructed me, got out and stood beside Sammy. I had
never noticed how quiet the lake could be. The only noise
came from the tiny waves tumbling gently onto the sand
at the lake's edge. The kids in the car weren't making
a sound. We listened. I prayed silently, "God, if ever
You have helped me, help me at this moment. Keep us
safe. . . ."*

*My prayer was interrupted when I heard a plane
engine. Sammy heard it at the same time. The plane flew
south across the lake. To myself I thought,* God, please help
me to get out of here today! I just don't want to stay around
here another day.

*The pilot circled the area once before he came in low
and circled above us. The first thing I noticed was that all
the numbers on the side of the plane were covered with
masking tape.* Good idea! *I thought to myself. The pilot
continued to circle overhead. I was growing concerned
that he would be spotted by someone if he didn't land
quickly. He continued to circle, and it looked as though he
was dipping the wing of the plane in a particular
direction. I watched as he circled again. He made the
same motion with the wing. What was he trying to tell
me? Had he spotted something or someone? Had we been
discovered? Were soldiers coming? Fear enveloped me like
a grave cloth. I squinted in the bright light, trying to see
if jeeps or other army vehicles were coming through the*

forest. I detected nothing. The pilot circled again very low. I saw him point toward a swamp a few yards away. "Get into the car, Sammy, Amaha! I think he is trying to tell us to cross that swamp."

I drove to the edge of the swamp. Everyone jumped out of the car. "Hurry!" I shouted above the noise of the low-flying aircraft. "The pilot wants us across this swamp!"

I grabbed my flight bag and ran into the swamp. The stench from the putrid sewage nearly choked me. "Hurry!" I called a second time. I sank into the ooze. When it reached the middle of my thigh, I hoped it wouldn't get much deeper. My shoes bogged me down. I reached into the rank mud, slipped off my shoes, and tossed them to the other side. As soon as I reached the bank, I set my case down and turned to see where the others were. I saw Aster struggling to lift Amaha. I knew she couldn't make it all the way across carrying him, so I waded back into the swamp toward her. I carried Amaha to the other side and returned to help Menen and Kokeb.

The kids were all giggling nervously and complaining about the horrible odor of the mud covering their legs. We had all climbed out of the mire onto the bank of the swamp when I saw a second plane circling. God help us! I thought instantaneously. What's that? *Before I had time to think, both planes set down right in front of us, taxied to the end of the open space, turned, and came back.* They arranged for a second plane, *I thought gratefully.* We'll all get out at once!

The pilot of the larger, first plane jumped from the cockpit and ran toward us. "Come on, quickly!" He motioned us toward the planes. I tried to think who should get aboard the first plane. "Sammy, you and Menen get on the big plane, quickly!" I knew their lives were in the most danger, Sammy because he was older and was a male heir to the throne, and Menen because of her father's efforts to overthrow the present government. "Meheret, Kokeb, Issac, and Bekere, go with Sammy and Menen. Loly, get Amaha into the small plane. Aster, go with Loly and Amaha!

I ran to make sure Sammy, Menen, and the others were aboard the larger plane. Menen was having difficulty getting aboard. I helped her and Kokeb into the plane. I ran back to get my bag and shoes and ran for the small plane as I heard the engine of the large plane revving up for takeoff. I climbed into the front seat of the smaller plane and watched breathlessly as the large plane lifted off. What a sight! *I thought. I felt the compression of our plane increasing as the pilot increased the throttle. My heart felt as if it was beating as fast as the plane engine. We were moving down the field. We were off the ground!* "Thank God, we've made it!" *I uttered. We were airborne!*

My intense nervousness didn't subside immediately. I listened as our pilot made radio contact with the pilot of the larger plane. Both men sounded British. I never learned their names. As we flew over a small town, the pilot said, "That's Arba Minch. We've just lost radio contact with the other plane. They can fly faster than we can, and they are out of radio range." *I sat up straighter and watched the countryside below.*

I lost all track of time. I wasn't certain how long we had been flying, when I sensed we were going to land. It didn't seem we had been flying long enough to arrive in Kenya.

"Where are we?" *I asked.*

"We are going to land in that dry lake bed down there," *he said, pointing below us.* "That is the Salt Lake. Half of it is in Ethiopia and half in Kenya. We will be landing on the Kenyan side, not that it would make much difference if we are caught!" *he added, not too reassuringly.* "The other pilot and I spent the night here last night. We hid fuel there in those bushes," *he said, nearly turning us all on our sides.*

I turned and looked at the children. Their eyes were huge with fear. Loly looked as though she might be sick.

"Are you all OK?" *I asked.*

"I feel kind of sick, Daddy," *Loly said, confirming my thoughts.*

"Hold on just a minute. We are landing right now," *the pilot said, as he brought the plane down in the dry lake bed.* "You can get out while we refuel the plane," *the pilot suggested.*

"The fuel is there, Mr. Collins, in the bushes," *the pilot* directed. "If you will bring the fuel, I'll turn the plane around."

I opened the door of the plane and jumped down. It felt good to stretch my legs. "Loly, do you guys want to get out?" I asked.

Her eyes as big as saucers, Loly said, "There's no way I'm getting off this plane. It still looks like Ethiopia out there to me." Obviously she had spoken for the other two as well. Amaha was sound asleep on Aster's lap.

I ran to the place the pilot had directed me and found the fuel hidden in the straggly sagebrush, beneath a cardboard cover. The pilot explained, saying the cardboard was to keep the fuel cans from reflecting the sun in case other planes flew over the area. I carried the heavy jerry cans to the plane. After he had turned the plane around, the pilot jumped from the cockpit to help me lift the cans and pour the fuel into the gas tank. We carried the cans back to their hiding place and left them without bothering to cover them again. We were both back in the plane within fifteen minutes after landing, and within seconds we had taken off once again.

A little of the tension seemed to have drained from my body once we were on our way for the second time. My joints didn't seem to ache as badly as they had earlier.

We had been flying another two hours when I felt the plane lose altitude once again. "Are we landing again?" I asked.

"Yes, we are meeting the others in that small fishing village," he said, pointing to a cluster of small thatched-roof huts beside another small lake. "I need to put some oil in the plane, too," he stated matter-of-factly.

It was good to see the other kids as they walked toward us. I think we were all finally beginning to realize we were out of Ethiopia. Even Loly got out of our plane. Amaha had awakened and raised his hands up to me so I would carry him. "Why don't you walk a little, big boy? It will be good for you to stretch. We have to get back on the plane in a few minutes."

All of the kids looked weary, but they were all smiling as we greeted each other again. The other plane was not *as comfortable as ours. All of the seats had been stripped out and a mattress had been placed in the fuselage to make room for everyone. They were all rubbing their cramped legs.*

We hadn't been on the ground more than fifteen minutes when the pilots told us to get back aboard the planes. We said goodbye to the other six kids and climbed back on board.

We had flown only about an hour when the pilot said to me, "Mr. Collins, we are going to land in a few minutes, and I am going to have to leave you and the children. In about four hours the other pilot will return and take you and these children the rest of the way."

He must have anticipated the shock that registered on my face, because he continued quickly.

"You see, Mr. Collins, your friends were desperate to find another airplane yesterday. I own this plane, but I had leased it to someone for the summer months. Last evening we went to the hangar and took it without telling anyone, hoping not to make anyone suspicious. But, if I don't get it back before the people who rented it go out and find it missing, they might report it stolen to the police, and everyone in Kenya will hear radio reports about a stolen airplane. We don't want that to happen, so I must return the plane as quickly as possible. Don't worry, Mr. Collins; the other pilot will know where to find you, and he should be back before nightfall."

And I had thought our problems were behind us! I didn't like this idea at all. We were all exhausted. The heat was stifling, and we had no water or food. I felt angry, but I didn't want to argue with this man who had tried to do us such a favor. In fact, I didn't even know whom I was angry with, but the last thing I wanted to do was wait in that desert for four hours with three children. I had no choice. He landed for the third time, reassured me one final time that the other pilot knew just where to find us, and he took off.

By late afternoon I was getting concerned that we might have to spend the night in the desert. In the distance, maybe five miles away, I saw what looked like a Catholic mission 'way up on a hill. I had just told the children we should start walking toward the mission. Kenyan children had seen our plane land and had come to see the strangers. They spoke Swahili, and I only understood their greeting, "Jumbo." When I answered "Jumbo," to them, they must have assumed that I knew Swahili, and they chattered away for several minutes before they realized that I was shrugging my shoulders and shaking my head because I didn't understand a word they were saying. Loly was getting annoyed by their persistent prattle and curiosity, and by the time I suggested that we walk toward the church, she was the most eager to leave. We had walked only about one-quarter of a mile when I heard a plane engine. I felt jubilant when I recognized the pilot and plane. He landed nearby, and we ran toward the plane. There was another man on board with him, and he jumped to the ground and introduced himself.

"Hello," he said in a friendlier tone than I had heard in weeks. "My name is Georgio." He shook hands with all of us, including Amaha. Amaha gave him a big smile. "Come," Georgio said to Ami, extending his arms. "Let me help you get onto the big airplane." Without reluctance, Amaha accepted Georgio's friendly invitation, and the two became fast friends. Amaha sat beside Georgio on the mattress. It didn't hurt their newly formed friendship when Georgio offered Amaha the only soft drink on board, a small bottle of Coca-Cola. He had brought box lunches for all of us, and we ate them with relish. The only other drink they had aboard was beer. I didn't normally drink beer, but we hadn't had a drink the entire day, and the four hours waiting in the desert sun had just about undone all of us. After I took a swallow from the bottle, I handed it back to Georgio. He handed it to Loly, and she looked at me. "If you can stand it, Loly, go ahead. I know how thirsty you must be." She screwed up her face preparing for the worst and took a big swallow. "Oh, that's horrible," she said, quickly handing it back to Georgio. He then handed it to Aster, and as hesitantly as Loly, she sipped the bitter liquid. She shuddered as she handed the empty bottle back to Georgio.

"Daddy, when we get to wherever we are going and Mommy is waiting there and I smell like cigarette smoke and beer, I hope you will explain all of this!"

Georgio laughed as he put out his cigarette. "Doesn't your mother drink beer and smoke?" he said, still grinning.

With great resolve, Loly shook her head and said "No, she doesn't. And she wouldn't like it if we did either," she concluded, nodding her head toward Aster and me. I couldn't help but smile.

We must have flown two more hours before we landed again. I hoped desperately that this was our final destination. As we disembarked for the fourth time that day, I saw a beige Volkswagen van beside the primitive airstrip.

"You will go with Georgio," the pilot instructed. "Good luck," he said, shaking my hand.

"Thank you very much," I said wearily. "I think we've just had a full day of it!" We shook hands, and I watched him taxi down the runway and take off. I turned and hurried toward the van. Georgio had gotten into the back seat with the kids, and waved me into the front seat. "You sit up there with Franco. Franco, this is Mr. Collins." A short, dark-haired man was behind the wheel. "Welcome to Kenya," he said, his voice rich with an Italian accent.

I heard Georgio say to the children, "Have you heard of the famous Treetop Resort here in Kenya?" They all shook their heads. "It is a very popular tourist attraction. People come from all over the world to stay there. There is a big sitting room that overlooks salt licks. All kinds of wild animals, elephant, deer, lions, all come there for salt. The visitors can watch them from the safety of the Treetop Hotel. It is like going on a safari right in your own living room, but better than television." The children all laughed at Georgio's description.

"We are very near to that hotel," he continued. "They don't let young children stay there, because they worry that if the children cry, it will scare away the animals. I'll bet you never cry, my big man," he said, teasing Amaha. Amaha, taking in every word, shook his head in complete

*agreement. Georgio was great for the kids. His friendly,
lighthearted manner entertained us all during the two-
hour drive to Nairobi, the capital city of Kenya. When we
pulled into the parking lot of a comfortable-looking hotel,
I think I felt more relieved than I had felt the entire day,
and it had been one long day!*

*Franco already had keys for our rooms, and as we
walked into the lobby, he explained, "You and the children
have five different rooms. We thought it would be safer
that way. I have explained to the hotel management that
you are a teacher traveling with a group of school
children. No one should ask you any questions. They know
me here, and if they ask you anything, just tell them to
see me unless you feel it is all right to answer them. You
can just sign for your food in the restaurant. I have told
them I will cover all your charges. I will be back to see
you tomorrow around noon. That will give you plenty of
time to rest and relax a bit. There is a swimming pool if
you and the children like to swim. I think you will be safe
here. Here is my telephone number if you need to get in
touch with me. Call me any time, night or day. Do you
have any questions?"*

*I was too tired to think of anything except a hot shower,
maybe some food and something to drink, and a good
night's sleep. I wasn't even sure I would have the energy to
walk to the restaurant after a hot shower.*

*Franco gave Aster and Loly a key and told Georgio to
walk them to their room. "Be sure to keep your door
locked, girls," Georgio instructed. "Turn the key half way
after it is locked and leave it in the door, so no one can
use another key to open it. By turning it sideways after
you lock it, no one can push it out of the lock. Do you
understand?" Loly and Aster just looked at each other
and started giggling. I knew they were nearly slap-happy,
and if they were half as tired as I was, they could hardly
focus their minds on what Georgio was trying to explain.
"Come with me," he said patiently. "I will show you when
I take you to your room."*

*"Good night, girls," I said, taking my case from Franco
in one hand and lifting Amaha with the other. He had*

been such a good little fellow all day, but he didn't look as if he could walk another step. "Daddy, I'm thirsty," he said as I picked him up. "OK, big boy. As soon as we get to the room we will get you a big drink of cold water. How does that sound?"

"Good," he said, putting his head down on my shoulder.

Amaha must have drunk five glasses of water before his thirst was finally quenched. I bathed him and tucked him under the covers of one of the twin beds. As I kissed him good night, he whispered sleepily, "Daddy, it's fun to be in this nice country." Such a perceptive little guy, *I thought as I pulled the covers up around him. "It sure is, Ami," I assured him. I can't remember when a shower ever felt better. The dried mud from the swamp we had waded through early this morning was still caked to my legs. It smelled nearly as bad as I scrubbed my legs to get it off.*

When I came out of the shower, Amaha was sound asleep. I was glad, because I was too tired to go downstairs to the restaurant. I couldn't remember a night in my life when I had felt more exhausted! But what a day! I closed my eyes and thanked God for the miracle He had performed that day. Moses had nothing on me!

Monday, July 18: *Today was a relaxing day. All the kids slept late. I met Sammy, Bekere, and Issac when I went to the dining room for lunch. We had all just gotten up, and Sammy said the girls were getting ready to come to the dining room. I think it will be days before we unwind. Our hotel accommodations are very comfortable, but I am eager to be clear out of Africa. I don't know why, but I don't feel entirely safe even in Kenya. I have no idea where Jodie is. Franco seemed rather unclear about the next step, but he said he would be back again tomorrow. He came for just a short time as we finished our lunch in the dining room. He had a cup of coffee and asked us if we were comfortable. It is almost like we are on hold again. I went swimming with Amaha this afternoon. The water was a little cold, but refreshing. My muscles are still so tense, they ache. The swimming helped considerably, however.*

Franco left some money with me to buy the kids toothbrushes and a few toiletries. We didn't bring all the luggage out of the zebra van, because there wasn't room enough on the plane.

I am to meet Richard here in Kenya. He was supposed to fly to Nairobi on Saturday. I gave him my cameras to bring out with him. He is supposed to stay at the Mennonite Guest House. When I tried to telephone him this evening, he wasn't there, although he was registered. Perhaps I will reach him tomorrow. I am sure he is eager to be on his way to the States. He isn't the only one! I will be glad when I hear from Jodie. I actually thought she would be here when we arrived.

Tuesday, July 19: *Still no word from Jodie. I was able to contact Richard today. He came here to the Jacaranda Hotel to see me. He looked much more relaxed than the last time I saw him! He brought my cameras. I was happy to get them out of Addis. I had thought at first I would have to leave them behind, but Richard suggested he bring them out.*

The kids and I just stayed around the hotel today. They bought a few books and magazines yesterday. There is an English television station, and they enjoy watching television in a sitting room near the lobby. It isn't like the United States, where each hotel room has its own television set. Franco is very friendly, but not too informative. Georgio came with him today and offered to take all the kids to a drive-in movie. I thought it would be good for them to get out. We are all ready to climb the walls because of boredom. I am feeling a lot more rested, but I still feel tension in all my joints.

Wednesday, July 20: *The kids can talk about nothing but Georgio. They think he is great! They had a good time with him last night. Amaha went with them last night, so I was on my own. I read, watched some television, and wrote a couple of letters, one to my folks, and one to Mom and Ben, Jodie's folks. Oh, my goodness! Kokeb just came running to my door calling, "Daddy, Daddy, Mommy is here. Come quick!" I can't believe it! Jodie is here at last!*

CHAPTER TWENTY-TWO
"You're a Political Powder Keg"

I smiled to myself as I closed the cover of Denton's journal. What an appropriate ending, I thought, as I set the book on the side table. It sounds like a good novel! I picked up my travel clock and looked at the time. Oh no! Two o'clock in the morning. I'd get only four hours sleep before I had to get up and get ready to meet Denton for breakfast. I turned out the light and lay in the dark thinking about the emotional holocaust Denton had experienced during his final weeks in Addis. Regrettably, I had caused some of the turmoil he had suffered. I found solace only in thinking of the alternative: the children's imprisonment and their possible execution.

I hardly felt like moving when my alarm clock went off a brief four hours later. I dragged myself to the shower, lacking my usual early morning vitality. The beads of hot water eased some of the exhaustion from my muscles. I let the steamy streams of water massage my neck and back. I dressed quickly, hoping to have time to place a call to London before Denton arrived. I knew Michael and Seyfou would be eager to hear of my reunion with Denton and the kids, and to hear that I had been well received at the American embassy.

"Yes, Michael, I've been to the embassy, and if all goes according to plan, we could be on our way to the United States today or tomorrow at the latest. They said within twenty-four hours. Yes, it is exciting. Denton and the kids are excited and eager to be on their way. Yes, I'll call when I know something definite."

Denton arrived to have breakfast with me at the Norfolk. We had only two hours together before my appointment at the American embassy. We talked excitedly about how good it would seem to be safely back in the United States. Just before nine o'clock he returned to the Jacaranda and I headed for the American embassy.

Exuberant and full of confidence, I opened the embassy door and strode toward the receptionist, Mrs. West. Remembering me, she greeted me graciously, and without delay she rang for Mr. Bennett. Minutes later he greeted me warmly and led me to the elevator. I felt much more at ease today than I had yesterday as I walked down these same halls.

Just as we were being seated in the same large, comfortable office, Mr. Henning joined us. Both men seemed nervous and more subdued than they were yesterday. Mr. Bennett asked me about Denton and the children, and I told them about our reunion at the hotel.

"My husband looks very worn out. Actually, the children look more relaxed than he does. I guess that is understandable."

Mr. Bennett interrupted me and said, "Mrs. Collins, as we promised you yesterday morning, we have been in touch with the President, his assistant for National Security Affairs, Mr. Brzezinski, and the Secretary of State, Mr. Vance. I hope you will understand that this is the position of the State Department and does not reflect our own personal feelings."

His pause seemed interminable. I didn't comment, and he finally continued.

"Mrs. Collins, the State Department has decided that you, your husband, and the ten great-grandchildren of the late Emperor Haile Selassie are a political powder keg, and we've been instructed not to touch you with a ten-foot pole."

Both men looked embarrassed and neither had much more to say.

I sat up straight. "A political powder keg!" My disbelief and shock were not camouflaged. "Whatever does that mean? President Carter has been an advocate of human rights since he took office! How can a missionary couple and ten great-grandchildren of one of America's oldest allies possibly be considered a political powder keg? This doesn't make sense to me!"

"I'm sorry, Mrs. Collins. We can do nothing more. Our hands are tied. I can only suggest that you see the United Nations High Commissioner for Refugees. Perhaps he can be of some help to you."

Mr. Henning volunteered to take me to the High Commissioner's office the following morning. He asked me to meet him at the embassy at nine o'clock.

I was near tears when I left the embassy. I knew I couldn't go back to the Jacaranda immediately. What was I going to say to Denton and the kids? I walked in the direction of the main part of town. My cheeks were hot and flushed. Tears splashed down onto my jacket. "So here we are again, Lord! Another setback. Whatever am I going to say to Denton? I'm sure he and the kids are expecting to be on their way to the States within the next few hours, and now I have to go back and tell them that not only are we not going, I have no idea when or if we are ever going! What am I going to do?"

I remembered the articles I had cut out of the newspapers in London and the United States about President Carter's human rights campaign. *Political jargon,* I thought disgustedly. *When the chips are really down, where is his human rights policy?* The longer I walked and the more I thought about being called a political powder keg, the angrier I got.

As I walked up and down the tree-lined streets, I began to tire. Some of the rage subsided. The Bible verse came back to me once again, "Trust . . . Trust in the Lord."

"Lord, I've already trusted you. Remember in Oklahoma City? We've been through all this." As I continued to walk, it became a little clearer to me that the Lord didn't want me just to trust Him once. He wanted me to trust Him each day of my life, with each situation of my life, no matter how big or how small. *So I guess I have to decide again,* I thought. *Do I trust the Lord in this situation, too? Well, the President has let me down! The United States government has disappointed me! The officials at the embassy have no power to act independently. I guess I have a choice. I can trust in myself or in the Lord—and when I stop and think about it, I haven't accomplished too much on my own either.* I turned around and began to walk toward the Norfolk.

In my room I opened my Bible to the Psalms again. I scanned the pages for verses that would encourage me. I copied several verses into my prayer journal.

Thursday, July 21, 1977—Psalm 52:1b: *"The goodness of God endureth continually."*

Psalm 52:8b: *"I trust in the mercy of God for ever and ever."*

Psalm 52:9: *"I will praise thee for ever because thou hast done it: and I will wait on thy name."*

Psalm 54:6b, 7: *"I will praise thy name, O Lord; for it is good. For he hath delivered me out of all trouble: and mine eye hath seen his desire [not my own desire, but* His *desire] upon mine enemies."*

Feeling more fortified than I had since leaving the embassy, I left the Norfolk and returned to the Jacaranda to face Denton and the kids. It was lunch time, and I found them all seated around one big table in the dining room. My heart sank when I saw their expectant faces.

"How did it go?" Denton asked, almost before I was seated beside him.

The kids were all listening attentively.

I shook my head. "Well, there has been a delay. The American embassy is reluctant to get involved. As a matter of fact, the State Department, presumably the President, his assistant for National Security Affairs, Mr. Brzezinski, and Secretary Vance, have called us a political powder keg and have instructed the embassy not to get involved. The two gentlemen at the embassy are actually very nice, but they insist their hands are tied. I am going to see the United Nations High Commissioner for Refugees in the morning. Maybe I will bring you better news tomorrow."

The kids' disappointment was obvious. They hardly

talked as they ate their lunch. Denton seemed preoccupied, watching someone across the dining room. I looked in the direction of his gaze, and my heart nearly stopped. An Ethiopian man was being seated at a table by himself. What could that mean?

Denton looked at me to see if I had noticed. He quickly put his fingers to his lips, signaling me not to mention what I'd seen. I understood he did not want to alarm the children. I could tell by the expression on Sammy's face that he had seen the man.

"Kids," Denton said softly, as they all looked up from eating, "as soon as we are finished, I think we should go up to my room and talk over some things. Hurry up and finish."

Once we were safely in Denton's room, he explained that he had seen an Ethiopian and that everyone should stay close to his room until we knew what was going on. We all talked together for nearly an hour, and then I said I'd like to go back to my hotel to rest and to make some phone calls. I told everyone that I had talked to Michael and Seyfou, and that brought smiles to the kids' faces. It was like contact with the outside world.

"Mom," Loly asked curiously, "are you going to tell us how you planned the escape?"

"Of course, Loly. There will be time for that. I will try to explain everything. Right now my head is reeling and I feel dizzy with exhaustion. Let me get some sleep, and then I will try to sort out the details for you, all right?"

Denton opened the door to walk me downstairs to catch a cab. We both saw him at once. He was unlocking the door next to Denton's room. It was the same Ethiopian man we had seen in the dining room. As calmly as possible, Denton took my arm and pulled me back into the room and locked the door.

"I think I should telephone Franco." He placed the phone call and explained the situation to Franco. When he hung up, he told us, "Franco said to stay in the room until he gets here."

"Well, maybe this is a good time to begin telling you about the escape plan and how it all started," I said, as all the children made themselves comfortable. Amaha climbed onto

290 CODE WORD: CATHERINE

my lap and settled himself. I had only recounted my original trip to London to meet with Michael in July 1976, when Franco called our room from the lobby.

"You must be extremely careful," he warned Denton over the telephone. "I have just seen this man, and I know he is with Ethiopian Security. Be cautious, and tell the children to move about the hotel only in a group. Don't even let them go two by two."

Denton asked him if it was safe for me to return to my hotel. Franco said it would be fine, but warned me to keep a watchful eye. He offered to take me if I would come down to the lobby to meet him. Thirty minutes later I was back at the Norfolk. For the second time that day, I telephoned London and explained to Michael the reaction of the State Department. His shock was genuine, and he asked me to call him after my visit to the High Commissioner's office the following morning.

At ten-thirty that evening, I placed a call to Senator Frenzel's office. He had been helpful in writing letters of introduction for me. Maybe he could help me now. I talked with his aide, a woman who promised to get in touch with the Senator in Washington, D.C. She asked me to call her back again in a few hours.

I set my alarm clock for one o'clock in the morning and telephoned her again. She said that Senator Frenzel would see what contacts he could make on our behalf. She suggested that I keep her posted on any new developments. I thanked her, a little disappointed that something more substantial couldn't be done, and agreed to call her if I had any new information.

Anticipating more help from the High Commissioner for Refugees, I met Mr. Henning at the American embassy the next morning. Together we walked into the main part of town. We went into the lobby of a multistory building and took the elevator to the third floor, where we would find the Commissioner's office.

As we stepped off the elevator, I was shocked by the appalling mass of humanity lining the hallway. It looked as if some of the refugees had been sleeping there for days. We had to step over and around many of them. My heart went out to them, and I felt guilty that we were able to walk right into the Commissioner's office ahead of them. Mr. Henning had obviously called and arranged for us to meet with the Commissioner. As we were escorted into his office, his secretary, a thin, bald man, stood from his chair behind a large desk and came toward us. He looked like Gandhi. In a friendly manner, he introduced himself to me, before Mr. Henning had time to say anything. "I'm Mr. Kadry," he said, greeting me.

"Mr. Kadry, I would like you to meet Mrs. Collins. This is the lady I telephoned you about yesterday."

"Yes, of course, of course; please, have a seat," he said, arranging two chairs in front of his desk.

"I'm sorry, Mr. Kadry, but I must return to the embassy," Mr. Henning said apologetically. "I will leave Mrs. Collins with you. I do hope you are able to assist her."

We said goodbye, and Mr. Henning left the office.

Mr. Kadry motioned me toward a chair, and instead of sitting behind his desk, he sat beside me in the chair he had set out for Mr. Henning.

"Mr. Henning explained only briefly why you need my help. Perhaps you would like to tell me why you have come?"

During the next hour, Mr. Kadry listened carefully to my account of the escape. Occasionally he made a notation on a small tablet he had on his lap.

When I concluded, he asked to see the letters I had from Senator Frenzel and the Crown Prince. He asked if he might photocopy the letters, and when he left the room, I glanced around his office for the first time since I had entered. On the wall beside his desk there was a poster that said, "It is not your fault that a man becomes a refugee. It might be if he remains a refugee."

This was the first time I had stopped to think that the ten children in our care were now considered refugees. Suddenly I realized that they could just as easily be lined up with all of those other people on the floor outside Mr. Kadry's office. It was a very humbling thought and made me even more appreciative of Mr. Kadry.

When he reappeared, I told him about the Ethiopian man that had checked into the room next door to Denton's at the Jacaranda Hotel. He expressed great concern and said that we should go to the police commission immediately. Within the next hour we were in the office of the Kenyan police commissioner, and I was repeating my story for the second time.

The police commissioner, a large and heavy-set man, spoke gently and reassured me that he would have plain-clothesmen at the Jacaranda by evening. I was surprised when he asked if he could come to the hotel personally and meet Denton and the children. I was gratified by the commissioner's concern and interest in our family, and suggested that he come to the Jacaranda that evening.

When Mr. Kadry and I returned to his office, he gave me several forms to fill out for each child, and suggested that I complete them over the weekend and bring them to his office on Monday morning.

"I am going to issue each child a United Nations travel document. It is as valid as an American passport, possibly more so. You will have to take these documents to the West German embassy here in Nairobi and apply for visas for each child. In Frankfurt, West Germany, there is an American immigration office. I feel certain that once you are off the continent of Africa, you will have little difficulty getting the children into the United States. The situation between Ethiopia and America since the Americans' expulsion from Ethiopia is volatile. America desires to keep a skeleton crew at the American embassy in Ethiopia. I am certain that the embassy here wants to do nothing to upset that precarious situation. That might account for the State Department's reluctance to become involved while you are still in Africa. It is likely that the American immigration in Frankfurt will process the children's papers for entrance into the States in a matter of days."

"I hope so," I cut into Mr. Kadry's thoughts. "I am eager to return to the States. I left my two children with their grandparents, and school is going to start the first of September. I would like to get all the children home so we can get them settled for school. They have had quite a summer holiday!"

Mr. Kadry smiled and continued. "The trick will be getting the visas to enter West Germany," he emphasized. "The Germans are very particular about allowing refugees into their country. I understand that it has to do with a government policy to provide for a refugee's welfare once they do arrive. The government pays for their food, clothing, education, medicine. It is quite an undertaking. Therefore, they make sure very few refugees enter the country. The fact that you have the children's airline tickets to California and that your intent is to raise the ten children in the United States will be very helpful.

"I would also like you to bring Mr. Collins's passport to me on Monday morning as well as all these completed forms. Do you have any questions?" he asked, as he stood to conclude our meeting.

"No, not just now," I said, thanking him for all his help and genuine concern and encouragement. I gathered the papers together and put them in my attaché case.

My gait was brisker and my shoulders straighter as I hurried out of the office to catch a taxi.

"Jacaranda Hotel," I called to a taxi driver.

It was nearly one o'clock in the afternoon when I reached Denton's hotel. I expected to find everyone in the dining room eating lunch. I asked the headwaiter if Denton and the children had come downstairs yet, and he said he had not seen them since breakfast.

I hurried off toward Denton's room and as I turned the corner, I saw Denton and Amaha just coming out of the room toward me.

Denton looked unusually concerned as he walked toward me. I waited at the end of the corridor until they reached me.

"You aren't going to believe this," he said, his voice filled with concern. "Several more Ethiopians have checked into the hotel. Franco is getting quite concerned. He said he is going to arrange for us to leave here for the weekend. He'll arrange a safari to Tsavo National Park. We will leave early in the morning. It is between Nairobi and Mombasa."

Taken aback by all the sudden developments, I asked, "Does Franco think I should go with you?"

"I asked that, too, and he said there would be no problem. He thought it was better for all of us to clear out of here until late Sunday night. He hopes the Ethiopian agents will be gone by then. Perhaps they will think we have left for good."

The others joined us in the dining room, but we didn't discuss our plans for the weekend. We thought it was better not to tell the children right away lest they talk about it in the television room or somewhere they might be overheard.

After lunch Franco came to the hotel, and while Amaha napped, Franco, Denton, and I sat in Denton's room and discussed our plans for the next morning.

"I will have two safari vans here first thing in the morning. I will drive one and Georgio the other. I think it is best if we go in two different cars. We will take box lunches so we don't have to stop on the way. I have made reservations at a lodge in Tsavo National Park. I think you will all have a very nice time."

As Franco left the hotel, he told me he would pick me up at seven o'clock the next morning. "We want to get a very early start," he assured us. "I don't like all of these Ethiopians watching every move we make. Since you cannot do any more business until Monday, Mrs. Collins, it is best you join us on this little outing."

That evening after dinner, the police commissioner came to the hotel. We called the children from their rooms and introduced them to the commissioner. He was a jolly man, and was particularly taken by Amaha's charm. That wasn't unusual; nearly everyone was fascinated with this bright-eyed, intelligent little three-year-old.

We discussed our plans for the weekend with the commissioner, and he approved of Franco's idea. "That will also give my men the weekend off. They will be back here, however, Sunday evening when you return," he assured us both.

As the children left the room, Denton asked them to pack their few things for our departure the next morning. The commissioner and I were leaving at the same time, and he offered to drive me to the Norfolk.

When I returned to my hotel, I telephoned Michael and explained the developments of the day, the unexpected appearance of several Ethiopian Security men, and my meetings with Mr. Kadry and the police commissioner. I said I would call again after I had gone to the West German embassy to apply for the children's visas. He sounded pleased with the progress I was making, but expressed deep concern about the Ethiopian agents.

"The police commissioner feels he can provide adequate protection, Michael," I said, trying to put his fears to rest.

"Be extremely careful, Mrs. Collins. Take no unnecessary risks!" he admonished.

On Saturday morning, just four days after I had arrived in Kenya, we were on our way to Tsavo game reserve. It seemed a peculiar twist of events that right in the middle of our escape, we would go on an African safari, an opportunity that many people dream about all their lives. I remembered the Bible verse in Ephesians 3:20 where it says that God can do exceeding abundantly more than we ask or think! I would recall the same verse many more times during the next few weeks.

Franco had picked me up at the Norfolk at seven o'clock. I was always impressed with Franco's promptness. Living in Ethiopia, I had learned that things rarely were on time. As Franco and I drove to the Jacaranda, I told him about the police commissioner's visit the evening before. He looked pleased and said, "That is very good, Mrs. Collins. I have been worried about those Ethiopian men since the first one arrived."

The day couldn't have been more perfect for our trip. The sun shone brightly in the clear azure blue African sky. Thorn trees stretched their prickly branches upward like early morning risers reaching skyward for a morning stretch. I looked forward to the two-day break. My body was tired, and I hadn't really had time to slow down since I had arrived in Kenya four days ago.

Wildlife surrounded us almost as soon as we left the city. Gazelle, ostrich, wildebeest, zebra. We drove for several hours, finally stopping just long enough to enjoy our box lunches in a shady spot along a river filled with hippopotamuses and crocodiles. The trees seemed alive with monkeys squealing and fighting with one another in the leafy boughs.

The children could not resist tossing bits and pieces of their lunches to the chattering primates as they gathered around the car.

Late in the afternoon we turned off the main road and wound our way along a dusty dirt road into the Tsavo game park. Thirty minutes later we pulled up in front of a rustic-looking lodge. Masai warriors, clad in their single skimpy piece of red cloth hanging from their long, languid bodies, stood on one leg, leaning against their tall spears, watching us file into the lodge. The children were wide-eyed with fascination as they stared back at the Masai warriors. I was certain that in their sheltered environment, the children had never seen anything quite like the Masai.

After dinner, Franco and Georgio invited us to a large bonfire where we were entertained by tribal dances, the Masai among them.

Weary from our long journey, Amaha quickly fell asleep on my lap to the beat of the African drums. I carried him to our bungalow and tucked him into his bed, pulled the mosquito netting down tight around his bed, and collapsed onto my cot. The sounds of the buzzing mosquitos sent me diving for my own mosquito netting. Securely inside the net, I could still hear their loud buzzing outside. I pulled the sheet up around my shoulders and listened to the distant drums and chanting of the dancers until I drifted into sleep.

The next day we had a lovely breakfast at the lodge and set off for a full-day safari. We saw elephants, lions, cheetahs, water buffaloes, and many more zebras, wildebeests, and the more common African animals. The giraffes and zebras were my favorites. I reminded Denton about the zebra safari van he had rented to leave Addis, and we both chuckled about it.

"I wonder if anyone has found it yet?" he pondered. "I hope the tour company gets it back. I still have the keys, but I left a large deposit with the rental company—certainly enough to pay for another set of keys! I remember that I wanted to lock the van before I crossed the swamp for the last time, but the lock was broken, so I had to leave it open."

I laughed and said, "It seems like a funny thing to think about while you're trying to get ten children across a swamp and escape from the country!" Denton agreed.

Weary from the full day of animal watching, we were all happy when the vans pulled into the Jacaranda Hotel grounds late Sunday evening. Dust-covered and bone-tired, we all walked into the lobby. I wondered whether the plainclothes policemen were watching us come in. I would never know for certain who they were.

Franco dropped me at the Norfolk, and I couldn't remember when a hot shower ever felt so good.

CHAPTER TWENTY-THREE
An Open Door

Early Monday morning I met Mr. Kadry in his office. He glanced over the forms I had filled out for the children during our weekend safari. Mr. Kadry called his secretary into his office, and they set right to work issuing the travel documents for the children. I had brought a small New Testament in my purse, and while they worked, I sat in Mr. Kadry's office and read.

By ten o'clock the paperwork was complete and Mr. Kadry gave me instructions on how to get to the West German embassy. "You can walk if you wish. It isn't that difficult to find," he assured me.

I packed the ten documents into my attaché case as he thought of something else and dashed from the office. When he returned he handed me Denton's passport, and said, "There, I have taken care of that little matter. Mr. Collins is now in Kenya legally." I smiled and put Denton's passport alongside the other documents and snapped my attaché case closed. I was on my way.

The receptionist at the West German embassy reminded me a great deal of Mrs. West, the receptionist at the American embassy. *They are just doing their job, Jodie,* I tried to remind myself after I had sat in the waiting room for more than an hour before she returned to tell me I would have to come back after lunch. Exasperated, I left the embassy and walked toward downtown. My case was heavy, and my shoulder began to ache. I found a small cafe and decided to have lunch while I waited for the embassy to open again at three o'clock. As in Addis, all offices closed from one o'clock until three each afternoon.

I had gone only a few steps down the sidewalk from the cafe where I had eaten lunch when I realized I was in front of the Pan American Airlines office. I recalled that the tickets Seyfou had given me were Pan American tickets. Surprised to find them open, I decided to go in and ask a few questions about various flights leaving Nairobi.

An attractive young lady was busily working at her desk as I entered the office. She greeted me with a pleasant smile and asked if she could be of assistance to me. I told her I was interested in flights to West Germany. She opened a large black book and began looking for the listings. "When are you planning to leave?" she asked politely.

"I'm not certain yet; in fact, I already have our tickets. I just wondered if there is a flight each day and how many days in advance I would need to make reservations?"

"How many are traveling in your party?"

"Twelve."

"Twelve!" she repeated, her shock obvious.

"Yes, my husband and I are traveling with ten school children," I answered quickly, trying to sound calm.

I noticed the name plate on her desk. It said "Imelda Brown."

"Are you Imelda?" I asked her.

"Yes, I am."

"Well, I am Mrs. Collins," I said. "Do you mind if I sit down? I will show you the tickets I have, and you can tell me if everything is in order. We will be traveling to San Francisco, California, via Frankfurt, West Germany," I explained as I settled into the comfortable swivel chair in front of her cluttered desk.

She examined the tickets and assured me they were in order.

"Mrs. Collins, it isn't always easy to reserve twelve seats on one flight. Most flights leaving Nairobi are quite full. There are two flights a week to West Germany: one on Tuesday morning and one Thursday evening. It will be most helpful if you can tell me several days in advance so that I can be sure and reserve twelve seats."

"All right, Imelda, I will do my best. I thought it was best to check with you. I will come by tomorrow and let you know when we will be leaving."

I thanked her for her help, and resumed my walk back to the West German embassy. It was quite far to walk, but I thought it would help me continue to unwind after my tedious, unproductive morning.

I had thought I was frustrated the first time I talked to the German receptionist, but that was nothing compared to what happened when I went back to the embassy after lunch. I had been sitting in the waiting room for an hour and a half when she finally called me to her desk.

"I'm sorry, Mrs. Collins," she began in her deep voice. "No one is going to be able to see you today. The gentleman you really need to talk to is in a meeting for the day, and he cannot see you."

"Isn't there anyone else I can see today?" I asked urgently. "It is extremely important. Mr. Kadry, the High Commissioner for Refugees sent me," I pleaded.

Firmly she replied, "I'm sorry, Mrs. Collins; there is no one."

Terribly disappointed, I left the German embassy, caught a taxi, and went to the Norfolk. I was too exasperated to see Denton and the children just then.

The Norfolk served a lovely high tea each day, and I decided to treat myself. I put my attaché case in my room and returned to the dining room. Everything looked attractive, and several couples sat around sipping tea. *I don't want to sit here drinking tea alone*, I thought forlornly, and I returned to my room to telephone Denton.

"Do you think you could get away to join me for high tea?" I asked in my most polished British accent.

Without hesitation he agreed, and a half hour later we sat together, enjoying our tea and biscuits as I described my morning with Mr. Kadry and my frustrating afternoon at the German embassy.

"Perhaps it will be easier tomorrow morning, Jodie," he

consoled me. "I think it is marvelous that Mr. Kadry issued those travel documents for the children. What an immense help that should be!" His voice was enthusiastic, and it was good to see him appearing more at ease.

"Since you are now in Nairobi legally," I said, handing him his passport, "why don't we walk downtown and look in a few of the shops together?"

"That's a great idea. I'm sure not ready to go back to the Jacaranda. I could climb the walls when I sit around there for very long. It is much easier when I can get out like this," he said as he put his arms around me and kissed me.

It was a lovely, relaxed afternoon and evening. Denton went with me back to the Norfolk after our stroll through town. We had seen a carved head of a Masai that we would like to buy, and I had cast a wishful eye on a soapstone chess set in the open marketplace. We decided that we would wait to make any purchases until we had a chance to look around a bit more.

I was tired from all the walking, and Denton and I decided to have dinner at the Norfolk before he returned to the children.

When Denton left later that evening, I telephoned Michael and told him about my unsuccessful visit to the West German embassy.

"Do you think the Crown Prince would know anyone in West Germany or here who might be of help to us?" I asked hopefully.

"I will talk to him and see, Mrs. Collins."

I didn't see Mr. Kadry on Tuesday morning. I went directly to the West German embassy. It always seemed to help when the receptionist recognized me. The German woman at the desk greeted me, "Good morning, Mrs. Collins. Please have a seat. I will see if Mr. Wolfgang is in yet this morning."

A good German name, I thought, as I went back to my familiar chair in the waiting room and dug through my purse, looking for my New Testament. During my hours of waiting, reading the Bible helped to fortify me and give me the patience that I needed. I wasn't normally good at waiting or delays. Perhaps I was learning!

Nearly an hour later I was sitting across the desk from the German embassy official. He appeared unreasonably impatient as I explained our recent escape and my purpose for coming to him.

"I have the United Nations travel documents for the children and their airline tickets to the United States. My husband and I intend to raise the children. I am very eager to return to the States, especially because our own two children are staying with their grandparents," I said.

"Mrs. Collins," he began rather gruffly. "West Germany has a very strict policy about allowing refugees into the country. I am certain that there will be no problem, however, if the American government will give me some assurance that once you and the children arrive in West Germany, the immigration service there will indeed process the children's papers."

It took several seconds before the full implication of what he had said struck me.

"Mr. Wolfgang, the American embassy here does not want to get involved in this situation. In fact, they have asked me not to return to the American embassy. Mr. Kadry at the United Nations office has assured me that immigration in West Germany will undoubtedly be more lenient than officials here, and process our papers."

"I'm sorry, Mrs. Collins. The only condition for the visas is that I have the American embassy's word that the papers will be approved once you are in West Germany. Otherwise, my hands are tied, as you say in America," he said, obviously dismissing me.

Irritated by yet another delay, I left the embassy and caught a taxi. "American embassy," I told the driver.

I knew I had been asked by Mr. Bennett not to come back to the American embassy, but I didn't see that I had a choice. There was no delay today in getting to see Mr. Bennett. Mrs. West was cooperative and Mr. Bennett available. However, my spirits flagged when Mr. Bennett emphasized over and over that there was nothing more he could do on our behalf.

"But Mr. Bennett," I argued, "the West Germans have agreed to help us if you will just give them some assurance, that U.S. immigration services will process the children. It is that simple!"

"I'm sorry, Mrs. Collins. I cannot do that. I can't speak for American immigration in West Germany. They work independently of the State Department or our offices. I'm just not in a position to make a guarantee about what immigration will do regarding your case."

The tone of his voice made it plain that he would not change his mind. My patience was waning as I left his office and returned to the Norfolk.

I paced the floor of my hotel room, trying to calm myself. I was angry and upset with all those government officials. *They are worse than Pharaoh when he refused to let the children of Israel leave Egypt,* I raged to myself. I grabbed my big Bible off the desk as I paced. Not bothering to sit down, I turned the pages furiously, looking for the passage about the Egyptian king. I found the book of Exodus. As I read the fourteenth chapter it seemed to spell out our plight: "They are entangled in the land, the wilderness hath shut them in . . . " Exodus 14:3. I continued reading down the page and read Exodus 14:8 a second time: "And the Lord hardened the heart of Pharaoh king of Egypt, and he pursued after the children. . . ." I opened my prayer diary and began to copy the verses. After verse 8, I wrote in parentheses (just as the Ethiopians have pursued us here in Kenya!).

Sitting at the desk, I turned back to Exodus 13. As I read, I jotted several verses in my journal. "And it came to pass when Pharaoh had let the people go, that God led them not through the way of the land of the Philistines, although that was near" [as it would have been had we returned to the States twenty-four hours after our arrival in Kenya]. "For God said, Lest the people repent when they see war, and they return to Egypt. But God led the people about through the way of the wilderness of the Red Sea." And from verse 21 I wrote, "And the Lord went before them by day in a pillar of a cloud, to lead them the way, and by night in a pillar of fire, to give them light; to go by day and night."

I turned to the page in my prayer journal where I had made several notations about the escape, and added four new requests.

1. I pray that we will finish our business here quickly.

2. I pray that the children's relatives in Addis will be kept safe and that when they hear the news of their children's escape, they too will rejoice. I'm thinking particularly of Tsige who could easily be put in prison for this.

3. No harsh repercussions against anyone in Ethiopia, the parents, aunt, relatives, or our church members—particularly Joseph, since he worked so closely with Denton.

4. I pray that we may, as such a large family, make a smooth transition in life in America with sufficient income to provide for such a large family! To begin with, we are going to need a home large enough for fifteen people: ten Ethiopian children, Shellie, Brent, Denton, Guenet, and me.

As I thought about Guenet, I recalled that her graduation was Sunday. That's just yesterday, I thought. She will be leaving for California in the next couple of days to stay in our townhouse. I will try to remember to call her and tell her what is happening. Perhaps by then I will know more than I know right now.

I decided to call my mom and update her about our situation. I knew she would be concerned that she had not heard from me in nearly a week. When I looked at my watch I decided to wait until later in the evening. With a twelve-hour time difference, it was only one o'clock in the morning there.

I didn't feel like eating lunch, so I just continued to read. I knew I had to go back to the West German embassy and face Mr. Wolfgang at three o'clock, when the office reopened for the afternoon. I *had* to get those visas for the children!

I read again in Exodus 14:15: "And when Pharaoh drew nigh, the children of Israel lifted up their eyes, and behold, the Egyptians marched after them, and they were sore afraid, and the children of Israel cried out unto the Lord." I wrote in my journal, "Even though the Egyptians were close enough to see the children of Israel, Moses said, 'Fear ye not, stand still, and see the salvation of the Lord, which he will show to you today: The Lord shall fight for you, and ye shall hold your peace. . . .' "

I was beginning to unwind by two o'clock, so I decided to take a taxi to the small cafe near the Pan Am office and have a cup of coffee and see Imelda Brown about our plane reservations. It was Tuesday. The next plane left Thursday. I would make reservations and believe we would be ready to go by then.

Had I known as I rode back to the West German embassy that afternoon that I would not find Mr. Wolfgang that day or the next, I would have felt dismal indeed.

I returned to the embassy Tuesday afternoon, Wednesday morning, and Wednesday afternoon and was told each time that I would have to come back because Mr. Wolfgang was unavailable. I was beginning to think he was trying to avoid me.

On Wednesday I considered cancelling our flight reservations, but I reconsidered, thinking I would hold off until I saw Mr. Wolfgang Thursday morning.

The most difficult part of Tuesday and Wednesday was not being told by the receptionist that Mr. Wolfgang was busy or unavailable, although that was frustrating enough in itself. The hardest part was trying to encourage Denton and the children that things would work out soon, when I wasn't really certain they would. Everyone was restless even though Georgio took the kids to several movies and Denton and I enjoyed window shopping and decided to buy the hand-carved head of the Masai woman we had looked at during our first shopping trip on Monday. We also returned to the spacious open market and bought the soapstone chess set for me. I liked to collect chess sets from all the places we traveled, not just because I thought they were beautiful, but because I am an avid chess player.

After a good night's sleep Wednesday night, I awoke with new determination and energy Thursday morning. Surely we would get a break soon. It had been twelve days since the escape, and I'd been in Kenya for nine days.

I arrived at the German embassy for the seventh time in four days. I felt confident that our matter would be resolved, and I would be able to return to Denton and the children with good news by lunch time today.

As I sat across from Mr. Wolfgang, my optimism was extinguished when I heard him reiterate, "Mrs. Collins, without the American embassy's verification that you are going to be processed in West Germany, I cannot under any conditions recommend that you be issued German visas for the ten children in your care."

I wanted to argue with him, but it was clear to me by the set of his mouth and look in his eyes that my appeal would go unheard. My throat felt constricted as I said, "Just what am I supposed to do, Mr. Wolfgang?"

"I'm sorry, Mrs. Collins," he said, ignoring my question. "I can be of no further service to you."

I stood and it felt as if a new weight of responsibility had just been placed on my shoulders. I knew nothing had been added, it was that I didn't know where to go next.

Once outside the embassy, I telephoned Mr. Kadry. He kindly suggested I come to his office. It was like visiting an old friend. He was gracious as he welcomed me back into his office.

I explained my many visits to see Mr. Wolfgang and my subsequent visit to the U. S. embassy.

"In light of the United States' refusal to say they would assist you and process your case once you were in West Germany, I am not surprised at the West Germans' refusal to issue the visas. I mentioned earlier that they might be reluctant. It seems to me that the United States could give a quiet nod under the table, so to speak, and assure the West Germans of their willingness to cooperate."

"What am I going to do, Mr. Kadry?"

"I'm not certain at this point. There are a couple of other immigration points—Belgium, Guam. But I'm not certain it will be any easier to get visas to go there."

We sat quietly for a few minutes before I exclaimed, "Sweden! What about Sweden, Mr. Kadry?"

"Do you know someone there?" he asked.

"No, I'm just trying to think of where we could go and be safe until we resolve this puzzle. I am so concerned for the children's safety. The Ethiopians are still at the hotel, and they watch every move the children and Denton make. It's eerie!"

He considered my suggestion for several minutes before

he said, "Why don't you try going to the Swedish embassy?" He looked up the address in the telephone directory and drew me a small map.

Wearily, I picked up my attaché case. I felt as if it were another limb of my body. I carried it everywhere since it had the children's documents and other papers that seemed too important to risk leaving at the hotel.

"Call me after you leave the Swedish embassy and let me know how you fared," he said kindly.

I was too tired to walk, so I hailed a taxi. I decided that before going to the Swedish embassy, I would stop by the Pan Am office and cancel our plane reservations. "I'll come back when our plans are more certain," I explained to Imelda Brown.

Then I headed for the Swedish embassy. As the small taxi darted in and out of traffic down the busy metropolitan boulevard, I was absorbed in my own thoughts. *Lord, have mercy!* I thought abruptly. *Another receptionist! I'm going to face another receptionist. Make her nice,* I prayed inwardly, as the taxi jerked to a sudden stop. "Swedish embassy!" the taxi driver said, with a cheerful smile. I paid him and walked into the neat-looking building. When I opened the door, I found the waiting room empty and quiet. I noted the receptionist's desk. She was busy writing.

I decided to get right to the heart of the matter, and almost before she had asked if she could help me, I told her the nutshell version of our escape, the refusal of the West German embassy to issue us visas, and about Mr. Kadry and the police commissioner.

By the time I concluded, her mouth was open in dismay.

"Yes, I understand," she said, getting to her feet.

I hoped I hadn't frightened her off.

"I will get Mrs. Karlstrom, the Charge of Affairs," she said, backing out of her small office.

Moments later a tall, nicely dressed lady appeared.

"Hello," she began in a friendly manner, "I am Mrs. Karlstrom. May I be of assistance to you?"

"I do hope so," I began nervously.

"Follow me," she instructed.

Moments later we were seated in a spacious, comfortable

office. I wondered if it was her office, and she said, "This is the ambassador's office. We do not have a Swedish ambassador here in Nairobi at this time. I am in charge. How may I help you?"

For the second time within minutes I repeated my story, this time in greater detail. She listened with great interest as I talked for nearly an hour. She didn't interrupt once.

When I finished I was exhausted and felt as if I had relived the entire ordeal. My shoulders drooped.

She was thoughtful and began slowly at first. "Mrs. Collins, this is just remarkable! You and your husband have done a very courageous thing. I am overwhelmed by what you've told me."

She paused and then continued. "Mrs. Collins, I am supposed to attend a formal banquet this evening. It is for all the members of this embassy. However, I want to assure you that no one will leave the embassy tonight until I have some answer for you from our foreign minister in Sweden."

Her words fell upon grateful ears. "Oh, Mrs. Karlstrom, I don't know what to say!" I exclaimed, greatly relieved.

"Please, return to the Jacaranda and tell your husband and the children to be strong. I will telephone you there this evening or as quickly as I have an answer for you."

Just as Mrs. Karlstrom finished talking, the receptionist appeared with a glass tray laden with coffee cups, coffeepot, cookies, and cakes. She graciously poured cups of coffee and passed a dish of cookies to me. I smiled at her, remembering my urgent little appeal to the Lord for a friendly receptionist. Not only had she responded quickly and called Mrs. Karlstrom, but she was a thoughtful hostess.

Twenty minutes later I was on my way to the Jacaranda Hotel. I could almost have floated there, I was so happy, but I decided to take a taxi instead!

As usual, everyone was in the dining room. I was ready to burst with excitement. "Mom looks happy today," Loly noted as I approached the table smiling.

"I'm happy all right," I began, as I scooted in beside Denton in the big corner booth. The waiters left our large table intact after each meal rather than to have to rearrange it for each meal. Our waiter came to the table when he saw I was seated and asked to take my order. He knew Denton and me by name.

"Thank you, but I'm not going to have anything to eat. I'll just have a Coke."

I lowered my voice, and everyone huddled closer to hear what I had to say. "I have just come from the Swedish embassy. They may help us. I will know by this evening. The lady there is going to call me. She said to tell you all to be strong. She was very kind." Everyone looked pleased with the good news. While they finished eating their lunch, I telephoned Mr. Kadry with the good news. That afternoon Denton and I sat by the swimming pool while Amaha waded in the shallow end. We talked, for the first time, about what we would do when we returned to the States.

"I sent my transcripts and application form to Simpson College. No matter what, I want to finish my Bachelor of Arts degree. How many of your units did they accept from Bible college, Jodie?"

"I don't recall, but I do know that Baptist Bible College has been accredited in the last couple of years, and I understand it is retroactive. Most of your credits will transfer to Simpson. I had to make up a lot of units when I finished in 1975. Do you know what you'd like to do if we don't go back overseas?"

"I've been thinking about it a lot! I think I would like to study psychology and become a family, marriage, and child counselor."

"It sounds like something you would enjoy, and I think you would be a good counselor, Denton," I assured him.

"I'm not certain about taking a family of fourteen back overseas," I said lightly.

He smiled and said, "What mission board would ever approve a family of fourteen to go overseas? It would even be difficult to find a church that would accept a pastor with a dozen kids in the family!"

We both laughed, although I knew he was right. Today was a good day, and I didn't want to cloud it with the uncertainty of the future.

As Denton and I basked in the late afternoon sun, I thought about the first evening I had arrived at the Jacaranda.

"Denton," I asked, sitting up from the chaise lounge where I had been lying, "remember the first night I got here? I was walking into the hotel and Audrey, the woman I played softball with in Addis—married to the Kenyan man from the embassy in Addis—was staying here at the Jacaranda. When I came up the front walk, she yelled to me from her room on the second floor. I signaled for her to stop calling, and she disappeared inside the window and I didn't see her again. Did you ever see her around the hotel?"

"Yes, I did, as a matter of fact. The second morning we were here, she saw all of us at breakfast. She didn't act surprised, but she didn't ask any questions either. She just talked normally, as if we were meeting at the Hilton in Addis. She did say they were on a summer holiday here in Kenya and planned to go back to Addis in a few weeks. As she turned around to leave, I heard her daughter say, 'I can't wait to get back and see my friend Ababa, to tell her that I saw Loly, Kokeb, and Menen.' Her mother said sternly, 'I don't think you had better tell anyone, particularly Ababa, that you saw the children here.' So, I think Audrey knew something was going on, even though she didn't act as if she suspected anything. Ababa's father is a general in the present government. I would hope that Audrey's daughter, Appeyo, was discouraged from talking to Ababa about seeing our girls here. I saw them only from a distance the next day, and since you've come, I haven't seen them once. I think they might have checked out the morning after you arrived. It would be dangerous for her to be seen with us. With these Ethiopian Security men around here, they might think that Audrey and her husband engineered the whole escape plan and arrest them when they return to Addis Ababa.

"Yes," I said, "wouldn't that be horrible? Particularly when they had nothing to do with it. Audrey was so funny, though, when she hollered out that window, 'Jodie Collins, what are you doing here!' I couldn't believe my ears or eyes!"

Dinner was a happy gathering. It was good to see the children and Denton relaxing a bit. They were all looking more rested, and I had noticed that the children were beginning to put on some much needed weight. I had been particularly concerned about Kokeb. She was skeletal when I first saw her coming down the steps towards me the night I had arrived at their hotel. She had lost a great deal of weight after I left Ethiopia. I wasn't surprised at their weight gain. Most of the kids ordered two meals a night. I didn't know how we would ever pay the bill when it came time to leave the Jacaranda. *We might have to work off our bill,* I thought to myself half jokingly. I decided I wouldn't worry about paying bills, either.

My thoughts were interrupted when the maitre d' called me to the telephone. Everyone stopped eating and watched as I stood up.

"Keep eating, you guys!" I said, smiling. "And pray!"

They all chuckled nervously, knowing this was probably Mrs. Karlstrom's call, for which we had been waiting all day.

I hurried through the crowded dining room toward the desk.

"Hello. Oh, yes, Mrs. Karlstrom. Yes. Yes, of course I will. Yes. I'll tell him. Fine. Goodbye."

Within minutes I was seated at the table. I could barely contain myself. No one took a bite, and they were all staring at me.

"Stay calm!" I instructed them in my most serious voice. "We have our visas to go to Sweden."

I could see they all wanted to cheer, but I put my finger to my lips and nodded toward the opposite side of the room where three of our Ethiopian antagonists sat scrutinizing us.

"Denton, Mrs. Karlstrom told me to come immediately to the embassy. She will process all our papers this evening before she and other embassy officials leave for their dinner party. She suggested you take the kids to the airport and get as many of them vaccinated as possible. She said they give free vaccinations until nine o'clock tonight."

"Shots!" I heard several of the kids groan.

Smiling, I said, "Anyone who doesn't want to have shots can always stay behind when we leave Kenya."

I think I heard ten kids groan in unison.

I left moments later to get my attaché case from Denton's room, then headed for the Swedish embassy.

By eight o'clock Mrs. Karlstrom handed me the last travel

document. "There you are. Everything is complete. You are ready to leave Kenya whenever you like," she said graciously, extending her hand toward me. We shook hands, and I thanked her and ten other officials who had stayed behind that evening to help her. "I cannot thank you enough," I said from the depths of my heart. "I thank all of you."

"I hope you enjoy your visit to Sweden, and I do hope things work out for you and your family quickly so that you can return to your two children in the States. I know they must be eager to have you home again."

"Yes, and believe me, we are all just as eager to get home! This has been an extended holiday!" We all laughed, and I left to return to the Norfolk. I wondered if Denton had gotten all the children's vaccinations before the immunization service closed at nine o'clock.

Without undressing, I lay down on my bed and threw my *gabe* over me. I awoke several hours later, surprised that I had fallen asleep. When I looked at my travel clock, it was after midnight. I decided not to phone Denton. I'd just wait until morning and call him then. Instead, I placed a call to Guenet and told her the good news. She was thrilled to hear that I had gotten the visas to Sweden, but she asked, "When do you think you will be home?"

"I don't really know. I'm just so happy we will be off the continent of Africa and safe in Sweden. We still must find a way to get to one of the immigration points: West Germany, Brussels, or Guam. Can you see us going to Guam from here? Those are the only designated entrance points for refugees trying to enter the United States, according to the man I talked to here. He is the High Commissioner for Refugees here in Kenya, so I assume he knows where we can get the kids' papers processed. My main purpose for going to Sweden is just to find a safe place to pursue my efforts. I'm hoping, and Mr. Kadry is too, that once we are out of Africa, embassies will take a more lenient view of our situation and help us. Officials here, according to Mr. Kadry, are too emotionally involved. They are afraid to rock the boat, so to speak. I guess their diplomatic careers are on the line, and first things first," I said sarcastically.

"Guenet, would you call my mom and try to explain as

much of this as possible? Just tell her not to worry. I will write all of you from Sweden. Also, please give Jean and Moe a call. I know they will be wondering what happened to us. Have you gotten all the sleeping bags together yet?"

"No, not yet, but I'm working on it. I talked to Pastor Carlson the day after I got here, and he said he would help me by calling people and having them bring them to the church."

"That's fine, because we will need them soon, I hope!"

"Keep in touch, Jodie, and take care of yourself. We are all praying for your safe and soon return. I've talked to your mom several times, and she is worried about you. She will be happy to hear that you are going to leave Africa."

After I hung up, I was tempted to call Michael, but I changed my mind when I considered how late it would be in London. *I'll call him first thing in the morning,* I thought, as I climbed into my bed and turned off the light.

CHAPTER TWENTY-FOUR
Goodbye to Africa

I had decided my strategy before falling asleep Thursday night. When I awoke Friday morning, July 29, ten days after I had first arrived in Nairobi, I showered, dressed, and went to the hotel dining room for a quick bite of breakfast. I returned to my room to make two telephone calls: to Michael and Mr. Kadry.

I had already decided not to call Denton until I had run my errand. I wanted to surprise him. As it turned out, I was the one who was surprised, and my idea nearly backfired.

As I spoke to Mr. Kadry on the telephone that morning, I explained that we had been issued visas for Sweden.

"I can't thank you enough for all you have done for us, Mr. Kadry. I don't have words adequate to say how much I appreciate your encouragement and help during our days here in Kenya."

To Michael I said, "Yes! We are on our way to Sweden. Isn't it great?" I was amazed when he told me that he and Seyfou had been in touch with Mr. Stargne, the Swedish gentleman who had been in England visiting the Crown Prince and family when the news of the successful escape from Ethiopia had arrived. It was Mr. Stargne who had contacted Mr. Harry Lindquist, president of a Christian foundation in Sweden. The foundation had generously provided the twelve airline tickets for our family to return to the States. Michael carefully explained that Mr. Stargne had also been working to arrange for us to come to Sweden. "It's wonderful," Michael exclaimed, "how our plans have come together! If you can let me know when you are going to arrive in Stockholm, I will contact Mr. Stargne."

"I will call you this evening when everything is settled, Michael, and I know for sure when we will leave," I assured him.

Concluding my telephone calls for the morning, I caught a taxi. I glanced at my watch as I jumped into the taxi and said, "Pan American Airlines office, please." It was eight-thirty. I would probably be there before the office opened, but I didn't mind. I was eager to make our reservations and get to the Jacaranda to tell the kids and Denton when we were leaving.

As I leaned back in the seat to enjoy one of my last taxicab rides through the Nairobi streets, I thought, *Actually, I'm going to miss this place.* Under different circumstances, this would have been a lovely vacation. The streets were getting crowded with the early morning rush of working people headed for their offices.

My cab pulled up in front of the familiar Pan Am office. I paid my cab fare, and crossed the street to the offices. The lights were still off inside. I tried the door, but it was still locked.

Still a little embarrassed about having to cancel our twelve reservations for West Germany yesterday afternoon, I waited restlessly for Imelda to arrive. Finally I saw her coming down the sidewalk. She smiled warmly and waved in my direction.

As she got nearer, she called, "Good morning, Mrs. Collins. My, you are here early!"

"Yes, I am, Imelda. We have had a change in our plans. We are not going to West Germany, but to Sweden."

"Sweden?" She sounded a bit surprised.

"Yes. Can you tell me when there is a flight to Stockholm? The sooner, the better," I added as a postscript.

She took off her jacket, turned on the office lights, and settled behind her desk. It looked as cluttered as the first day I had met her.

She reached for her big black book and checked the flight

listings. I settled comfortably into the same swivel chair I had sat in the first day I wandered into the office. I could hardly believe it was only two days ago. It seemed as if I had known Imelda a long time.

"Hmmm," I heard her say. She continued running her finger up and down the page. I waited.

I wondered where Denton was. I was sure he was curious about where I was as well. I hadn't talked to him since we left each other at the Jacaranda last night when I hurried off to the Swedish embassy and he dashed to the airport with ten children to get them all vaccinated so they could leave the country.

"Yes, here it is," Imelda interrupted my thoughts. "There is only one flight a week from Nairobi to Stockholm, Mrs. Collins."

My heart sank with disappointment. Another week in Nairobi? Oh, no!

Smiling, as if she read my thoughts, she continued, "It leaves today!"

My insides felt as though they were already in flight. "Really!" I screamed.

"Yes! However, you will have to hurry. I'm not certain we can even write the twelve tickets in time. The plane leaves in an hour and a half. Actually, you and your family should be at the airport within the next half hour."

"A half hour! Oh, my goodness! May I use your telephone to call my husband? I had wanted to surprise him with the news of our departure, but I had not anticipated such a shock. Wait until he hears this!"

I dialed the Jacaranda Hotel's number by memory. "Room 204, please," I requested. "Denton? Listen! I'm at the Pan Am office. There is only one flight a week that goes to Stockholm."

I heard him groaning, undoubtedly thinking the same thing I had thought.

"It leaves today, Denton!" I said excitedly.

"Really? That's great!" he joined my enthusiasm.

"The only thing is, Denton, the plane leaves in an hour and a half. You and the kids need to be at the airport within a half hour!"

"Oh, no! I don't think we can make it, Jodie. Some of the kids are still sleeping."

"Let's try, Denton. Phone Franco right away. By the time you're ready, he should be there to help you get everyone to the airport. I have to wait here for Imelda to rewrite all the tickets. She isn't even sure if she can do it in the length of time we have. We're just going to try. I have to check out of my hotel, too. I'll meet you at the airport as soon as possible."

"OK, Jodie, but some of the kids didn't get their shots last night. The lady at the vaccination center was very curious about how the kids were able to get into Kenya without international vaccination booklets. She filled out and signed new shot books for the kids she vaccinated, but three of them weren't able to get their shots before she closed. She said we'd never be able to leave Kenya without their getting shots. I will try and get out there as quickly as possible and see if they are open."

"Do your best, Denton. That's all we can do."

"See you there! Good luck with the tickets," he said encouragingly.

As I set the receiver back into its place, I thought, "Fine surprise this turned out to be! I just never thought we would have to cut it this close!"

Imelda had called two other men who had just come to work and started them rewriting our tickets. She worked on several herself.

As I sat there anxiously watching them, a large limousine pulled up in front of the office. Mrs. Karlstrom jumped out of the back seat and came scurrying into the office.

"Wonderful! I've found you!" she exclaimed when she saw me.

"Is something wrong, Mrs. Karlstrom?" I asked, fearful of another delay.

"No! No! I knew you would be leaving today. I knew there was only one flight a week to Stockholm, and I wanted to tell you that it left today. I called your hotel earlier but I didn't find you there. I remembered from our conversation that you had Pan Am tickets, so I came directly here, hoping to find you. What can I do to help you? I know the plane leaves shortly. Doesn't it?" she said, addressing Imelda.

"Yes, in approximately one hour," Imelda confirmed. "However, let me telephone the airport and see if the flight is on time."

Minutes later she said, "Yes, the flight is on time. I guess if I had ever wished for one to be delayed, it was this morning," she laughed good-naturedly.

Imelda was very kind. She knew nothing of our personal plight, and yet she had been so patient and willing to help.

"The Norfolk said you hadn't checked out yet, Mrs. Collins. May I take you there to check out while Mrs. Brown finishes writing up your tickets?"

"That would be wonderful, and would save considerable time," I assured her.

The chauffeur raced toward the Norfolk. Sitting in the back seat with Mrs. Karlstrom, I decided I preferred the luxury of the limousine to the small taxis I had used during the last ten days.

I checked out of the Norfolk, using my American Express card. I wondered how Denton would ever cover the immense bill at the Jacaranda. *I hope Franco will help him,* I thought, as I dashed back outside to the waiting car. The chauffeur held the door open for me and I clumsily collapsed into the back seat. The chauffeur and bellhop put my suitcase into the trunk. I had my attaché case and all the papers beside me on the seat.

Just as we pulled away from our parking place, I saw Franco with several of the kids in his car. I lowered my electric window and called to him. He finally saw me and pulled alongside our car. "Mr. Collins and the other children went with Georgio to the airport. We came by to see if you needed a ride, Mrs. Collins," he called.

"I'll ride with Mrs. Karlstrom," I said, and he waved me on.

Just as the driver pulled up in front of the Pan Am office, Imelda ran out of the office, waving the completed tickets in the air.

Mrs. Karlstrom retrieved them as I thanked Imelda. She whispered breathlessly, "Good luck, Mrs. Collins," as we pulled away from the curb and made our dash for the airport.

Seconds later the driver turned onto the Uhuru Highway

leading toward the Nairobi airport. *Will we make it?* I thought nervously, as the driver swerved to miss villagers herding their laden donkeys toward the market place. I looked at my watch. It would be close; we had only twenty minutes.

With only ten minutes to spare, the chauffeur swung the large car up to the front of the terminal. Mrs. Karlstrom jumped out of the car almost before it had stopped, calling over her shoulder, "I'll be right back. Get your luggage and come into the terminal building!" She was gone.

As I hurried into the building, I was shocked to see Mr. Kadry. "Mrs. Karlstrom telephoned me earlier and said it was likely that you and your family would be leaving on today's flight. I took a chance and came out here. I recognized your husband from his passport picture. He is with the children at the vaccination center, but he'll be here shortly."

Just then I saw Denton coming down the corridor, Loly, Aster, and Amaha were rubbing their arms and looking rather distressed. It was clear they had just had their shots.

Mrs. Karlstrom emerged from a swinging door and called to us, "Come this way; come with me!"

"Where are Franco and his carload?" I asked.

"He's already in here," Mrs. Karlstrom called, poking her head back through the swinging doors a second time.

We all followed her into a large, nicely furnished VIP lounge.

I had only heard about such places. It was my first time to see one. It was lovely, with large comfortable chairs and couches. A waiter dressed in a freshly starched uniform was busy pouring soft drinks for several of the children. They looked relaxed as they took small tea cakes and cookies from the silver tray on the table in front of them.

Finally catching up with Mrs. Karlstrom as she hovered around the children, encouraging them to help themselves to more cookies, I said, "Won't we miss the airplane if we don't hurry?"

"Oh, no, Mrs. Collins. You can relax now. I've requested that the airplane be delayed briefly while you and your family have time to catch your breath and have a little refreshment! Please, just relax now, and enjoy some of the refreshment we have prepared for you. I will see that you get out to the airplane on time and that you all get aboard safely."

I sank into one of the huge, soft chairs while the waiter hurried to pour me a cup of coffee and filled a plate with cakes and cookies. Denton fell into a chair beside mine. We were both too shaken to eat anything. It had been quite a morning. I thought of asking him if he liked my surprise, but considering the look on his face, I decided it wasn't the time.

I relaxed momentarily and began sipping my coffee as I watched the children across the room. Georgio was talking with them, and they were smiling and enjoying his company as they had from the beginning. Franco stood beside Denton. Denton stood to talk with Franco.

"I don't know how Jodie and I can thank you for everything, Franco. You have gone beyond the call of duty to help us. Thank you!" Denton said sincerely. I stood beside Denton now, and added my thanks. Mrs. Karlstrom joined us. We shook hands, and I said, "And you, Mrs. Karlstrom, have moved mountains to help us. Thank you for everything. Thank you so much."

At the last moment, Mrs. Karlstrom gave me a big hug, and I could not hold back my tears.

Ten minutes later we were all aboard an East African Airlines jet bound for Stockholm, Sweden.

My goodness, I thought as I helped the younger children fasten their seat belts. *There are ten children on this flight—and they are all mine!*

I collapsed into my narrow seat and fastened my own seat belt.

As the plane revved its large engines and lifted skyward, I sighed deeply and thought, our own freedom flight, a new beginning, a new life. I knew I wasn't going to have to go through the years ahead alone. I had Denton, Shellie, Brent, and ten more children besides. But most important, I knew I had the Lord! I had found Him trustworthy. Little did I know how often I would be put to the test again in the days ahead, but each time I would hear those words, "Trust me!" from the 37th Psalm, and each new day, regardless of what I faced, I knew I would have to make a choice whether or not I would trust God or whether I would try, in my own strength, to work out the delays, frustrations, and heartaches of that day.

Epilogue

God's faithfulness never failed. During our two-week stay in Sweden, God miraculously provided us with a home, a car, new clothes for Denton and the children, boat trips, and a visit to Skansen, a quaint Scandinavian recreation center. During this time, I met with embassy and government officials, pursuing entry into West Germany, the immigration point for African refugees into the United States. A small legal technicality enabled me to leave Sweden with six children who were under sixteen years old and enter West Germany without visas. Denton and the four oldest young people had to remain in Sweden until the West German government felt certain that the United States immigration service in Frankfurt would process the papers of the younger children.

Within one week of our arrival in Frankfurt, the immigration paper work was well underway for the younger children. The West German government sent a telegram to their embassy in Stockholm as well as to the American embassy, and Denton and the four young people still with him were able to join us in West Germany. Another wonderful reunion!

After nearly two weeks of filling out forms and completing mounds of paper work, we were ready to return to the United States. A few days prior to our departure, an uncle of the six brothers and sisters we had agreed to bring out and raise, flew from his home in New York to Frankfurt, West Germany, where he met with Denton and me. He asked if he could take his sister's six children to New York and raise them himself.

Undoubtedly this was best for all of us, although we felt very sad saying goodbye to the six of them.

I completed the paper work for the young children a week earlier than the paper work for the older ones. Anxious to return to Shellie and Brent, who had been with Denton's parents in Kansas, Denton and I decided that I would fly to the United States ahead of him and get the children settled into school, which would open within one week. I flew from Stockholm to London, England, where we had a six-hour layover. Family members were going to come to Heathrow Airport to meet us during our layover, but were inadvertently delayed, a great disappointment to all.

Disappointed, but very eager to get the children home, we began the last leg of our journey, London to San Francisco. We arrived home to the cheers of Shellie, Brent, Mom and Ben, Jean, Moe, Michelle, and Guenet, who had managed at last to find ten sleeping bags! It was a happy day, clouded only by the fact that Denton was not home yet. A week later, the other young people's paper work completed, Denton joined us.

We had definitely outgrown our two bedroom townhouse, and we began immediately to search for a home large enough to accommodate our large family. Again God was faithful to provide "exceeding abundantly above what we could ask or think," and we found a lovely five-bedroom home with three baths in a small community in northern California.

Denton entered college during our first year home and graduated with honors from Simpson College a year later. Working, going to college, and providing for a family of nine people, Denton successfully completed his Master's Degree in psychology and is a marriage, family, and child counselor in the San Francisco Bay area.

During our first two years in the United States I worked to help provide a comfortable home for our family. In January 1979, I began working as Director of Financial Aid for

Simpson College, my alma mater, in San Francisco. I became the Director of Student Recruitment the following year and traveled extensively for the college until I had the opportunity to write this book for publication. As an aspiring writer, it was a dream come true. Again, my God had given me the desire of my heart, and He reminds me daily to "trust in the Lord, and do good; dwell in the land and cultivate faithfulness. Delight yourself in the Lord; and He will give you the desires of your heart. Commit your way to the Lord, trust also in Him, and He will do it. And He will bring forth your righteousness as the light, and your judgment as the noonday. Rest in the Lord and wait patiently for Him; fret not . . . " Psalm 37:3-7, NASB.